THE
YEATS
COMPANION

THE
YEATS
COMPANION

With a Biographical
Portrait by

ULICK
O'CONNOR

PAVILION
MICHAEL JOSEPH

For A. L. P.

I would like to thank A. T. Cross, Company for the sponsorship and
help they gave me in enabling me to complete this book.
Also Patricia Nolan, Eleanor Ashe, Gerald and
Lelia O'Flaherty, Jane Knechtel and Judith Sheppard.

First published in 1990 by
PAVILION BOOKS LIMITED
196 Shaftesbury Avenue, London WC2H 8JL

Front cover portrait of W. B. Yeats
painted by J. B. Yeats reproduced by
courtesy of The National Gallery of
Ireland, Dublin

Designed by Tom Sawyer

A CIP catalogue record for this book is
available from the British Library

ISBN 1 85145 360 1

10 9 8 7 6 5 4 3 2 1

Printed and bound in Great Britain
by Billing and Sons Ltd, Worcester

Contents

Preface

I have chosen such selections from Yeats's poetry and prose which I hope will convey some measure of his greatness as an artist and entertain the reader as well.

I have arranged the material with the intention of showing how much his works relate to the events of his life and the many remarkable people who were his friends and who influenced him.

There will inevitably be some readers who will feel I have excluded some favourite poem or piece of prose that they cherish. But I have tried to give *The Yeats Companion* a fabric of its own, and in the weaving inevitably some jaunty piece must be laid aside because it does not fit the image of the whole cloth.

Ulick O'Connor
Dublin 1989

Biographical Portrait

When he died at Roquebrune, France in 1939, William Butler Yeats was already recognized as a major poet. Eliot, Auden, Ezra Pound, harbingers of Modernism, looked on him as a master, as well as those who found themselves unable to comprehend trends in modern verse. Yeats's greatness lay in that he had renewed his creative imagination, and expressed it in his work at each stage of his life: the period of the young Yeats of the early lyrics and symbolist verse; the middle period when he was the 'smiling public man' involved in the affairs of the nation; and the last period when he turned to the intellect of the eighteenth century to strengthen his thought, while he set up those great poems of defiance against death and decay – all demonstrate that he never deviated in his determination to express what he termed 'things discovered in the deep'.

He received world-wide recognition when in 1923, at the age of fifty-eight, he was awarded the Nobel Prize for Literature. Two other Dubliners have received the same award, and in fact Dublin is the only city in the world to have produced three Nobel Prize winners for Literature.

The Dublin in which Yeats was born and spent a large part of his life was in fact the centre of the last Literary Renaissance in Europe. It was to produce the greatest prose writer in English of the century in Joyce, the greatest poet in Yeats and writers of world influence in George Moore, John Millington Synge, Seán O'Casey, as well as James Stephens, George Russell, Pádraic Colum, Oliver St John Gogarty, Lady Gregory and a later generation, Liam O'Flaherty, Seán Ó Faoláin, Frank O'Connor, Monk Gibbon, Patrick Kavanagh and Austin Clarke. The Irish Literary Renaissance was created out of that fusion of two cultures that had been separated for centuries. Anglo-Ireland and native Irish had existed side by side since the sixteenth century. But by the nineteenth century the barriers between the two races began to weaken. Both races began to share common characteristics of temperament and outlook. Just as Norman, Celt and Saxon had fused into one blinding Elizabethan flash to produce the greatest literature in the world, so too a new Irishman was coming into existence, neither Anglo-Irish nor Gaelic but a blend of both races. The image of the new nation was naked in the air, and as all moments of conception are accompanied by elation so too there was an excitement in Ireland then that would never be found again. Yeats sought the principle of unity that would bind 'the peasant visionaries that are, the landlord duellists that were in one Celtic phantasmagoria', while George Russell prepared to hail 'the first born of the coming race', the new Irishman, ı composite of Gael and Gall (foreigner):

> One river born from many streams,
> Roll in one blaze of blinding light.

Thus it was in an Ireland in which vital changes were occurring in the national psyche that Yeats grew up and would spend the greater part of his youth and early manhood. He was born in 1865 in Sandymount Avenue in Dublin. His father John Butler Yeats was a barrister turned painter and his mother Elizabeth Pollexfen was from a Sligo merchant family. The Yeatses were Protestant Anglo-Irish. Among the poet's paternal ancestors had been small gentry, rectors and Jacobite adventurers; while the Pollexfens and Middletons, Yeats's mother's people, owned large shipping and milling businesses in Sligo town.

John Butler Yeats has so far not received the recognition he deserves as a painter. Henry Lamb thought him 'by far the greatest painter Ireland has produced'; while the American critic Charles Henri once went so far as to say that 'J.B. Yeats is the greatest British portrait painter of the Victorian era.'

His conversation astonished G.K. Chesterton, who thought it so brilliant that he felt it must be a survival of an earlier style of social communication, in which one thought up one's sentences the night before, to introduce them at an appropriate time the following day under the guise of spontaneity.

In 1870 the Yeatses moved to London, where John Butler Yeats intended to earn his living as a portrait painter. Willie attended the Godolphin School in Hammersmith. He was never happy there and always longed for the Sligo he lived in as a small boy and used to return to for his holidays. Impoverished though the Yeatses were, travel was easy for them because their Middleton uncles in Sligo owned steamers which plied to and from Liverpool and Willie always had a free passage back as well as the comfort of a berth in the captain's cabin.

The countryside around Sligo always loomed darkling in his mind:

Drumcliff, the Rosses, Lough Gill and Ben Bulben with its crown of megalithic graves. As a young man Willie would go back to Sligo town to stay for periods with his uncle George Pollexfen, a rich unmarried merchant who, uncommonly among men of commerce, was the possessor of a physic gift. If one wanted to think of any single incident to provide an insight into the nature of the Anglo-Irish character it would be that of Yeats and his uncle walking by the sea, one on a cliff, the other on land, imagining symbols which they would successfully transmit to each other through the mind's eye. Also in Sligo as a young man Yeats had contact with the landed gentry. In those days it was unusual for the merchant classes to be received by the landed gentry. But with Yeats it was different – he was a writer. Sir Henry Gore-Booth welcomed him warmly at Lissadell, a Georgian mansion just outside Sligo 'with a sitting room as high as a church', and long French lawns stretching to the twilight where the two beautiful daughters of the house, Constance and Eva, used to walk. The girls were famous for their dash and bravura on the hunting field, and Constance was a fine painter as well. Later she would be condemned to death as one of the leaders of the Rebellion against England in 1916 and, after having been reprieved, would become the first woman elected to Westminster. Her sister Eva, a poetess, devoted her life to social work in the North of England. One of Yeats's greatest poems commemorates these two sisters: 'In Memory of Eva Gore-Booth and Con Markiewicz.'

After attending the High School in Dublin, Willie studied art at the Metropolitan School and worked in his father's studios in York Street cleaning brushes and pallettes in between writing poetry. He would read his verse to the young writers who came into the studios, or read out their own verse to them beating time with his hands and chanting with his head on one side. When one young visitor, the poetess Katherine Tynan, gave him chlorodyne lozenges for a bad cough, Willie absent-mindedly ate the whole lot in one go and slept for thirty hours.

He had such a temper at this time that he sometimes had to be put to bed by his sisters to calm down his fits. His father was not much better in this respect and he would engage in ferocious arguments with his son. One day Yeats senior challenged Willie to a fistfight and when his son said he could not fight his father that extraordinary man asked him simply why not. One fear of his father's was that Willie would obtain regular employment which would interfere with his artistic life, and he was always relieved when the lad would return and tell him he had failed to obtain the job he had applied for. The father would comfort the son with: 'You know the Dublin definition of a gentleman is someone not wholly interested in getting on in life.'

At the Dublin School of Art Willie met a student who was to influence the whole of his life. This was George Russell, painter and poet, who wrote under the pseudonym AE. As Russell would draw the model of a male figure at the school something else would emerge on the drawing sheet, perhaps an image of St John, almost as if it had intruded itself from outside. Yeats was intrigued by such gifts and soon became a friend of Russell's who introduced him to the rituals of the psychic world. As he was in reaction against the Positivist and Darwinian notions of his father, and felt his mission should be to lead 'the revolt of the soul against the intellect', Yeats found Russell an ideal companion and soulmate. Together at week-ends they would head out for the nearby Dublin hills and conjure up there visions of Aengus, the Irish God of Love, with a fiery plumage of birds about his golden hair, or Mananaan the Sea God or Bo Dearg whom they believed were part of a universal hierarchy of gods related to Hindu or Oriental Deities.

One day AE even claimed to have seen an airship, steered by a young man with black hair blown back from his forehead, that passed so close he could have stretched out his hand and touched it.

Yeats now wrote poetry somewhat in the style of William Morris and the Pre-Raphaelites, who had sought to revive the spirit of medieval England in literature and art.

In looking for financial assistance to help him publish his first poem, 'The Wanderings of Oisin', written in Pre-Raphaelite manner, Yeats encountered a man who was to have a profound influence on his life. This was John O'Leary, a former revolutionary, who had been imprisoned for his part in Fenian activities, and on being released on ticket of leave, had lived for some years in Paris, sharpening his mind in the cafés and numbering among his friends, Turgenev, Swinburne, Kropotkin and George Du Maurier. Now back home in Dublin, he lived in rooms on Leinster Road, on a private income he derived from land he owned. In Dublin he lived very much according to his Paris routine, spending the morning writing letters, cutting clippings from papers to send to his friends and covering postcards with indomitable comments which sometimes finished up around the stamp. He spent his afternoons fishing in the bookshops, and his evenings were given over to people who would drop in to see him. His rooms had become a meeting place for young poets, writers and revolutionaries. Katherine Tynan and the poet T.W. Rolleston were among the regular visitors. Tea was served by his sister Ellen, who was thought to resemble Christina Rossetti, with her eyes set wide under her brow and her large eyelids. It was here through O'Leary that Yeats met perhaps the most powerful figure in the whole revival, Douglas Hyde, the landed son of a Roscommon rector who 'had brought a new force into literature' with his exquisite translation of native Gaelic poetry into English in his 'Love Songs of Connacht'.

O'Leary believed that a political revolution would not succeed without a cultural revival. When his instinct told him one evening in the Contemporary Club that here was the great poet Ireland awaited, he determined at all costs to get young Yeats along to his evenings. He succeeded and in a short time the two had become close friends. Yeats was fascinated by this Irish patriot who rejected most of the nineteenth-century Irish poetry because it was bad literature. Propaganda had no interest for him. It was the awakening of the national soul that concerned him. O'Leary steered Yeats towards the poets who had translated from Irish, Callanan, Walsh, O'Curry, that he might devise a new rhythm that had not yet come into English. Above all he encouraged him to read the works of Sir Samuel Ferguson, who had put into verse the same sagas and tales that O'Grady had written in prose.

It was from this period on that a new quality creeps into Yeats's work. With his uncanny ear for rhythm he began to pick up metres that were not in the English tradition but which had grown out of the structure of verse in the Irish language. A long couplet of Ferguson with its gapped rhythms could give him a lead.

My bitter woe it is, love, that we are not far away,
In Cashel town, though the bare deal board were our marriage
    bed this day.

Or Callanan's:

My bed was the ground, my roof the greenwood above
And the wealth that I sought – one far kind glance from my love.

It was O'Leary's moral force that captivated Yeats. The old man would never abuse his English jailers, though he had an impaired digestion as a result of his treatment in prison and had to live mainly on milk and biscuits. 'Why should I complain?' he said, 'I was in the hands of my enemies.' And when a politician who had gone on hunger strike in Mullingar railed about his predicament, O'Leary's comment was that 'there are some things a man should not do to save a country, one is to cry in public'. He had long dismissed the Church as a possible ally in the fight for freedom and used to say, 'My religion is the old Persian one – to pull the bow and tell the truth.' He admired Parnell because 'of the man's character,' but would follow him only in so far as he went for Irish freedom and no more.

Through O'Leary's influence Yeats finally made contact with the two thousand-year-old culture of Gaelic Ireland which had lain almost unknown about him. He read Standish O'Grady's *History of Ireland* which recounted in sterling English for the first time the tales of Cuchulain and Deirdre, tales which belonged with the *Odyssey* and the *Nibelungenlied* and to the heroic literature of Europe.

It was John O'Leary who introduced Yeats to Maud Gonne. He was staying at Bedford Park at the time in June 1899 when she arrived, telling the poet that John O'Leary had sent her. To Yeats she seemed like a being from another world. Her complexion was 'like apple blossom . . . luminous like that of a blossom through which the light falls'. Yeats's sister Lolly didn't like the way she smiled on everyone 'with a royal smile', and his youngest sister Lily noticed disapprovingly that she was wearing slippers. But their brother was mesmerized by this statuesque girl who told them her name was Maud Gonne. She took Willie to dine that evening and they spent the following eight evenings together. Yeats couldn't get her out of his mind. He discovered that despite her voice – she spoke with a Dublin Castle voice and not in the easy-going Dublin drawl of the Yeats family – and manner, which suggested an aristocratic background, Maud Gonne was an Irish revolutionary. O'Leary had directed her energy to the cause of Ireland and she had become a legendary figure in the West, organizing the peasants to resist evictions, setting up soup kitchens and temporary camps for those who had been unhoused, and on one occasion putting weedkiller in an unpleasant bailiff's soup in an attempt to polish him off. Country people reached out to touch the hem of her coat as if to draw strength from her. She left Ireland for Paris, where she edited a propaganda magazine, *L'Irlande Libre*, which detailed British injustices in Ireland and which was sent free to French, English and American newspapers. She lectured in Paris, Amsterdam and Brussels, and her great beauty and histrionic ability drew large audiences wherever she went. On one of her revolutionary missions she had travelled to Moscow with secret documents sewn into the hem of her dress and a revolver in her bag. There she met Wickham Steed of the *Review of Reviews*, who described her as 'one of the most beautiful women in the world'.

Her early years had been spent in quite a different atmosphere. Her father had been brigade-major of the cavalry in Dublin, and she had grown up insulated from the life of ordinary people. It was said that Kitchener of Khartoum, not noted for his interest in the opposite sex, had proposed to her. But Maud had no ambitions for social success. She had turned away from a life of hunt balls and riding to hounds, and had decided to dedicate herself to the dispossessed. The combination of beauty, breeding and rebellion proved irresistible to Yeats. 'From this time the troubling of my life began,' he wrote shortly after meeting her. Though Maud obviously liked him, Yeats sensed a barrier between them. He was not to know till ten years later that she had another lover, Lucien Millevoye, a French journalist and politician by whom she had a child in 1891. No matter how long she would remain away on revolutionary activities, she always went back to Paris and her Lucien.

Driven nearly mad by her indifference, Yeats seized on every opportunity to plead his cause. Once he hurried to Dublin to confide that he had a dream that he had seen her and himself as brother and sister in the Arabian desert centuries before. Maud, who was a believer in the occult, was impressed by this, but now she told him that she would never marry him and that henceforth it would be a spiritual friendship between them.

When she changed flats (as she frequently did), Willie was her willing slave in transporting her numerous pets to the new premises. She had many birds, and he would walk behind her carrying the cages, loudly declaiming over the birdsong while her pet marmoset nestled at her neck. Yeats was not hostile to the birdsong (after all, did not Aengus, the Irish God of Love, have a halo of birds about his head?) but he had a decided dislike of the marmoset, whom Maud would use as a confidant, just as the poet was winning an argument, by talking to the clinging monkey as if it were a human being.

Together Maud and Willie experienced Blake-like visions. She would lie on a green couch in his room in Woburn Buildings surrounded by candlesticks and, with a bowl of water between them, would go into a trance. She never could decide whether these visions were transferred from Willie's mind to hers or whether they had come out of some shared subconscious.

He was to write plays and poems for her, make her the touchstone of his inspiration, but Maud would remain resolute in her refusal to become his lover. When he complained that she made life unbearable for him, she replied with a sweet smile, 'You are making beautiful poetry out of what you call your unhappiness and you are happy in that.'

Throughout his life he would write poetry to her. Even after his marriage her beauty and personality continued to haunt him. When she had become an almost skeleton-like figure, moving through the Dublin streets murmuring beneath her breath of revolution, she still could exert a magic influence over him. She is one of the three themes that continually re-surface through his collected poems; the other two being the affairs of his country and his confrontation with the inevitability of death.

Between 1887 and 1900 Yeats spent a great deal of his time in London. The capital of the Empire was to have an important influence on him. There he was to mingle with William Morris's Pre-Raphaelite group, and with The Rhymers Club, which he founded with Ernest Rhys and which included

Aubrey Beardsley, Ernest Dowson and Lionel Johnson as its members, and to make contact with his fellow countrymen Oscar Wilde and Bernard Shaw, who were beginning to make an impression on the London literary scene.

Oscar was kind to Yeats and encouraged him to maintain his Irish identity by telling him: 'We Irish are too poetical to be poets, we are a nation of brilliant failures. We are the greatest talkers since the Greeks.'

By an extraordinary coincidence Yeats and Shaw shared the same bill at the Comedy Theatre in June 1895. Yeats's one-act play *The Land of Heart's Desire* (his first dramatic piece) was to precede John Todhunter's full-length *A Comedy of Sighs* at the Comedy Theatre: but Todhunter's play failed and was replaced after its first week by Shaw's *Arms and the Man*. This was Shaw's first theatre success and he revelled in it with his Dublin flair for exhibitionistic wit, while Yeats each night strode up and down the back of the theatre enjoying his own play dressed in a black cape and wide-brimmed hat and at the same time torn between admiration and hate for his fellow Dubliner's play, because it caused him to have nightmares in which he was 'haunted by a sewing machine that clicked and shone but the incredible thing was that the machine smiled and smiled perpetually.'

William Morris attracted Yeats much more, and he made frequent visits to Kelmscott House, where he would eat supper on Sunday evenings and attend meetings. But though Morris wore a blue smock to show his identity with the working class, his philosophy was light years away from the folk-world Yeats had touched on. They soon broke over a religious argument, when at a public meeting Morris refused to allow Yeats to go on about his revolt of the soul against the dominance of science and the intellect.

Yeats's most important friend in this English period was Arthur Symons, who has never really got the credit he deserves as a critic. Alone among English critics (though George Moore had written on the French Impressionists and the Realist novelists) Symons was in touch with contemporary trends in French literature. He and Yeats found a mutual interest in the work of Stephen Mallarmé and Villier de L'Isle Adam, and it was through Symons's influence that Yeats managed to attend one of the few performances ever given of Villier's seminal play *Axel* in Paris. In February 1884 Yeats watched the play with Maud Gonne sitting beside him to translate the difficult passages, and noted:

The infinite is alone worth retaining, and the infinite is in the possession of the dead. Such appears to be the moral of this play. Seldom has utmost pessimism found a more magnificent expression.

Axel, with its origins in Rosicrucian beliefs, was to be a vital influence on Yeats's development, side by side with Mallarmé's dictum that

> to name an object is to do away with three-quarters of the enjoyment – to suggest it, to evoke it, that is what charms the imagination.

Yeats's interest in magic, Rosicrucianism and the Order of the Golden Dawn, which he had joined, was a search for something that he felt the scientific revolution had failed to provide, an understanding of the mystical side of human nature. He had long since discounted the idea that alchemy was concerned with turning common metal into gold and recognized that those medieval seekers after truth who had their origins in the philosophers of Alexandria were seeking a universal transportation of being into an imperishable substance. The Rosicrucian doctrines on which the Golden Dawn cult was based seemed to Yeats an ideal blend between the essential truths of Christianity and Paganism – the rose, symbol of beauty and pressed upon the cross of time, the Celtic Gods entwined with universal Deities.

> Far off most secret and inviolate rose
> Enfold me in my hour of hours.

Using the Rose because of its double meaning as a symbol of love, he hoped to penetrate beyond the brim of the real world.

But it was in 1897 that Yeats was to meet the person who was to have the greatest influence on his life. This was Lady Gregory, the widow of a former Colonial Governor of Ceylon, Sir William Gregory. She had come from a landed Galway family, the Persses, and as a young girl had reacted against the Philistine and puritan background of her family to find relief and release in literature and a natural sympathy with the people. After she had married Sir William Gregory (who was 62 while she was only 27), a new life began for her at Coole Mansion in Gort. This was a fine Georgian house built in extremely beautiful surroundings with seven woods and a number of lakes on the estate. The house was approached through an avenue of arching ilexes, and here for a number of years Lady Gregory led the life of a country lady. Sir William's duties had taken him round the world and she had been involved at one time in Egyptian politics, working for the release of nationalists who had sided against the government. She was thus, when Yeats met her, a young widow in the flower of her womanhood seeking an outlet for the intellectual power that had convinced her that some time or other she should write. Her first book had been a life of her husband, and she had had some literary success in London. In fact the Gregorys had a house in London and she had an entree to the top echelons of English society. Now back living in Coole, she was looking for some movement which would unite the genius of the native Irish people among whom she moved and the Anglo-Irish culture into which she had grown up. Quite fortuitously she was to meet Yeats in 1897. Edward Martyn, a landlord who lived at Tulira Castle near Coole, asked Yeats one afternoon whether he would care to come on a visit to his cousin Count de Basterot, whose villa lay on an inlet of the sea about six miles away at Duras. When they arrived Lady Gregory was having tea there. When Edward arrived with Yeats, it turned out that the Count wanted to have a talk with his cousin about some business matters which were private. Leaving the pair alone, Yeats and Lady Gregory went into the steward's office for a cup of tea. We can see the two of them: the poet with his raven black hair and intense dark eyes and olive skin sitting opposite this small demure lady with her quick mind and eager response to ideas. Did she fall in love with him then? Maybe. Many women had done before. When she found that his heart was already elsewhere, she was to work for him in recognition of his greatness as a poet and completely without jealousy.

Yeats told her how he had wanted a theatre in Ireland because politics and the Church had created listeners. The intellectual communion he wanted between writer and people could come in this way, as it could not through the novel or verse. Dublin was in the grip of the commercial theatre: English touring companies or local groups performing melodrama on popular national subjects; at best Boucicault with his ear for dialogue. But there was no intellectual commitment such as the theatre of Scandinavia had or the movements led by Lugné Poe and Antoine in Paris, and J.T. Grein and William Archer in London. His own play *The Countess Cathleen* was ready for production, he told her. He wanted to form a company in London to present it. Edward Martyn, in despair of getting his *The Heather Field* produced in an English-speaking milieu, had proposed a German production of his play.

Lady Gregory was thrilled. Here was her chance to work for 'the intellectual movement'. Tentatively she suggested putting on the plays in Ireland. Yeats would at first have dismissed the idea as unworkable. Some years before he had wanted to tour Ireland presenting Irish plays, but had been unable to get his project off the ground. But as Lady Gregory explained her plan to him, he, with his practical mind, could foresee possibilities. As wife of the former Governor of Ceylon she had friends in high places. During her travels and as hostess for Sir William in London she had met many who could help just the sort of project Yeats and Martyn wished to launch: Lord Dufferin, the Viceroy of India; Lord Ardilaun; the Duchess of St Alban's; the

Lord Chief Justice of Ireland, the Right Honourable Horace Plunkett; William Hartpole Lecky, the historian and MP, were some of the names she mentioned. Lady Gregory's plan was to hire a theatre in Dublin by public subscription to present the plays. She would subscribe the first £25 and other subscribers would be asked to guarantee £300 to enable the group to present a season of plays every year for three seasons. By the time Edward and his cousin emerged from their business affairs, Yeats had been converted to the scheme by Lady Gregory's enthusiasm and commonsense approach. The four of them went out to the lawn as the rain had cleared. It was one of those Irish days when the sun continually breaks through the rainclouds, and across the lonely inlet they could see the green-washed mountains changing colour under the drifting clouds. There Yeats explained what Augusta proposed to do. Edward agreed almost immediately and the Irish Literary Theatre was born.

The first performance of the Irish Literary Theatre was Yeats's *Countess Cathleen*, performed with an English cast at the Antient Concert Rooms in May 1899. In 1901, *Diarmuid and Grainne*, written by Yeats in collaboration with George Moore, was presented by Sir Frank Benson's company at the Gaiety Theatre. Then the success of a little folk play of Yeats's, *Cathleen Ni Houlihan*, performed by a company of Irish actors organized by the Fay brothers, pushed the idea of an Irish theatre a stage further. By great good fortune an English heiress, Miss Horniman, was interested in the theatre, and not at all uninterested in W.B. Yeats. One day, after a performance of the *Shadowy Waters*, when Yeats had come before the audience and made an impassioned speech in favour of freedom of ideas in theatre, Miss Horniman came up afterwards and said with a smile, 'I will give you a theatre.'

She made good her promise, hiring the architect and theatre lover Joseph Holloway to convert the Mechanics Institute, a former music hall in Abbey Street, in the centre of Dublin, into a theatre – the Abbey Theatre – with a full proscenium stage, a pit and balcony which would hold nearly 600 people.

So the Abbey Theatre opened in December 1904 with three one-act plays: *Spreading the News* by Lady Gregory, *On Baile's Strand* by Yeats, and *Riders to the Sea* by John Millington Synge. The plays were acted by the Fays' company. Synge was the important addition to the group. Yeats, sniffing around like a retriever for additions to his theatre trove, had spotted Synge some years before in a Paris hotel. Synge came from landed background – his family drew their wealth from lands in Galway – and had intended to become a concert pianist and composer. But when Yeats heard that Synge had studied the Irish language at Trinity College he immediately saw an opportunity to recruit an important figure to his movement. 'Give up Paris and go to the Aran Islands. Live there as one of the people themselves, express a life that has never found expression,' he had told Synge. In the few years between the meeting in Paris and the opening of the Abbey, Synge had taken his advice and found in the Aran Isles and the Gaelic-speaking West of Ireland a language untouched by nineteenth-century commercial usage and capable in its English expression of bringing a new melody and imagery into dramatic verse. His *Riders to the Sea* has been called the finest one-act play in the English language, and *The Playboy of the Western World* is in the classical repertoire of world theatre.

It was one of Yeats's proudest boasts that he could read a balance sheet at a glance – a gift acquired from his merchant forebears. He, Synge and Lady Gregory were an ideal combination to achieve what is rare enough in Irish life, the creation of an institution that would survive the death of its founders. Synge would die in a few years, and though Yeats was always ready to confront controversy if it was threatening his beloved Abbey, it was Lady Gregory's extraordinary tenacity that helped to make the theatre into one which had world recognition, with playwrights like himself, Synge, O'Casey, T.C. Murray, Lennox Robinson and Brian Friel, and actors like Barry Fitzgerald, F.J. McCormick, Cyril Cusack, Sarah Allgood, Maire O'Neill and Arthur Sinclair.

It was not too much to call Lady Gregory the Diaghilev of the Irish theatre. It is also possible that Yeats might never have achieved what he did without her help. She loaned him money over long periods in order to make it possible for him to survive as a poet and not have to work at things which would detract from his imaginative energy. She was a true Maecenas for him. A great deal of his composition at this period was achieved under her mothering influence at Coole. He would arrive at the mansion through the long avenue of arching ilexes and would be settled in upstairs by Lady Gregory. He was to discover there the Seven Woods, all with different names.

It was in such an atmosphere that Yeats's troubled temperament found itself at rest. The continuity, the sense of order, the decorum, steadied that side of him which might have gone askew with his magical practices and his preoccupation with fairy lore. Lady Gregory was a constant strength to him. Every day she had soup sent up to his rooms at intervals to make sure that his strength was kept up. Nobody was allowed to disturb the poet. His whole day was organized. When he came down for meals she would remain silent if he seemed too exhausted to converse, an heroic gesture in someone as anxious as she must have been for literary talk. He spent much of his time walking by the woods and the lake. 'I was to know later,' Yeats said, 'the edges of that lake better than any spot on earth, to know it in all the changes of the seasons, to find there always some new beauty.' Here he first saw the 'nine-and-fifty swans'. Augusta was probably in love with him, but she never allowed his lack of response to her love to interfere with what she felt was her duty to him as an artist. She was the rock to which he would cling during the storms of his life over the next nineteen years until he married, and even that marriage was partly arranged by Lady Gregory.

'I cannot realize the world without her,' he wrote once. 'She had been to me mother, friend, sister and brother. She brought to my wavering thoughts steadfast nobility – all night the thought of losing her is a conflagration in the rafters.'

Yeats is largely remembered as a poet, and it has become customary to denigrate his contribution to the drama. Yet he was to anticipate in his use of total theatre – dance, music, chorus, verse and mask – many of the developments that were to take place in the Sixties, when the impact of television and cinema would make it imperative for a theatre audience to undergo an experience which would be unique to live drama. In fact the English critic Katherine Worth has gone so far as to say:

> In the last twenty years since *Waiting for Godot* first appeared the entire European theatre has expressed the revolution which Yeats carried through singlehandedly in Dublin in the first two decades of the century. He carved out of nothing the form the theatre at large would not see for almost fifty years.

That Beckett himself is in agreement with this statement is clear from something he wrote when he was asked to contribute a note to a Bernard Shaw Centenary programme.

> I wouldn't suggest that GBS is not a great playwright, whatever that is when it's at home. What I would do is give the whole unupsettable apple-cart for a sup of *The Hawk's Well*.

Katherine Worth points out that though we have become accustomed to the ideas of Artaud and Grotowski and Peter Brooke's 'empty spaces' we forget how much Yeats anticipated the use of silence and stillness to create dramatic effect on the stage. His ideal was Maeterlinck's recipe: 'An old man sitting in his armchair waiting patiently with his lamp beside him.'

Yeats early spotted the value of chorus, music and gesture in enabling the playwright to dispense with the conventions of the theatre. With the rattle of a drum and a choral chant, a character could be moved back and forward in time. Through the heightened effect of verse, hints of the unreal world beyond consciousness could be suggested to an audience. Through the use of a mask it might be possible to achieve an effect with an audience that would jolt them out of conventional perceptions of reality.

He was the first dramatist to recognize the possibilities of the Japanese Noh form, with its ritual blend of dance, drama, music and chorus. Though he only once or twice achieved the true impact of the form, which does not lead to catharsis in the Western sense, but to Yügen, an emotion connected with the concept of Zen Buddhism and reincarnation, nevertheless plays like *The Hawk's Well*, *The Only Jealousy of Emer* and *The Dreaming of the Bones* have a specifically modern impact.

He was also ahead of his time in lighting and design. Gordon Craig, the inventor of modern design, once told the author that nothing in his life gave him more pleasure than Yeats's praise for his design for *Acis and Galatea*. Yeats himself was dazzled by Craig's purple backcloth for *Dido and Aneas* that 'made them seem wandering on the edge of eternity'. He and Craig together designed a set of screens on wheels which could be arranged to represent various lighting designs and which were used in the Abbey before the first war. Altogether it is nonsense to dismiss Yeats as a great poet, as some academics do, who tried but failed to write good plays. Lennox Robinson, that most skilful of dramatic craftsmen, has said:

> Anyone who can read Yeats's plays and not say he is a dramatist is a fool . . . In play after play from the *Countess Cathleen* on down the years he has proved his mastery over his instrument, testing it, developing it, learning from it and teaching it to obey.

A major attraction of the theatre for Yeats was that he believed that through his plays he could insinuate images into the popular consciousness, through 'a nationwide multiform reverie, every mind passing through a stream of suggestion and all streams acting and reacting upon one another no matter how distant the mind or dumb the lips.'

That explains why he continually turned to drama to express himself, and how with his uncanny instinct he could use a modernist composer like George Antheil to compose the music for *Fighting the Waves* and have the young Ninette de Valois arrange the choreography. It was precisely because he was so modern in his concept of what the threatre might become that it has taken until now to recognize his importance as a dramatist.

Of course Maud Gonne's rejection continued to obsess him. But by now another beautiful and talented Englishwoman, who was well-read and could communicate with him as an intellectual equal, had become his lover. This was Olivia Shakespear, the wife of an elderly solicitor, who had been introduced to Yeats by her cousin Lionel Johnson. In his letters to Olivia Shakespear, written over forty years, is to be found much evidence of his intellectual growth and an intimate account of the expansion of the inner life of his imagination.

Not everyone had hailed the emergence of the Abbey Theatre with unrestrained enthusiasm. Young James Joyce, lately qualified in the University College, had looked on the whole Irish Literary Renaissance with suspicion. He referred to Yeats and Lady Gregory's work as 'dwarf drama' and lampooned her ladyship with limericks. On one occasion when he met Yeats for tea he imperiously enquired about the poet's age and having been told it, replied 'I thought as much. I met you too late. You are too old'.

But Yeats did not allow himself to be put off by this youthful arrogance and he arranged introductions for Joyce with leading English publishers which were helpful to him. Later he was to support the publication of Joyce's *A Portrait of the Artist as a Young Man*, and he was among the first to recognize Joyce's *Ulysses* as a work of genius.

But being a genius in Dublin at that time was not easy. There were too many people looking for the post, without being prepared to put their shoulder to the wheel to achieve it.

When the Abbey presented John Millington Synge's *The Playboy of the Western World* in January 1907 there were riots in the auditorium. The mob had taken as a libel what was in fact a hymn to the majesty of language often used unconsciously by Irishmen, simply because the leading character, Christy Mahon, in a fit of fury has slain his tyrannical Da, and becomes as a result a Don Juaneen to the girls of a distant barony who are dazzled by any lad who would perpetrate such a fearful deed. However the directors, Yeats, Lady Gregory and Synge, stood firm and refused to take the play off. Yeats even faced the mob in an open debate. 'I never witnessed a human being fight as Yeats did that night,' remembered Mary Colum, the poet's wife, 'or knew another with such weapons in his armoury for controversy.'

Yeats's physical presence helped on the stage. The tall figure with the high cheekbones, bronzed face, black hair thrown back and the resonant commanding voice was not easy to defy. But it was also his courage and his sense of savage indignation in the tradition of Swift that were to bring him through many such battles when he entered the public arena as a controversial figure.

In April 1907 Yeats, Lady Gregory and her son Robert went to stay in

Venice at Lady Layard's palazzo, Ca Capello. There he found some peace from the riotous Dublin scene, and Lady Gregory arranged for him to have his own writing room where he could look out on the dancing light that seemed to hover on the wave tops as the gondolas drifted by. Together he and Lady Gregory visited Florence, Urbino, Ferrara and Ravenna. Duke Guidobaldo's reign at Urbino and the primacy of the poet and artist under his regime, commemorated by Castiglione in his book *The Courtier*, fascinated Yeats. In moods of despair he had often longed to have been part of such an advanced society. From Castiglione he took much of his thinking on the evolution of the imaginative arts and was delighted with the word *Sprezzatura*, as applied to the perfect courtier, capturing for Yeats the blend of nonchalance and style allied with insight and imagination which he felt was necessary for the complete human personality.

After John O'Leary's death in 1907, Yeats began to feel increasingly the nature of the conflict between the artist and those who were fashioning society without taking into account the functions of the imagination in the community's life. He had returned to Ireland because he believed that the people might find a unity that would enable artist and politician to influence one another. Now it seemed that materialism had weakened many of the ideals he had hoped to see realized in the national life. The mustering of the Philistines had begun with the 'Playboy' riots. Then Hugh Lane (Lady Gregory's nephew) had offered his collection of French Impressionist paintings (the largest outside the Luxembourg) to the Modern Art Gallery in Dublin on condition that they were properly housed. Yeats's poem, 'To a Wealthy Man Who Promised a Second Subscription to the Dublin Municipal Gallery if it Were Proved the People Wanted Pictures', was addressed to a well-known Dublin merchant who was not noted for his interest in the arts. Then, in 'To a Shade', written at Parnell's grave, he lashed out at Lord Ardilaun, one of the Guinness brewing family, for his failure to appreciate the work of a man who, like Parnell, was of the 'passionate serving kind'.

Lane, rebuffed, left the portraits to the National Gallery in London. Later, however, he revoked his will and bequeathed his collection to the Dublin gallery. Shortly afterwards he was drowned in the *Lusitania*. The codicil of the will had not been properly witnessed, however, and the ownership of the paintings is still a subject of controversy between the Irish and the English governments.

But at Easter 1916 Yeats was to discover that the unselfish serving spirit of the race had not been totally submerged in 'paudeen's pence'. A group of professors, schoolteachers, clerks and working men took over the General Post Office in the centre of Dublin (the Rebellion was intended to be nationwide, but poor organization had confined it to the metropolis) and declared an Irish Republic. They demanded that England should withdraw and leave Irishmen to govern themselves. Their belief was that constitutional means had failed and that it was only through physical force that England would let go her grip on the country.

Yeats was on familiar terms with a number of the leaders. Patrick Pearse, the Commander-in-Chief of the rebels, had actually only a short while before the insurrection directed his own plays at the Abbey with masks created by his brother Willie, who, along with Patrick, was executed after the insurrection. During the 'Playboy' riots Pearse had strongly defended Yeats, holding him to be the greatest living Irish poet and maintaining that Synge's work, whatever its flaws, was a 'gníomh' ('a deed'). Thomas MacDonagh, another of the executed leaders, was a sensitive poet who had published a book on English metres in Irish verse, while Joseph Plunkett, also a poet, had edited *The Irish Review*, which Yeats wrote for along with AE and Edward Martyn.

By a ferocious irony, Maud Gonne's husband John MacBride (who had fought as a major for the Boers against England), though not officially accredited to the insurrectionary forces, turned up at the General Post Office to take part in the Rising. To have escaped death after one Rebellion against England seems to have been regarded by the authorities as fair enough, but now he was regarded as having exceeded the limit. So after this second foray MacBride was executed along with the other leaders.

The mood of the country was against the rebels at the time, but some butchery by the occupying forces and the subsequent execution of seventeen of the leaders turned the population in favour of the rebels. By 1918 Sinn Fein, as the rebel party had become known, had gained an overwhelming majority in the general election. They refused to take their places in Parliament but created their own phantom one in Dublin. This sat regularly in secret, created law courts, authorized tax collections and organized labour relations, with the agreeable result that the British administration was to disintegrate and become a farce.

The elected Sinn Feiners claimed to have a mandate to support an army, and the IRA initiated a campaign of urban guerilla warfare and rural flying columns to create the first successful resistance to colonial rule – an example which would be followed by numerous other countries in the decolonization process which took place after the Second World War.

The Anglo-Irish war was a particularly bitter one. Yeats, 'a nationalist of the old school of O'Leary' as he liked to describe himself, sided with Sinn Fein. As early as 1918 he had written to Lord Haldene, a member of the cabinet, warning of the consequences if Conscription was imposed on Ireland.

I was ordering some coal yesterday and I said I shall be in such and such a house for the next four months. The man at the counter, a stranger to me, muttered: 'Who in Ireland can say where he will be in four months?' Another man almost a stranger used nearly those very words to me some weeks ago. There is a danger of a popular hysteria that may go to any height or any whither. There is a return to that sense of crisis which followed the Rising.

After the death of Kevin Barry (an eighteen-year-old medical student hanged for his Republican activities in 1920) Yeats addressed the Oxford Union on the motion: 'This house has no confidence in the Irish policy of the government.' He electrified the students by leaving the platform and walking up and down among the audience waving his fists as he unleashed a tirade against the government's misdeeds in Ireland. The motion was passed by an overwhelming majority amid scenes of 'unexampled enthusiasm'.

Meanwhile he had not relinquished his love for Maud Gonne. After her husband's execution he had gone over to Normandy, where she was living, to set about the process of re-wooing. Incredibly, after she had refused him once more he turned this time to her daughter, Iseult. Iseult was amused and perhaps startled but predictably refused him.

How could she mate with fifty years that was so wildly bred,
Let the caged bird and the caged bird mate, and the wild bird mate in the wild.

Now he decided to marry George Hyde-Lees, whom he had first met at Stone Cottage when he was staying there with Ezra Pound. She was 32, young, tall, good-looking, highly intelligent and also rich. Sisters are often a good judge of a new sister-in-law, and after their marriage Lily Yeats, on meeting George and Willie together for the first time, thought that she never saw 'Willie looking so well'. It was some time after their marriage that his wife discovered that she could do spirit writing, which was a bonus for Yeats. Though she was marrying one of the most difficult men in the world to manage, the relationship worked like a dream. She seemed to have some instinct into Yeats's inner needs, infinite patience and a belief in his privacy as a poet. So much so that she may have given too much of herself and after his death not had the happiness she otherwise might have enjoyed.

The pair lived for a while after their marrage in a restored Norman tower at Ballylee near Coole. It was to be a symbol for Yeats, the poet's tower.

> I the poet William Yeats
> With old mill boards and sea-green slates
> And smithy work from the Gort forge
> Restore this tower for my wife George
> And up here these characters remain
> When all is ruin once again.

Of course the Dublin wits had to say that he had married his wife to find a rhyme for 'forge' – but then Dublin wits do say many things.

In 1921, after a truce between Sinn Fein and the English Government, the British Administration moved out of Ireland. After a counter-revolution and a civil war a new state had been set up by the more conservative elements of Sinn Fein. There was now a Parliament (Dáil) and Senate (Seanad). Yeats was chosen as one of the new Senators – a tribute to his nationalist loyalties and to his constant participation in the political affairs of his country. He took his duties as a Senator seriously. He had himself appointed head of the committee to draw up a new design for the Irish coinage and after conducting a competition selected the most beautiful designs for the coins. He was less successful, however, in his efforts to reform the lawyers' garb. The judges, who wanted to hold on to their wigs and gowns, were not at all enthusiastic when Yeats produced drawings of elegant Venetian robes sketched by his friend Ricketts. Bar and Bench managed to retain a similar garb to that of their English counterparts.

It was dangerous being a Senator at that time. Thirty-seven homes of Senators were burnt one day during the Civil War in January 1922. The arsonists were those who had opposed the Treaty. Yeats had a bodyguard but he pooh-poohed the danger. His fellow Senator and poet Oliver St John Gogarty was less fortunate. One evening as Gogarty was having his bath he felt a revolver pressed in the back of his neck. It was a pair of anti-Treaty men, who took him out to a boathouse near Island Bridge on the outskirts of the city and on the River Liffey where he was to be held as a hostage against the execution of an anti-Treaty man in Dundalk. Pleading a natural necessity, Gogarty slipped his arms out of a coat and plunged into the foaming Liffey forty feet below. Up to his neck in the broiling flood he vowed if he survived to present two swans to the Liffey.

This vow delighted Yeats and may have been one of the reasons why he put the seventeen Gogarty poems into his *Oxford Book of Modern Verse* fifteen years later.

Gogarty's poetry fits the incident, a gay, stoical – no, I will not withhold the word – heroic song – and I think him one of the great lyric poets of the age.

Yeats of course had to be present at the presentation of the swans to the Liffey, a ceremony which he conducted with great panache. 'It would be terrible, Gogarty, if a vow was to be unfulfilled,' he intoned, as the swans refused to budge from their box. Gogarty was red in the face trying to get the birds out of the box and eventually gave them a hefty kick with his left foot, whereupon they flew up the river like a pair of torpedoes as Yeats continued his chant. He was now 'the smiling public man'. Joseph Hone, his first biographer, has recalled that:

> The Senators of the group often sought his advice on practical matters and one of them said 'Yeats would have made an admirable banker' and another 'a great lawyer was lost in the poet'.

Of course his new role caused the usual Dublin remarks.

'Yeats is getting so aristocratic he is evicting imaginary tenants,' Gogarty told a friend one day. And later on, when the poet had the Steinach operation to renew his sexual powers, Gogarty remarked:

> Yeats is in his post-prostatic period of prose. He is writing a new play called 'The Dreaming of the Stones'.

Yeats had expanded his sexual awareness considerably, and on learning that his friend Lady Dorothy Wellesley probably had Sapphic tastes he was not in the least put out. On the contrary the idea excited him:

> My dear, my dear – when you crossed the room with that boyish movement, it was no man who looked at you, it was the woman in me. It seems that I can make a women express herself as never before. I have looked out of her eyes. I have shared her desire.

In 1923 Yeats was awarded the Nobel Prize for Literature. The following evening he gave a celebratory dinner in the Shelbourne Hotel and was much gratified to receive during the meal a telegram from James Joyce congratulating him on the award. He received the Diploma and Medal in the splendid hall of the Swedish Academy. Back in Dublin on the whole there was much rejoicing, but the usual cautionary tales had already begun to circulate. One of the best was the account by Bertie Smyllie, the Editor of the *Irish Times*.

I think I was the first person, certainly the first person in this country, to know that Yeats had won the Nobel Prize. I was on duty at the *Irish Times* office that night, when the message came over the Creed machine to say that for the first time an Irish poet had won the prize, which amounted to quite a considerable sum, I think between seven and eight thousand pounds. I was rather friendly with Yeats at the time, and it was fairly late in the evening, getting on to eleven o'clock I suppose, and I rang him up at his house, hoping that he didn't know the news. He came to the phone himself – he didn't know the news. I said, 'Mr Yeats, I've got very good news for you; a very great honour has been conferred upon you,' and I was rather enthusiastic and gushing at the time, and I said, 'This is a great honour not only for you but for the country,' and I could tell he was getting slightly impatient to know what it was all about, so I said, 'You've been awarded the Nobel Prize, a very great honour to you and a very great honour to Ireland,' and to my amazement the only question he asked was, 'How much, Smyllie, how much is it?'

Yeats's Pollexfen and Middleton blood was never far from the surface. A while before, when he had sent money to his father in New York to help out, the old man had replied with an acute comment.

It was like a Yeats to send money and make no fuss about it. It was like a Pollexfen to have the money to send.

His public activity was now intense. In the Abbey, where he had succeeded in arranging that his theatre would become the first to be State subsidised in the English-speaking world, he dominated the board, a gift he felt he inherited from his Middleton ancestors. Lennox Robinson, a fellow member of the Abbey board, has recalled how Yeats's presence 'stiffened a directors meeting'.

He could understand and cross-examine an auditor. Kind by nature he could be as pitiless as Lady Gregory.

When the mob turned to try to break up the theatre in the first week of O'Casey's *Plough and the Stars* (as they had done with Synge's *Playboy of the Western World*), Yeats was at the front of the stage fearlessly facing them like a Roman emperor. The mob had become increasingly violent. As one of them tried to climb on the stage to get at the actors, Barry Fitzgerald, who was playing Fluther Good, knocked the intruder back into the audience with a punch on the jaw. Then the curtain was temporarily lowered. Gabriel Fallon, who was in the cast that night told me:

> Yeats loved every minute of it. He was in his element. 'I am sending for the police, Fallon,' he said, 'and this time it will be their *own* police.'

(This was a reference to the fact that when the police had been called at the *Playboy* riots, Yeats had been pilloried because, it was alleged, he had called in English constabulary to deal with Irishmen.)

Fallon never forgot how Yeats, like a general directing his troops, turned to the stage director and said: 'Don't raise the curtain till I say so.'

Then, listening with his ear close to the curtain, like a fox listening in a covert, he judged the exact moment when the tumult subsided and with an imperious wave of his arm had the curtain raised instantly. Then he faced the audience with, as Fallon said, 'every gesture, every phrase, every inflection geared to subdue an angry mob.'

In the Senate he worked very hard, involving himself in various issues, perhaps remembering Castiglione's admonition that a poet should take part in public affairs. He devoted considerable energy towards having a number of bills put through the Upper House, which were to have their effect later on when the new State began to get into gear.

Now he was entering the last period of his writing. He had become fascinated with Plotinus and wanted to unite the intellect of Berkeley, Swift and Burke with his own imaginative discoveries and through the blend perhaps bring forth something new. He sought to express himself in geometrical terms, and he began to work on *A Vision*, to give an exposition 'of the twenty-eight typical incarnations or phases of the moon,' after which a 'cone or gyre was drawn, expressive of the soul's judgement after death'. His first biographer, Joseph Hone (who was also the biographer of Berkeley), considers that in *A Vision* 'the Yeatsian Anschaung condescended to mathematical formulae'.

He had frequent bursts of ill health, but he could usually find an imaginative means of dealing with them. One day his doctor came to him with a letter which contained what amounted to a death sentence. A Spanish colleague had written a report on Yeats's condition, couched in quaint medical jargon, including the comment: 'We have here an antique cardio sclerotic of advanced years.'

The doctor tried to withhold the letter from Yeats at first, but the poet insisted on hearing the truth.

'It is my letter and I must see it.'

As he read it he rolled the word cardio sclerotic lovingly on his tongue. He looked up, his great shock of white hair tumbling over his bronzed features.

'You know I'd rather be called cardio sclerotic than Lord of Lower Egypt.'

In 1932 he founded with Shaw the Irish Academy of Letters to prevent what he felt were intrusions on the liberty of the writer in Ireland by right-wing and pious organizations. He included Frank O'Connor, Sean Ó Faoláin, Liam O'Flaherty and others among the invitees and was charmed when T.E. Lawrence wrote saying how much he appreciated being invited to become an associate member.

In 1933 the Clarendon Press asked Yeats to compile the *Oxford Book of Modern Verse*. Yeats set about the task enthusiastically and produced one of the best selling poetry anthologies of all time. It was eccentric in its taste and, while it may have omitted certain writers who in retrospect should have had more prominence, what Yeats had brought to the surface may have been of more value. The introduction contained his summing-up of the modern movement in verse.

> Eliot has produced his great effect upon his generation because he has described men and women that get out of bed or into it from mere habit; in describing this life that has lost heart his own heart seems grey, cold, dry. He is an Alexander Pope, working without apparent imagination, producing his effects by a rejection of all rhythms and metaphors used by the more popular romantics rather than by the discovery of his own, this rejection giving his work an unexaggerated plainness that has the effect of novelty. He has the rhythmical flatness of *The Essay on Man* – despite Miss Sitwell's advocacy I see Pope as Blake and Keats saw him – later, in 'The Waste Land', amid much that is moving in symbol and imagery there is much monotony of accent:

> > When lovely woman stoops to folly and
> > Paces about her room again, alone,
> > She smooths her hair with automatic hand
> > And puts a record on the gramophone.

> I was affected, as I am by these lines, when I saw for the first time a painting by Manet. I longed for the vivid colour and light of Rousseau and Courbet, I could not endure the grey middletint – and even today Manet gives me an incomplete pleasure; he had left the procession.

He admired 'Day Lewis, Madge and MacNeice' because

> They are modern to the character of their intellectual passion. No matter
> how great a reformer's energy a still greater is required to face, all
> activities expended in vain, the unreformed. 'God,' said an old
> countrywoman, 'smiles alike when regarding the good and condemning
> the lost.' MacNeice, the anti-Communist, expecting some descent of
> barbarism next turn of the wheel, contemplates the modern world with
> even greater horror than the communist Day Lewis, although with less
> lyrical beauty. More often I cannot tell whether the poet is communist
> or anti-communist. On what side is Madge? Indeed I know of no school
> where the poets so closely resemble each other. Spender has said that
> the poetry of belief must supercede that of personality, and it is perhaps
> a belief shared that has created their intensity, their resemblance; but
> this belief is not political. I would if I could have dealt at some length
> with George Barker, who, like MacNeice, Auden, Day Lewis, handled
> their traditional metres with a new freedom – vers libre lost much of its
> vogue some years ago – but has not their social passion, their sense of
> suffering.

He, however, only included seven of Eliot's poems, four from Auden, left out
Wilfred Owen altogether and put in seventeen of Gogarty's. This could not be
considered a balanced assessment. His most eccentric contribution was to take
Pater's famous preface to *The Renaissance* and extract the passage on Leonardo,
allegedly written in prose, and set it down here in verse form.

Perhaps the very success of Yeats's *Oxford Book of Modern Verse* was the
reason why some who had been wrongfully excluded reacted so violently.
Lord Alfred Douglas sent Yeats a telegram (with copies to the leading
newspapers and leading literary figures):

> Your omission of my work from the absurdly named Oxford Book of
> Modern Verse is exactly typical of the attitude of the minor to the major
> poet. For example Thomas Moore, the Yeats of the nineteenth century,
> would undoubtedly have excluded Keats and Shelley from any anthology
> he had compiled. But why drag in Oxford. Would not Shoneen Irish be
> more correct description?

Yeats was undoubtedly wrong about Wilfred Owen, whom he considered
'unworthy of the poet's corner of a country newspaper'.

But it was hard to please everyone. An enraged English schoolmaster wrote to him abusing him for saying nothing in his introduction about Rupert Brooke, who was 'the truest and, if he had lived, unquestionably would have been the finest poet ever produced by England', and confessing fury because he had included the 'senseless twaddle' of Auden, Day Lewis and the others.

Yeats, too, from what he wrote in his introduction about Gerald Manley Hopkins, seems either to have misjudged what the Jesuit poet was trying to do or to have failed to understand the structural rules on which stressed metres are based. He was not at any rate particularly sympathetic towards Hopkins, whom he once referred to in speaking to Oliver Edwards, the professor and critic as 'that inherent absurdity, a religious Englishman'.

Yeats's last poems are an exploration of his past and a last prodigious effort to probe the mystery of the separation of flesh and spirit. He was active to the end. In 1938 in the Hotel Carlton he had written *The Herne's Egg*, in the author's view the most powerful of all his plays. It tells the story of two factions fighting over a Virgin Priestess, Attracta, who is impregnated by a God. It seems to be Yeats's comment on the futility of organized religions. In the end all that is brought forth is a donkey.

> ATTRACTA: I thought that I
> Could give a human form to Congal,
> But now he must be born a donkey.

> CORNEY: All that trouble and nothing to show for it.
> Nothing but just another donkey.

It was said that he was murmuring poetry on his lips as he slid into unconsciousness. He died at Cap D'Ail in the South of France on Saturday 28 January 1939. A while before he had written to Ethel Mannin:

> All men with subjective natures move towards the possible ecstasy, all with objective natures towards a possible wisdom. When all the sensuous images are dissolved we meet true death. Painters of the Zen school of Japanese Buddhism have the idea of the concordance of achievement and death, and connect both with what they call poverty. To explain poverty they point to those paintings where they have suggested peace and loneliness by some single object or by a few strokes of the brush.

He was buried at the nearby cemetery of Roquebrune. There his remains lay until after the war, when they were brought back to Ireland on the Irish

Government Corvette *Macha*. Maud Gonne was still alive and it is difficult to imagine that she had not something to do with the return of Yeats's body to his native land, as her son Seán had become Minister of Foreign Affairs in the new government.

He is buried, as he wished, at Drumcliff:

> In Drumcliff churchyard Yeats is laid.
> An ancestor was rector there
> Long years ago, a church stands near,
> By the road an ancient cross.
> No marble, no conventional phrase;
> On limestone quarried near the spot,
> By his command these words are cut:
>
> Cast a cold eye
> On life, on death.
> Horseman, pass by!

These last three lines are inscribed on his gravestone.

ULICK O'CONNOR

Poetry

1883–1889

*F*or this first selection of Yeats's poetry, I have chosen from three books: *Crossways* (1889), *The Rose* (1893) and *The Wind Among the Reeds* (1899).

There are many beautiful poems in these three books, but I have tried to bring to the reader those which particularly illustrate the evolving mind of the poet and, may I say also, those which please me most. Yeats's early poems don't belong entirely to the style he was working towards; there is a leap forward, however, in *The Rose*, when he begins to see the rose as a symbol of love that could mean two things at once, which shows the influence of the symbolist beliefs of Mallarmé. This book contains one of the most beautiful love poems in any language, 'When you are Old', written for Maud Gonne. There is a definite similarity between it and Ronsard's 'Quand vous serez bien vieille', but Yeats claims that he had not read the French poet before he wrote his own poem. The similarities at least in the first four lines are so remarkable, however, that it seems that Yeats must in some way, even unknown to himself, have been influenced by the Ronsard poem.

At the end of *The Rose* Yeats makes it clear that he identifies now with Ireland.

> Know, that I would accounted be
> True brother of a company
> That sang, to sweeten Ireland's wrong,
> Ballad and story, rann and song,
> Nor be I any less of them,
> Because the red-rose-bordered hem
> Of her, whose history began
> Before God made the angelic clan,
> Trails all about the written page,
> When Time began to rant and rage.

Though there are clearly attempts early on in his work to loose himself from the shackles of the English iambic, it is not until the third book that the halting rhythm underlying Gaelic verse begins to creep in with poems like 'He Wishes for the Cloths of Heaven' and 'He bids his Beloved be at Peace'. In the 'Song of Wandering Aengus' the last three lines rove off into splendid counterpoint that holds together only because the poet has stitched it, with his ear close to the initial melody.

THE STOLEN CHILD

There is a belief in the Irish countryside that sometimes children are stolen by the fairies and taken off to live in Fairyland, and that in the child's place a changeling is left. It was this theme which Yeats took for the first poem in his collected poems, published in 1938.

> Where dips the rocky highland
> Of Sleuth Wood in the lake,
> There lies a leafy island
> Where flapping herons wake
> The drowsy water-rats;
> There we've hid our faery vats,
> Full of berries
> And of reddest stolen cherries.
> *Come away, O human child!*
> *To the waters and the wild*
> *With a faery, hand in hand,*
> *For the world's more full of weeping than you*
>   *can understand.*
>
> Where the wave of moonlight glosses
> The dim grey sands with light,
> Far off by furthest Rosses
> We foot it all the night,
> Weaving olden dances,
> Mingling hands and mingling glances
> Till the moon has taken flight;

To and fro we leap
And chase the frothy bubbles,
While the world is full of troubles
And is anxious in its sleep.
Come away, O human child!
To the waters and the wild
With a faery, hand in hand,
For the world's more full of weeping than you
*   can understand.*

Where the wandering water gushes
From the hills above Glen-Car,
In pools among the rushes
That scarce could bathe a star;
We seek for slumbering trout
And whispering in their ears
Give them unquiet dreams;
Leaning softly out
From ferns that drop their tears
Over the young streams.
Come away, O human child!
To the waters and the wild
With a faery, hand in hand,
For the world's more full of weeping than you
*   can understand.*

Away with us he's going,
The solemn-eyed:
He'll hear no more the lowing
Of the calves on the warm hillside
Or the kettle on the hob
Sing peace into his breast,
Or see the brown mice bob
Round and round the oatmeal-chest.
For he comes, the human child,
To the waters and the wild
With a faery, hand in hand,
From a world more full of weeping than he
*   can understand.*

DOWN BY THE SALLEY GARDENS

One day when my nanny was scrubbing my fingernails, I started to sing 'Down by the Salley Gardens'. She was from County Tyrone in Ulster, and when she remarked, 'That's a come-all-ye', I indignantly replied that it was by the poet Yeats. (A 'come-all-ye' means a ballad of the type sung at fairs and markets, and is always introduced by a first line, 'Come all ye noble people and listen to my song').

But in fact nanny was right. 'The Salley Gardens' is an old folk song which Yeats altered but slightly to make it his own. Such is the alchemy of the poet that that alteration has made it into a wonderful lyric.

> Down by the salley gardens my love and I did meet;
> She passed the salley gardens with little snow-white feet.
> She bid me take love easy, as the leaves grow on the tree;
> But I, being young and foolish, with her would not agree.
> In a field by the river my love and I did stand,
> And on my leaning shoulder she laid her snow-white hand.
> She bid me take life easy, as the grass grows on the weirs;
> But I was young and foolish, and now am full of tears.

TO THE ROSE UPON THE ROOD OF TIME (1893)

In the symbol of the rose Yeats hoped to find the Ireland that he believed the poetic imagination might some day help to realize itself. The Cuchulain referred to in the poem is the heroic figure of the Irish sagas – the equivalent of Ulysses or Siegfried – whose deeds are recorded in the *Táin*, while Fergus was the son of Fionn Mac Cumhaill, the leader of the Fianna, a sort of early version of the Knights of the Round Table for whom Fergus was bard.

> Red Rose, proud Rose, sad Rose of all my days!
> Come near me, while I sing the ancient ways:
> Cuchulain battling with the bitter tide;
> The Druid, grey, wood-nurtured, quiet-eyed,
> Who cast round Fergus dreams, and ruin untold;
> And thine own sadness, whereof stars, grown old
> In dancing silver-sandalled on the sea,
> Sing in their high and lonely melody.
> Come near, that no more blinded by man's fate,

I find under the boughs of love and hate,
In all poor foolish things that live a day,
Eternal beauty wandering on her way.

Come near, come near, come near – Ah, leave me still
A little space for the rose-breath to fill!
Lest I no more hear common things that crave;
The weak worm hiding down in its small cave,
The field-mouse running by me in the grass,
And heavy mortal hopes that toil and pass;
But seek alone to hear the strange things said
By God to the bright hearts of those long dead,
And learn to chaunt a tongue men do not know.
Come near; I would, before my time to go,
Sing of old Eire and the ancient ways:
Red Rose, proud Rose, sad Rose of all my days.

THE ROSE OF THE WORLD

Here Yeats compares the Trojan War, fought over a woman, with the Irish theme of the Sons of Usna who were destroyed by King Connor of Ulster because their brother Naoise had eloped with Deirdre, the King's ward.

Who dreamed that beauty passes like a dream?
For these red lips, with all their mournful pride,
Mournful that no new wonder may betide,
Troy passed away in one high funeral gleam,
And Usna's children died.

We and the labouring world are passing by:
Amid men's souls, that waver and give place
Like the pale waters in their wintry race,
Under the passing stars, foam of the sky,
Lives on this lonely face.

Bow down, archangels, in your dim abode:
Before you were, or any hearts to beat,
Weary and kind one lingered by His seat;
He made the world to be a grassy road
Before her wandering feet.

THE LAKE ISLE OF INNISFREE

This is Yeats's best known poem and perhaps because of its popularity he came to dislike it somewhat and was inclined to be put out if it was mentioned to him. He has described himself how one day, as a young man lonely for Sligo, he was walking in a London street when he noticed in the window of a shop a little ball hopping up and down on top of an artificial fountain. In a Proustian flash his mind returned to the West of Ireland and Lough Gill on which there is a small island, Innisfree, a few hundred yards from the shore. In this way the poem came about. In 'Reveries of Childhood' Yeats has recorded how Mary Battle, his uncle's servant, thought that the young poet, in going out to spend a night on the Isle of Innisfree in search of poetic inspiration, was on a somewhat different mission which she archly suggested was connected with a certain young lady.

In many ways this is an astonishing poem which no one else but Yeats could have got away with. 'Nine bean-rows' and 'cricket sings' and 'purple glow' are phrases that should spell disaster for any poet. But Yeats, with a poet's song always in his ear, was able to rescue the banal and turn it so that it would form part of what this poem is – lasting literature.

> I will arise and go now, and go to Innisfree,
> And a small cabin build there, of clay and wattles made:
> Nine bean-rows will I have there, a hive for the honey-bee,
> And live alone in the bee-loud glade.
>
> And I shall have some peace there, for peace comes dropping slow,
> Dropping from the veils of the morning to where the cricket sings;
> There midnight's all a glimmer, and noon a purple glow,
> And evening full of the linnet's wings.
>
> I will arise and go now, for always night and day
> I hear lake water lapping with low sounds by the shore;
> While I stand on the roadway, or on the pavements grey,
> I hear it in the deep heart's core.

WHEN YOU ARE OLD

This is Maud Gonne's poem.

When you are old and grey and full of sleep,
And nodding by the fire, take down this book,
And slowly read, and dream of the soft look
Your eyes had once, and of their shadows deep;

How many loved your moments of glad grace,
And loved your beauty with love false or true,
But one man loved the pilgrim soul in you,
And loved the sorrows of your changing face;

And bending down beside the glowing bars,
Murmur, a little sadly, how Love fled
And paced upon the mountains overhead
And hid his face amid a crowd of stars.

WHO GOES WITH FERGUS?

Fergus was the bard of the Fianna warriors.

Who will go drive with Fergus now,
And pierce the deep wood's woven shade,
And dance upon the level shore,
Young man, lift up your russet brow,
And lift your tender eyelids, maid,
And brood on hopes and fear no more.

And no more turn aside and brood
Upon love's bitter mystery;
For Fergus rules the brazen cars,
And rules the shadows of the wood,
And the white breast of the dim sea
And all dishevelled wandering stars.

THE MAN WHO DREAMED OF FAERYLAND

He stood among a crowd at Dromahair;
His heart hung all upon a silken dress,
And he had known at last some tenderness,
Before earth took him to her stony care;
But when a man poured fish into a pile;
It seemed they raised their little silver heads,
And sang what gold morning or evening sheds
Upon a woven world-forgotten isle
Where people love beside the ravelled seas;
That Time can never mar a lover's vows
Under that woven changeless roof of boughs:
The singing shook him out of his new ease.

He wandered by the sands of Lissadell;
His mind ran all on money cares and fears,
And he had known at last some prudent years
Before they heaped his grave under the hill;
But while he passed before a plashy place
A lug-worm with its grey and muddy mouth
Sang that somewhere to north or west or south
There dwelt a gay, exulting, gentle race
Under the golden or the silver skies;
That if a dancer stayed his hungry foot
It seemed the sun and moon were in the fruit:
And at that singing he was no more wise.

He mused beside the well of Scanavin,
He mused upon his mockers: without fail
His sudden vengeance were a country tale,
When earthy night had drunk his body in;
But one small knot-grass growing by the pool
Sang where – unnecessary cruel voice –
Old silence bids its chosen race rejoice,
Whatever ravelled waters rise and fall
Or stormy silver fret the gold of day,
And midnight there enfold them like a fleece
And lover there by lover be at peace.
The tale drove his fine angry mood away.

He slept under the hill of Lugnagall;
And might have known at last unhaunted sleep
Under that cold and vapour-turbaned steep,
Now that the earth had taken man and all:
Did not the worms that spired about his bones
Proclaim with that unwearied, reedy cry
That God has laid His fingers on the sky,
That from those fingers glittering summer runs
Upon the dancer by the dreamless wave.
Why should those lovers that no lovers miss
Dream, until God burn Nature with a kiss?
The man has found no comfort in the grave.

THE BALLAD OF FATHER GILLIGAN

The old priest Peter Gilligan
Was weary night and day;
For half his flock were in their beds,
Or under green sods lay.

Once, while he nodded on a chair,
At the moth-hour of eve,
Another poor man sent for him,
And he began to grieve.

'I have no rest, nor joy, nor peace,
For people die and die';
And after cried he, 'God forgive!
My body spake, not I!'

He knelt, and leaning on the chair
He prayed and fell asleep;
And the moth-hour went from the fields,
And stars began to peep.

They slowly into millions grew,
And leaves shook in the wind;
And God covered the world with shade,
And whispered to mankind.

Upon the time of sparrow-chirp
When the moths came once more,
The old priest Peter Gilligan
Stood upright on the floor.

'Mavrone, mavrone! the man has died
While I slept on the chair';
He roused his horse out of its sleep,
And rode with little care.

He rode now as he never rode,
By rocky lane and fen;
The sick man's wife opened the door:
'Father! you come again!'

'And is the poor man dead?' he cried.
'He died an hour ago.'
The old priest Peter Gilligan
In grief swayed to and fro.

'When you were gone, he turned and died
As merry as a bird.'
The old priest Peter Gilligan
He knelt him at that word.

'He Who hath made the night of stars
For souls who tire and bleed,
Sent one of His great angels down
To help me in my need.

'He Who is wrapped in purple robes,
With planets in His care,
Had pity on the least of things
Asleep upon a chair.'

TO IRELAND IN THE COMING TIMES

Know, that I would accounted be
True brother of a company
That sang, to sweeten Ireland's wrong,
Ballad and story, rann and song;
Nor be I any less of them,
Because the red-rose-bordered hem
Of her, whose history began
Before God made the angelic clan,
Trails all about the written page
When Time began to rant and rage
The measure of her flying feet
Made Ireland's heart begin to beat;
And Time bade all his candles flare
To light a measure here and there;
And may the thoughts of Ireland brood
Upon a measured quietude.

Nor may I less be counted one
With Davis, Mangan, Ferguson,
Because, to him who ponders well,
My rhymes more than their rhyming tell
Of things discovered in the deep,
Where only body's laid asleep.
For the elemental creatures go
About my table to and fro,
That hurry from unmeasured mind
To rant and rage in flood and wind;
Yet he who treads in measured ways
May surely barter gaze for gaze.
Man ever journeys on with them
After the red-rose-bordered hem.
Ah, faeries, dancing under the moon.
A Druid land, a Druid tune!

While still I may, I write for you
The love I lived, the dream I knew.
From our birthday, until we die,
Is but the winking of an eye;

And we, our singing and our love,
What measurer Time has lit above,
And all benighted things that go
About my table to and fro,
Are passing on to where may be,
In truth's consuming ecstasy,
No place for love and dream at all;
For God goes by with white footfall.
I cast my heart into my rhymes,
That you, in the dim coming times,
May know how my heart went with them
After the red-rose-bordered hem.

THE SONG OF WANDERING AENGUS

I went out to the hazel wood,
Because a fire was in my head,
And cut and peeled a hazel wand,
And hooked a berry to a thread;
And when white moths were on the wing,
And moth-like stars were flickering out,
I dropped the berry in a stream
And caught a little silver trout.

When I had laid it on the floor
I went to blow the fire aflame,
But something rustled on the floor,
And some one called me by my name:
It had become a glimmering girl
With apple blossom in her hair
Who called me by my name and ran
And faded through the brightening air.

Though I am old with wandering
Through hollow lands and hilly lands,
I will find out where she has gone,
And kiss her lips and take her hands;
And walk among long dappled grass,
And pluck till time and times are done

The silver apples of the moon,
The golden apples of the sun.

HE BIDS HIS BELOVED BE AT PEACE

As the critic Denis Donoghue has pointed out, James Joyce clearly got inspiration for his finest poem, 'I Hear an Army' (written in 1904 when he was 23), from this poem of Yeats's. The rhythmic structure and dreamlike submission to the subsconscious indicates similarities. It is worth noting that when Yeats read *Chamber Music*, in which 'I Hear an Army' appeared as the last poem, he described it as 'a technical and emotional masterpiece'.

> I hear the Shadowy Horses, their long manes a-shake,
> Their hoofs heavy with tumult, their eyes glimmering white;
> The North unfolds above them clinging, creeping night,
> The East her hidden joy before the morning break,
> The West weeps in pale dew and sighs passing away,
> The South is pouring down roses of crimson fire:
> O vanity of Sleep, Hope, Dream, endless Desire,
> The Horses of Disaster plunge in the heavy clay:
> Beloved, let your eyes half close, and your heart beat
> Over my heart, and your hair fall over my breast,
> Drowning love's lonely hour in deep twilight of rest,
> And hiding their tossing manes and their tumultuous feet.

THE SECRET ROSE

> Far-off, most secret, and inviolate Rose,
> Enfold me in my hour of hours; where those
> Who sought thee in the Holy Sepulchre,
> Or in the wine-vat, dwell beyond the stir
> And tumult of defeated dreams; and deep
> Among pale eyelids, heavy with the sleep
> Men have named beauty. Thy great leaves enfold
> The ancient beards, the helms of ruby and gold
> Of the crowned Magi; and the king whose eyes
> Saw the Pierced Hands and Rood of elder rise
> In Druid vapour and make the torches dim;

Till vain frenzy awoke and he died; and him
Who met Fand walking among flaming dew
By a grey shore where the wind never blew,
And lost the world and Emer for a kiss;
And him who drove the gods out of their liss,
And till a hundred morns had flowered red
Feasted, and wept the barrows of his dead;
And the proud dreaming king who flung the crown
And sorrow away, and calling bard and clown
Dwelt among wine-stained wanderers in deep woods;
And him who sold tillage, and house, and goods,
And sought through lands and islands numberless years,
Until he found, with laughter and with tears,
A woman of so shining loveliness
That men threshed corn at midnight by a tress,
A little stolen tress. I, too, await
The hour of thy great wind of love and hate.
When shall the stars be blown about the sky,
Like the sparks blown out of a smithy, and die?
Surely thine hour has come, thy great wind blows,
Far-off, most secret, and inviolate Rose?

HE WISHES FOR THE CLOTHS OF HEAVEN

Had I the heavens' embroidered cloths,
Enwrought with golden and silver light,
The blue and the dim and the dark cloths
Of night and light and the half-light,
I would spread the cloths under your feet:
But I, being poor, have only my dreams;
I have spread my dreams under your feet;
Tread softly because you tread on my dreams.

Reveries Over Childhood and Youth – 1914

*T*he first of Yeats's autobiographies, published in 1914, recalled his childhood days in Sligo, and the year he spent as a boy and young man in London and Dublin. There is also a striking word portrait of his uncle George Pollexfen, which I have abstracted from a later volume, *The Trembling of the Veil*, because it seems to fit perfectly in this context.

From his book *The Celtic Twilight*, first published in 1893 with additions that run up to the end of the century, I have selected some of the tales which Yeats heard from the folk of the countryside and wrote down to illustrate their beliefs and customs, and through which he came to draw close to the imagination of his own people.

Rosa Alchemica is from his mystical symbolist period. Who is Michael Robartes? It is hard to say. But through the pages of *Rosa Alchemica* surely stalks the spirit of the Symbolist writer Villier de L'Isle Adam, who, wrapped in his great cloak, used to plague the Paris cafés with his plans for substituting automatons for a real woman, or for a house he was going to build to provide a choice of exits, including crucifixion, for those who tired of being men and wanted to become Gods. First, however, here is an extract from *Reveries Over Childhood and Youth*.

My first memories are fragmentary and isolated and contemporaneous, as though one remembered some first moments of the Seven Days. It seems as if time had not yet been created, for all thoughts are connected with emotion and place without sequence.

I remember sitting upon somebody's knee, looking out of an Irish window at a wall covered with cracked and falling plaster, but what wall I do not remember, and being told that some relation once lived there. I am looking out of a window in London. It is in Fitzroy Road. Some boys are playing in the road and among them a boy in uniform, a telegraph-boy perhaps. When I ask who the boy is, a servant tells me that he is going to blow the town up, and I go to sleep in terror.

After that come memories of Sligo, where I live with my grandparents. I am sitting on the ground looking at a mastless toy boat with the paint rubbed and scratched, and I say to myself in great melancholy, 'It is further away than it used to be', and while I am saying it I am looking at a long scratch in the stern, for it is especially the scratch which is further away. Then one day at dinner my great-uncle, William Middleton, says, 'We should not make light of the troubles of children. They are worse than ours, because we can see the end of our trouble and they can never see any end', and I feel grateful, for I know that I am very unhappy and have often said to myself, 'When you grow up, never talk as grown-up people do of the happiness of childhood'. I may have already had the night of misery when, having prayed for several days that I might die, I began to be afraid that I was dying and prayed that I might live. There was no reason for my unhappiness. Nobody was unkind, and my grandmother has still after so many years my gratitude and my reverence. The house was so big that there was always a room to hide in, and I had a red pony and a garden where I could wander, and there were two dogs to follow at my heels, one white with some black spots on his head and the other with long black hair all over him. I used to think about God and fancy that I was very wicked, and one day when I threw a stone and hit a duck in the yard by mischance and broke its wing, I was full of wonder when I was told that the duck would be cooked for dinner and that I should not be punished.

Some of my misery was loneliness and some of it fear of old William Pollexfen, my grandfather. He was never unkind, and I cannot remember that he ever spoke harshly to me, but it was the custom to fear and admire him. He had won the freedom of some Spanish city, for saving life perhaps, but was so silent that his wife never knew it till he was near eighty, and then from the chance visit of an old sailor. She asked him if it was true and he said it was true, but she knew him too well to question and his old shipmate had left the town. She too had the habit of fear. We knew that he had been in many parts of the world, for there was a great scar on his hand made by a whaling-hook, and in the dining-room was a cabinet with bits of coral in it and a jar of water from the Jordan for the baptizing of his children and Chinese pictures upon rice-paper and an ivory walking-stick from India that came to me after his death. He had great physical strength and had the reputation of never ordering a man to do anything he would not do himself. He owned many sailing-ships and once, when a captain just come to anchor at Rosses Point reported something wrong with the rudder, had sent a messenger to say, 'Send a man down to find out what's wrong'. 'The crew all refuse' was the answer, and to that my grandfather answered, 'Go down yourself', and not being obeyed, he dived from the main deck, all the neighbourhood lined along the pebbles of the shore. He came up with his skin torn but well informed about the rudder. He had a violent temper and kept a hatchet at his bedside for burglars and would knock a man down instead of going to law, and I once saw him hunt a party of men with a horsewhip. He had no relation, for he was an only child, and, being solitary and silent, he had few friends. He corresponded with Campbell of Islay who had befriended him and his crew after a shipwreck, and Captain Webb, the first man who had swum the Channel and who was drowned swimming the Niagara Rapids, had been a mate in his employ and a close friend. That is all the friends I can remember, and yet he was so looked up to and admired that when he returned from taking the waters of Bath his men would light bonfires along the railway line for miles; while his partner, William Middleton, whose father after the great famine had attended the sick for weeks, and taken cholera from a man he carried in his arms into his own house and died of it, and was himself civil to everybody and a cleverer man than my grandfather, came and went without notice. I think I confused my grandfather with God, for I remember in one of my attacks of melancholy praying that he might punish me for my sins, and I was shocked and astonished when a daring little girl – a cousin, I think – having waited under a group of trees in the avenue, where she knew he would pass near four o'clock on the way to his dinner, said to him, 'If I were you and you were a little girl, I would give you a doll'.

Yet for all my admiration and alarm, neither I nor any one else thought it wrong to outwit his violence or his rigour; and his lack of suspicion and something helpless about him made that easy while it stirred our affection. When I must have been still a very little boy, seven or eight years old perhaps, an uncle called me out of bed one night, to ride the five or six miles to Rosses Point to borrow a railway-pass from a cousin. My grandfather had one, but thought it dishonest to let another use it, but the cousin was not so particular. I was let out through a gate that opened upon a little lane beside the garden away from earshot of the house, and rode delighted through the moonlight, and awoke my cousin in the small hours by tapping on his window with a whip. I was home again by two or three in the morning and found the coachman waiting in the little lane. My grandfather would not have thought such an adventure possible, for every night at eight he believed that the stable-yard was locked, and he knew that he was brought the key. Some servant had once got into trouble at night and so he had arranged that they should all be locked in. He never knew, what everybody else in the house knew, that for all the ceremonious bringing of the key the gate was never locked.

Even to-day when I read *King Lear* his image is always before me, and I often wonder if the delight in passionate men in my plays and in my poetry is more than his memory. He must have been ignorant, though I could not judge him in my childhood, for he had run away to sea when a boy, 'gone to sea through the hawse-hole' as he phrased it, and I can but remember him with two books – his Bible and Falconer's *Shipwreck*, a little green-covered book that lay always upon his table; he belonged to some younger branch of an old Cornish family. His father had been in the Army, had retired to become an owner of sailing-ships, and an engraving of some old family place my grandfather thought should have been his hung next a painted coat of arms in the little back parlour. His mother had been a Wexford woman, and there was a tradition that his family had been linked with Ireland for generations and once had their share in the old Spanish trade with Galway. He had a good deal of pride and disliked his neighbours, whereas his wife, a Middleton, was gentle and patient and did many charities in the little back parlour among frieze coats and shawled heads, and every night when she saw him asleep went the round of the house alone with a candle to make certain there was no burglar in danger of the hatchet. She was a true lover of her garden, and before the care of her house had grown upon her, would choose some favourite among her flowers and copy it upon rice-paper. I saw some of her handiwork the other day and I wondered at the delicacy of form and colour and at a handling that may have needed a magnifying-glass it was so minute. I can remember no other pictures but the Chinese paintings, and some coloured prints of battles in the Crimea upon the wall of a passage, and the painting of a ship at the passage end darkened by time.

My grown-up uncles and aunts, my grandfather's many sons and daughters, came and went, and almost all they said or did has faded from my memory, except a few harsh words that convince me by a vividness out of proportion to their harshness that all were habitually kind and considerate. The youngest of my uncles was stout and humorous and had a tongue of leather over the keyhole of his door to keep the draught out, and another whose bedroom was at the end of a long stone passage had a model turret-ship in a glass case. He was a clever man and had designed the Sligo quays, but was now going mad and inventing a vessel of war that could not be sunk, his pamphlet explained, because of a hull of solid wood. Only six months ago my sister awoke dreaming that she held a wingless sea-bird in her arms and presently she heard that he had died in his madhouse, for a sea-bird is the omen that announces the death or danger of a Pollexfen. An uncle, George Pollexfen, afterwards astrologer and mystic, and my dear friend, came but seldom from Ballina, once to a race-meeting with two postilions dressed in green; and there was that younger uncle who sent me for the railway pass. He was my grandmother's favourite, and had, the servants told me, been sent away from school for taking a crowbar to a bully.

I can only remember my grandmother punishing me once. I was playing in the kitchen and a servant in horseplay pulled my shirt out of my trousers in front just as my grandmother came in, and I, accused of I knew not what childish indecency, was given my dinner in a room by myself. But I was always afraid of my uncles and aunts, and once the uncle who had taken the crowbar to the bully found me eating lunch which my grandmother had given me and reproved me for it and made me ashamed. We breakfasted at nine and dined at four and it was considered self-indulgent to eat anything between meals; and once an aunt told me that I had reined in my pony and struck it at the same moment that I might show it off as I rode through the town, and I, because I had been accused of what I thought a very dark crime, had a night of misery. Indeed I remember little of childhood but its pain. I have grown happier with every year of life as though gradually conquering something in myself, for certainly my miseries were not made by others but were a part of my own mind.

II

One day some one spoke to me of the voice of the conscience, and as I brooded over the phrase I came to think that my soul, because I did not hear an articulate voice, was lost. I had some wretched days until being alone with one of my aunts I heard a whisper in my ear, 'What a tease you are!' At first I thought my aunt must have spoken, but when I found she had not, I concluded it was the voice of my conscience and was happy again. From that day the voice has come to me at moments of crisis, but now it is a voice in my head that is sudden and startling. It does not tell me what to do, but often reproves me. It will say perhaps, 'That is unjust' of some thought; and once when I complained that a prayer had not been heard, it said, 'You have been helped'. I had a little flagstaff in front of the house and a red flag with the Union Jack in the corner. Every night I pulled my flag down and folded it up and laid it on a shelf in my bedroom, and one morning before breakfast I found it, though I knew I had folded it up the night before, knotted round the bottom of the flagstaff so that it was touching the grass. I must have heard the servants talking of the faeries, for I concluded at once that a faery had tied those four knots and from then on believed that one had whispered in my ear. I have been told, though I do not remember it myself, that I saw, whether once or many times I do not know, a supernatural bird in the corner of the room. Once, too, I was driving with my grandmother a little after dark close to the Channel that runs for some five miles from Sligo to the sea, and my grandmother showed me the red light of an outward-bound steamer and told me that my grandfather was on board, and that night in my sleep I screamed out and described the steamer's wreck. The next morning my grandfather arrived on a blind horse found for him by grateful passengers. He had, as I remember the story, been asleep when the captain aroused him to say they were going on the rocks. He said, 'Have you tried sail on her?' and judging from some answer that the captain was demoralized took over the command and, when the ship could not be saved, got the crew and passengers into the boats. His own boat was upset and he saved himself and some others by swimming; some women had drifted ashore, buoyed up by their crinolines. 'I was not so much afraid of the sea as of that terrible man with his oar', was the comment of a schoolmaster who was among the survivors. Eight men were, however, drowned and my grandfather suffered from that memory at intervals of his life, and if asked to read family prayers never read anything but the shipwreck of Saint Paul.

I remember the dogs more clearly than any one except my grandfather and grandmother. The black hairy one had no tail because it had been sliced off, if I was told the truth, by a railway train. I think I followed at their heels more than they did at mine, and that their journeys ended at a rabbit-warren behind the garden; and sometimes they had savage fights, the black hairy dog, being well protected by its hair, suffering least. I can remember one so savage that the white dog would not take his teeth out of the black dog's hair till the coachman hung them over the side of a water-butt, one outside and one in the water. My grandmother once told the coachman to cut the hair like a lion's hair and, after a long consultation with the stable-boy, he cut it all over the head and shoulders and left it on the lower part of the body. The dog disappeared for a few days and I did not doubt that its heart was broken.

There was a large garden behind the house full of apple-trees, with flower-beds and grass-plots in the centre, and two figure-heads of ships, one among the strawberry plants under a wall covered with fruit-trees and one among the flowers. The one among the flowers was a white lady in flowing robes, while the other, a stalwart man in uniform, had been taken from a three-masted ship of my grandfather's called the *Russia*, and there was a belief among the servants that the stalwart man represented the Tsar and had been presented by the Tsar himself. The avenue, or as they say in England the drive, that went from the hall door through a clump of big trees to an insignificant gate and a road bordered by broken and dirty cottages, was but two or three hundred yards, and I often thought it should have been made to wind more, for I judged people's social importance mainly by the length of their avenues. This idea may have come from the stable-boy, for he was my principal friend. He had a book of Orange rhymes, and the days when we read them together in the hayloft gave me the pleasure of rhyme for the first time. Later on I can remember being told, when there was a rumour of a Fenian rising, that rifles had been served out to the Orangemen; and presently, when I had begun to dream of my future life, I thought I would like to die fighting the Fenians. I was to build a very fast and beautiful ship and to have under my command a company of young men who were always to be in training like athletes and so become as brave and handsome as the young men in the story-books, and there was to be a big battle on the sea-shore near Rosses and I was to be killed. I collected little pieces of wood and piled them up in a corner of the yard, and there was an old rotten log in the distant field I often went to look at becuase I thought it would go a long way in the making of the ship. All my dreams were of ships; and one day a sea-captain who had come to dine with my grandfather put a hand on each side of my head and lifted me up to show me Africa, and another day a sea-captain pointed to the smoke from the pern-mill on the quays rising up beyond the trees of the lawn, as though it came from the mountain, and asked me if Ben Bulben was a burning mountain.

Once every few months I used to go to Rosses Point or Ballisodare to see another little boy, who had a piebald pony that had once been in a circus and sometimes forgot where it was and went round and round. He was George Middleton, son of my great-uncle William Middleton. Old Middleton had bought land, then believed a safe investment, at Ballisodare and at Rosses, and spent the winter at Ballisodare and the summer at Rosses. The Middleton and Pollexfen flour mills were at Ballisodare, and a great salmon weir, rapids, and a waterfall, but it was more often at Rosses that I saw my cousin. We rowed in the river-mouth or were taken sailing in a heavy slow schooner yacht or in a big ship's boat that had been rigged and decked. There were great cellars under the house, for it had been a smuggler's house a hundred years before, and sometimes three loud raps would come upon the drawing-room window at sundown, setting all the dogs barking: some dead smuggler giving his accustomed signal. One night I heard them very distinctly and my cousins often heard them, and later on my sister. A pilot had told me that, after dreaming three times of a treasure buried in my uncle's garden, he had climbed the wall in the middle of the night and begun to dig but grew disheartened 'because there was so much earth'. I told somebody what he had said and was told that it was well he did not find it, for it was guarded by a spirit that looked like a flat-iron. At Ballisodare there was a cleft among the rocks that I passed with terror because I believed that a murderous monster lived there that made a buzzing sound like a bee.

It was through the Middletons perhaps that I got my interest in country stories, and certainly the first faery-stories that I heard were in the cottages about their houses. The Middletons took the nearest for friends and were always in and out of the cottages of pilots and of tenants. They were practical, always doing something with their hands, making boats, feeding chickens, and without ambition. One of them had designed a steamer many years before my birth and, long after I had grown to manhood, one could hear it – it had some sort of obsolete engine – many miles off wheezing in the Channel like an asthmatic person. It had been built on the lake and dragged through the town by many horses, stopping before the windows where my mother was learning her lessons, and plunging the whole school into candlelight for five days, and was still patched and repatched mainly because it was believed to be a bringer of good luck. It had been called after the betrothed of its builder *Janet*, long corrupted into the more familiar *Jennet*, and the betrothed died in my youth having passed her eightieth year and been her husband's plague because of the violence of her temper. Another Middleton who was but a year or two older than myself used to shock me by running after hens to know by their feel if they were on the point of dropping an egg. They let their houses decay and the glass fall from the windows of their greenhouses, but one among them at any rate had the second sight. They were liked but had not the pride and reserve, the sense of decorum and order, the instinctive playing before themselves that belongs to those who strike the popular imagination.

Sometimes my grandmother would bring me to see some old Sligo gentlewoman whose garden ran down to the river, ending there in a low wall full of wall-flowers, and I would sit up upon my chair, very bored, while my elders ate their seed-cake and drank their sherry. My walks with the servants were more interesting; sometimes we would pass a little fat girl, and a servant persuaded me to write her a love-letter, and the next time she passed she put her tongue out. But it was the servants' stories that interested me. At such-and-such a corner a man had got a shilling from a recruiting sergeant by standing in a barrel and had then rolled out of it and shown his crippled legs. And in such-and-such a house an old woman had hid herself under the bed of her guests, an officer and his wife, and on hearing them abuse her beaten them with a broomstick. All the well-known families had their grotesque or tragic or romantic legends, and I often said to myself how terrible it would be to go away and die where nobody would know my story. Years afterwards, when I was ten or twelve years old and in Lonodn, I would remember Sligo with tears, and when I began to write, it was there I hoped to find my audience. Next to Merville where I lived was another tree-surrounded house while I sometimes went to see a little boy who stayed there occasionally with his grandmother, whose name I forgot and who seemed to me kind and friendly, though when I went to see her in my thirteenth or fourteenth year I discovered that she only cared for very little boys. When the visitors called I hid in the hay-loft and lay hidden behind the great heap of hay while a servant was calling my name in the yard.

I do not know how old I was (for all these events seem at the same distance) when I was made drunk. I had been out yachting with an uncle and my cousins and it had come on very rough. I had lain on deck between the mast and the bowsprit and a wave had burst over me and I had seen green water over my head. I was very proud and very wet. When we got into Rosses again, I was dressed up in an older boy's clothes so that the trousers came down below my boots, and a pilot gave me a little raw whiskey. I drove home on an outside car and was so pleased with the strange state in which I found myself that for all my uncle could do I cried to every passer-by that I was drunk, and went on crying it through the town and everywhere until I was put to bed by my grandmother and given something to drink that tasted of blackcurrants and so fell asleep.

III

Some six miles off towards Ben Bulben and beyond the Channel, as we call the tidal river between Sligo and the Rosses, and on top of a hill there was a little square two-storeyed house covered with creepers and looking out upon a garden where the box borders were larger than any I had ever seen, and where I saw for the first time the crimson streak of the gladiolus and awaited its blossom with excitement. Under one gable a dark thicket of small trees made a shut-in mysterious place, where one played and believed that something was going to happen. My great-aunt Micky lived there. Micky was not her right name, for she was Mary Yeats, and her father had been my great-grandfather, John Yeats, who had been Rector of Drumcliff, a few miles further off, and died in 1847. She was a spare, high-coloured, elderly woman and had the oldest-looking cat I had ever seen, for its hair had grown into matted locks of yellowy white. She farmed and had one old man-servant, but could not have farmed at all, had not neighbouring farmers helped to gather in the crops, in return for the loan of her farm implements and 'out of respect for the family', for as Johnny MacGurk, the Sligo barber, said to me, 'The Yeats's were always very respectable'. She was full of family history; all her dinner-knives were pointed like daggers through much cleaning, and there was a little James I cream-jug with the Yeats motto and crest, and on her dining-room mantelpiece a beautiful silver cup that had belonged to my great-great-grandfather, who had married a certain Mary Butler. It had upon it the Butler crest and had been already old at the date 1534, when the initials of some bride and bridegroom were engraved under the lip. All its history for generations was rolled up inside it upon a piece of paper yellow with age, until some caller took the paper to light his pipe.

Another family of Yeats, a widow and her two children on whom I called sometimes with my grandmother, lived near in a long low cottage, and owned a very fierce turkey-cock that did battle with their visitors; and some miles away lived the secretary to the Grand Jury and land agent, my great-uncle, Mat Yeats, and his big family of boys and girls; but I think it was only in later years that I came to know them well. I do not think any of these liked the Pollexfens, who were well off and seemed to them purse-proud, whereas they themselves had come down in the world. I remember them as very well-bred and very religious in the Evangelical way and thinking a good deal of Aunt Micky's old histories. There had been among our ancestors a King's County soldier, one of Marlborough's generals, and when his nephew came to dine he gave him boiled pork, and when the nephew said he disliked boiled pork he had asked him to dine again and promised him something he would like better. However, he gave him boiled pork again and the nephew took the hint in silence. The other day as I was coming home from America, I met one of his descendants whose family has not another discoverable link with ours, and he too knew the boiled pork story and nothing else. We have the General's portrait, and he looks very fine in his armour and his long curly wig, and underneath it, after his name, are many honours that have left no tradition among us. Were we country people, we could have summarized his life in a legend. Other ancestors or great-uncles bore a part in Irish history; one saved the life of Sarsfield at the battle of Sedgemoor; another, taken prisoner by King James's army, owed his to Sarsfield's gratitude; another, a century later, roused the gentlemen of Meath against some local Jacquerie, and was shot dead upon a country road, and yet another 'chased the United Irishmen for a fortnight, fell into their hands and was hanged'. The notorious Major Sirr, who arrested Lord Edward Fitzgerald and gave him the bullet-wound he died of in the jail, was godfather to several of my great-great-grandfather's children; while, to make a balance, my great-grandfather had been Robert Emmet's friend and was suspected and imprisoned though but for a few hours. One great-uncle fell at New Orleans in 1813, while another, who became Governor of Penang, led the forlorn hope at the taking of Rangoon, and even in the last generation of all there had been lives of some power and pleasure. An old man who had entertained many famous people in his eighteenth-century house, where battlement and tower showed the influence of Horace Walpole, had but lately, after losing all his money, drowned himself, first taking off his rings and chain and watch as became a collector of many beautiful things; and once, to remind us of more passionate life, a gunboat put into Rosses, commanded by the illegitimate son of some great-uncle or other. Now that I can look at their miniatures, turning them over to find the name of soldier, or lawyer, or Castle official, and wondering if they cared for good books or good music, I am delighted with all that joins my life to those who had power in Ireland or with those anywhere that were good servants and poor bargainers, but I cared nothing as a child for Micky's tales. I could see my grandfather's ships come up the bay or the river, and his sailors treated me with deference, and a ship's carpenter made and mended my toy boats and I thought that nobody could be so important as my grandfather. Perhaps, too, it is only now that I can value those more gentle natures so unlike his passion and violence. An old Sligo priest has told me how my great-grandfather, John Yeats, always went into his kitchen rattling the keys, so much did he fear finding some one doing wrong, and of a speech of his when the agent of the great land-owner of his parish brought him from cottage to cottage to bid the women send their children to the Protestant school. All promised till they came to one who cried, 'Child of mine will never darken your door'. 'Thank you, my woman,' he said, 'you are the first honest woman I have met to-day.' My uncle, Mat Yeats, the land agent, had once waited up every night for a week to catch some boys who stole his apples and when he caught them had given them sixpence and told them not to do it again. Perhaps it is only fancy or the softening touch of the miniaturist that makes me discover in their faces some courtesy and much gentleness. Two eighteenth-century faces interest me the most, one that of a great-great-grandfather, for both have under their powdered curling wigs a half-feminine charm, and as I look at them I discover a something clumsy and heavy in myself. Yet it was a Yeats who spoke the only eulogy that turns my head: 'We have ideas and no passions, but by marriage with a Pollexfen we have given a tongue to the sea cliffs'.

Among the miniatures there is a larger picture, an admirable drawing by I know not what master, that is too harsh and merry for its company. He was a connection and close friend of my great-grandmother Corbet, and though we spoke of him as 'Uncle Beattie' in our childhood, no blood relation. My great-grandmother who died at ninety-three had many memories of him. He was the friend of Goldsmith and was accustomed to boast, clergyman though he was, that he belonged to a hunt-club of which every member but himself had been hanged or transported for treason, and that it was not possible to ask him a question he could not reply to with a perfectly appropriate blasphemy or indecency.

IV

Because I had found it hard to attend to anything less interesting than my thoughts, I was difficult to teach. Several of my uncles and aunts had tried to teach me to read, and because they could not, and because I was much older than children who read easily, had come to think, as I have learnt since, that I had not all my faculties. But for an accident they might have thought it for a long time. My father was staying in the house and never went to church and that gave me the courage to refuse to set out one Sunday morning. I was often devout, my eyes filling with tears at the thought of God and my own sins, but I hated church. My grandmother tried to teach me to put my toes first to the ground because I suppose I stumped on my heels, and that took my pleasure out of the way there. Later on when I had learnt to read I took pleasure in the words of the hymn, but never understood why the choir took three times as long as I did in getting to the end; and the part of the service I liked, the sermon and passages of the Apocalypse and Ecclesiastes, were no compensation for all the repetitions and for the fatigue of so much standing. My father said if I would not go to church he would teach me to read. I think now that he wanted to make me go for my grandmother's sake and could think of no other way. He was an angry and impatient teacher and flung the reading-book at my head, and next Sunday I decided to go to church. My father had, however, got interested in teaching me, and only shifted the lesson to a week-day till he had conquered my wandering mind. My first clear image of him was fixed on my imagination, I believe, but a few days before the first lesson. He had just arrived from London and was walking up and down the nursery floor. He had a very black beard and hair, and one cheek bulged out with a fig that was there to draw the pain out of a bad tooth. One of the nurses (a nurse had come from London with my brothers and sisters) said to the other that a live frog, she had heard, was best of all. Then I was sent to a dame-school kept by an old woman who stood us in rows and had a long stick like a billiard cue to get at the back rows. My father was still at Sligo when I came back from my first lesson and asked me what I had been taught. I said I had been taught to sing, and he said, 'Sing then,' and I sang –

> Little drops of water,
> Little grains of sand,

58

Make the mighty ocean
And the pleasant land

high up in my head. So my father wrote to the old woman that I was never to be taught to sing again, and afterwards other teachers were told the same thing. Presently my elder sister came on a long visit and she and I went to a little two-storeyed house in a poor street where an old gentlewoman taught us spelling and grammar. When we had learned our lesson well, we were allowed to look at a sword presented to her father who had led troops in India or China and to spell out a long complimentary inscription on the silver scabbard. As we walked to her house or home again we held a large umbrella before us, both gripping the handle and guiding ourselves by looking out of a round hole gnawed in the cover by a mouse. When I had got beyond books of one syllable, I began to spend my time in a room called the library, though there were no books in it that I can remember except some old novels I never opened and a many-volumed encyclopaedia published towards the end of the eighteenth century. I read this encyclopaedia a great deal and can remember a long passage considering whether fossil wood despite its appearance might not be only a curiously shaped stone.

My father's unbelief had set me thinking about the evidences of religion and I weighed the matter perpetually with great anxiety, for I did not think I could live without religion. All my religious emotions were, I think, connected with clouds and cloudy glimpses of luminous sky, perhaps because of some Bible picture of God's speaking to Abraham or the like. At least I can remember the sight moving me to tears. One day I got a decisive argument for belief. A cow was about to calve, and I went to the field where the cow was with some farm-hands who carried a lantern, and next day heard that the cow had calved in the early morning. I asked everybody how calves were born, and because nobody would tell me, made up my mind that nobody knew. They were the gift of God, that much was certain, but it was plain that nobody had ever dared to see them come, and children must come in the same way. I made up my mind that when I was a man I would wait up till calf or child had come. I was certain there would be a cloud and a burst of light and God would bring the calf in the cloud out of the light. That thought made me content until a boy of twelve or thirteen, who had come on a visit for the day, sat beside me in a hay-loft and explained all the mechanism of sex. He had learnt all about it from an elder boy whose pathic he was (to use a term he would not have understood) and his description, given, as I can see now, as if he were telling of any other factor of physical life, made me miserable for weeks. After the first impression wore off, I began to doubt if he had spoken truth, but one day I discovered a passage in the encyclopaedia that, though I only partly understood its long words, confirmed what he had said. I did not know enough to be shocked at his relation to the elder boy, but it was the first breaking of the dream of childhood.

My realization of death came when my father and mother and my two brothers and my two sisters were on a visit. I was in the library when I heard feet running past and heard somebody say in the passage that my younger brother, Robert, had died. He had been ill for some days. A little later my sister and I sat at the table, very happy, drawing ships with their flags half-mast high. We must have heard or seen that the ships in the harbour had their flags at half-mast. Next day at breakfast I heard people telling how my mother and the servant had heard the banshee crying the night before he died. It must have been after this that I told my grandmother I did not want to go with her when she went to see old bed-ridden people because they would soon die.

v

At length when I was eight or nine an aunt said to me, 'You are going to London. Here you are somebody. There you will be nobody at all.' I knew at the time that her words were a blow at my father, not at me, but it was some years before I knew her reason. She thought so able a man as my father could have found out some way of painting more popular pictures if he had set his mind to it and that it was wrong of him 'to spend every evening at his club'. She had mistaken, for what she would have considered a place of wantonness, Heatherley's Art School.

My mother and brother and sister were at Sligo perhaps when I was sent to England, for my father and I and a group of landscape-painters lodged at Burnham Beeches with an old Mr and Mrs Earle. My father was painting the first big pond you come to if you have driven from Slough through Farnham Royal. He began it in spring and painted all through the year, the picture changing with the seasons, and gave it up unfinished when he had painted the snow upon the heath-covered banks. He is never satisfied and can never make himself say that any picture is finished. In the evening he heard me my lessons or read me some novel of Fenimore Cooper's. I found delightful adventures in the woods – one day a blindworm and an adder fighting in a green hollow – and sometimes Mrs Earle would be afraid to tidy the room because I had put a bottle full of newts on the mantelpiece. Now and then a boy from a farm on the other side of the road threw a pebble at my window at daybreak, and he and I went fishing in the big second pond. Now and then another farmer's boy and I shot sparrows with an old pepper-box revolver and the boy would roast them on a string. There was an old horse one of the painters called The Scaffolding, and sometimes a son of old Earle's drove with me to Slough and once to Windsor, and at Windsor we made our lunch of cold sausages bought from a public-house. I did not know what it was to be alone, for I could wander in pleasant alarm through the enclosed parts of the Beeches, then very large, or round some pond imagining ships going in and out among the reeds and thinking of Sligo or of strange seafaring adventures in the fine ship I should launch when I grew up. I had always a lesson to learn before night and that was a continual misery, for I could very rarely, with so much to remember, set my thoughts upon it and then only in fear. One day my father told me that a painter had said I was very thick-skinned and did not mind what was said to me, and I could not understand how anybody could be so unjust. It made me wretched to be idle, but one could not help it. I was once surprised and shocked. All but my father and myself had been to London, and Kennedy and Farrar and Page, I remember the names vaguely, arrived laughing and talking. One of them had carried off a card of texts from the waiting-room of the station and hung it up on the wall. I thought, 'He has stolen it', but my father and all made it a theme of merry conversation.

Then I returned to Sligo for a few weeks as I was to do once or twice in every year for years, and after that we settled in London. Perhaps my mother and the other children had been there all the time, for I remember my father now and again going to London. The first house we lived in was close to Burne-Jones's house at North End, but we moved after a year or two to Bedford Park. At North End we had a pear-tree in the garden and plenty of pears, but the pears used to be full of maggots, and almost opposite lived a schoolmaster called O'Neill, and when a little boy told me that the schoolmaster's great-grandfather had been a king I did not doubt it. I was sitting against the hedge and iron railing of some villa-garden there, when I heard one boy say to another it was something wrong with my liver that gave me such a dark complexion and that I could not live more than a year. I said to myself, 'A year is a very long time, one can do such a lot of things in a year', and put it out of my head. When my father gave me a holiday and later when I had a holiday from school I took my schooner boat to the Round Pond, sailing it very commonly against the two cutter yachts of an old naval officer. He would sometimes look at the ducks and say, 'I would like to take that fellow home for my dinner', and he sang me a sailor's song about a 'coffin ship' which left Sligo after the great famine, that made me feel very important. The servants at Sligo had told me the story. When she was moved from the berth she had laid in, an unknown dead man's body had floated up, a very evil omen;

and my grandfather, who was Lloyd's agent, had condemned her, but she slipped out in the night. The pond had its own legends; and a boy who had seen a certain model steamer 'burned to the water's edge' was greatly valued as a friend. There was a little boy I was kind to because I knew his father had done something disgraceful though I did not know what. It was years before I discovered that his father was but the maker of certain popular statues, many of which are now in public places. I had heard my father's friends speak of him. Sometimes my sister came with me, and we would look into all the sweet-shops and toy-shops on our way home, especially into one opposite Holland House because there was a cutter yacht made of sugar in the window, and we drank at all the fountains. Once a stranger spoke to us and bought us sweets and came with us almost to our door. We asked him to come in and told him our father's name. He would not come in, but laughed and said, 'Oh, that is the painter who scrapes out every day what he painted the day before'. A poignant memory came upon me the other day while I was passing the drinking-fountain near Holland Park, for there I and my sister had spoken together of our longing for Sligo and our hatred of London. I know we were both very close to tears and remember with wonder, for I had never known any one that cared for such mementoes, that I longed for a sod of earth from some field I knew, something of Sligo to hold in my hand. It was some old race instinct like that of a savage, for we had been brought up to laugh at all display of emotion. Yet it was our mother, who would have thought its display a vulgarity, who kept alive that love. She would spend hours listening to stories or telling stories of the pilots and fishing-people of Rosses Point, or of her own Sligo girlhood, and it was always assumed between her and us that Sligo was more beautiful than other places. I can see now that she had great depth of feeling, that she was her father's daughter. My memory of what she was like in those days has grown very dim, but I think her sense of personality, her desire of any life of her own, had disappeared in her care for us and in much anxiety about money. I always see her sewing or knitting in spectacles and wearing some plain dress. Yet ten years ago when I was in San Francisco, an old cripple came to see me who had left Sligo before her marriage; he came to tell me, he said, that my mother 'had been the most beautiful girl in Sligo'.

The only lessons I had ever learned were those my father taught me, for he terrified me by descriptions of my moral degradation and he humiliated me by my likeness to disagreeable people; but presently I was sent to school at Hammersmith. It was a Gothic building of yellow brick: a large hall full of desks, some small classrooms, and a separate house for boarders, all built perhaps in 1860 or 1870. I thought it an ancient building and that it had belonged to the founder of the school, Lord Godolphin, who was romantic to me because there was a novel about him. I never read the novel, but I thought only romantic people were put in books. On one side, there was a piano factory of yellow brick, upon two sides half-finished rows of little shops and villas all yellow brick, and on the fourth side, outside the wall of our playing-field, a brick-field of cinders and piles of half-burned yellow bricks. All the names and faces of my schoolfellows have faded from me except one name without a face and the face and name of one friend, mainly no doubt because it was all so long ago, but partly because I only seem to remember things dramatic in themselves or that are somehow associated with unforgettable places.

For some days, as I walked homeward along the Hammersmith Road, I told myself that whatever I most cared for had been taken away. I had found a small, green-covered book given to my father by a Dublin man of science; it gave an account of the strange sea creatures the man of science had discovered among the rocks at Howth or dredged out of Dublin Bay. It had long been my favourite book; and when I read it I believed that I was growing very wise, but now I should have no time for it nor for my own thoughts. Every moment would be taken up learning or saying lessons, or in walking between school and home four times a day, for I came home in the middle of the day for dinner. But presently I forgot my trouble, absorbed in two things I had never known, companionship and enmity. After my first day's lesson, a circle of boys had got around me in a playing-field and asked me questions, 'Who's your father?' 'What does he do?' 'How much money has he?' Presently a boy said something insulting. I had never struck anybody or been struck, and now all in a minute, without any intention upon my side, but as if I had been a doll moved by a string, I was hitting at the boys within reach and being hit. After that I was called names for being Irish, and had many fights and never, for years, got the better in any one of them; for I was delicate and had no muscles. Sometimes, however, I found means of retaliation, even of aggression. There was a boy with a big stride, much feared by little boys, and finding him alone in the playing-field, I went up to him and said, 'Rise upon Sugaun and sink upon Gad'. 'What does that mean?' he said. 'Rise upon hay-leg and sink upon straw,' I answered, and told him that in Ireland the sergeant tied straw and hay to the ankles of a stupid recruit to show him the difference between his legs. My ears were boxed, and when I complained to my friends, they said I had brought it upon myself; and that I deserved all I got. I probably dared myself to other feats of a like sort, for I did not think English people intelligent or well-behaved unless they were artists. Every one I knew well in Sligo despised Nationalists and Catholics, but all disliked England with a prejudice that had come down perhaps from the days of the Irish Parliament. I knew stories to the discredit of England, and took them all seriously. My mother had met some Englishwoman who did not like Dublin because the legs of the men were too straight, and at Sligo, as everybody knew, an Englishman had once said to a car-driver, 'If you people were not so lazy, you would pull down the mountain and spread it out over the sand and that would give you acres of good fields'. At Sligo there is a wide river-mouth and at ebb tide most of it is dry sand, but all Sligo knew that in some way I cannot remember it was the spreading of the tide over the sand that left the narrow Channel fit for shipping. At any rate the carman had gone chuckling all over Sligo with his tale. People would tell it to prove that Englishmen were always grumbling. 'They grumble about their dinners and everything – there was an Englishman who wanted to pull down Knocknarea', and so on. My mother had shown them to me kissing at railway stations, and taught me to feel disgust at their lack of reserve, and my father told how my grandfather, William Yeats, who had died before I was born, when he came home to his Rectory in County Down from an English visit, spoke of some man he had met on a coach road who 'Englishman-like' told him all his affairs. My father explained that an Englishman generally believed that his private affairs did him credit, while an Irishman, being poor and probably in debt, had no such confidence. I, however, did not believe in this explanation. My Sligo nurses, who had in all likelihood the Irish Catholic political hatred, had never spoken well of any Englishman. Once when walking in the town of Sligo I had turned to look after an English man and woman whose clothes attracted me. The man, I remember, had grey clothes and knee-breeches and the woman a grey dress, and my nurse had said contemptuously, 'Tow-rows' – perhaps, before my time, there had been some English song with the burden 'tow row row' – and everybody had told me that English people ate skate and even dog-fish, and I myself had only just arrived in England when I saw an old man put marmalade on his porridge.

I was divided from all those boys, not merely by the anecdotes that are everywhere perhaps a chief expression of the distrust of races, but because our mental images were different. I read their boys' books and they excited me, but if I read of some English victory, I did not believe that I read of my own people. They thought of Cressy and Agincourt and the Union Jack and were all very patriotic, and I, without those memories of Limerick and the Yellow Ford that would have strengthened an Irish Catholic, thought of mountain and lake, of my grandfather and of ships. Anti-Irish feeling was running high, for the Land League had been founded and landlords had been shot, and I, who had no politics, was yet full of pride, for it is romantic to live in a dangerous country.

I daresay I thought the rough manners of a cheap school, as my grandfather Yeats had those of a chance companion, typical of all England. At any rate I had a harassed life and got many a black eye and had many outbursts of grief and rage. Once a boy, the son of a great Bohemian glass-maker, who was older than the rest of us, and had been sent out of his country because of a love affair, beat a boy for me because we were 'both foreigners'. And a boy who grew to be the school athlete and my chief friend beat a great many. His are the face and name that I remember – his name was of Huguenot origin and his face like his gaunt and lithe body had something of the American Indian in colour and lineament.

I was very much afraid of the other boys, and that made me doubt myself for the first time. When I had gathered pieces of wood in the corner for my great ship, I was confident that I could keep calm among the storms and die fighting when the great battle came. But now I was ashamed of my lack of courage; for I wanted to be like my grandfather, who thought so little of danger that he had jumped overboard in the Bay of Biscay after an old hat. I was very much afraid of physical pain, and one day when I had made some noise in class, my friend the athlete was accused and I allowed him to get two strokes of the cane before I gave myself up. He had held out his hands without flinching and had not rubbed them on his sides afterwards. I was not caned, but was made to stand up for the rest of the lesson. I suffered very much afterwards when the thought came to me, but he did not reproach me.

I had been some years at school before I had my last fight. My friend, the athlete, had given me many months of peace, but at last refused to beat any more and said I must learn to box, and not go near the other boys till I knew how. I went home with him every day and boxed in his room, and the bouts had always the same ending. My excitability gave me an advantage at first and I would drive him across the room, and then he would drive me across and it would end very commonly with my nose bleeding. One day his father, an elderly banker, brought us out into the garden and tried to make us box in a cold-blooded, courteous way, but it was no use. At last he said I might go near the boys again and I was no sooner inside the gate of the playing-field than a boy flung a handful of mud and cried out, 'Mad Irishman'. I hit him several times on the face without being hit, till the boys round said we should make friends. I held out my hand in fear, for I knew if we went on I should be beaten, and he took it sullenly. I had so poor a reputation as a fighter that it was a great disgrace to him, and even the masters made fun of his swollen face; and though some little boys came in a deputation to ask me to lick a boy they named, I had never another fight with a school-fellow. We had a great many fights with the street boys and the boys of a neighbouring charity school. We had always the better because we were not allowed to fling stones, and that compelled us to close or do our best to close. The monitors had been told to report any boy who fought in the street, but they only reported those who flung stones. I always ran at the athlete's heels, but I never hit any one. My father considered these fights absurd, and even that they were an English absurdity, and so I could not get angry enough to like hitting and being hit; and then, too, my friend drove the enemy before him. He had no doubts or speculations to lighten his fist upon an enemy that, being of low behaviour, should be beaten as often as possible, and there were real wrongs to avenge: one of our boys had been killed by the blow of a stone hid in a snowball.

I had one reputation that I valued. At first when I went to the Hammersmith swimming-baths with the other boys, I was afraid to plunge in until I had gone so far down the ladder that the water came up to my thighs; but one day when I was alone I fell from the spring-board which was five or six feet above the water. After that I would dive from a greater height than the others and I practised swimming under water and pretending not to be out of breath when I came up. And then, if I ran a race, I took care not to pant or show any sign of strain. And in this I had an advantage even over the athlete, for though he could run faster and was harder to tire than anybody else he grew very pale; and I was often paid compliments. I used to run with my friend when he was training to keep him in company. He would give me a long start and soon overtake me.

I followed the career of a certain professional runner for months, buying papers that would tell me if he had won or lost. I had seen him described as 'the bright particular star of American athletics', and the wonderful phrase had thrown enchantment over him. Had he been called the particular bright star, I should have cared nothing for him. I did not understand the symptom for years after. I was nursing my own dream, my form of the common schoolboy dream, though I was no longer gathering the little pieces of broken and rotting wood. Often, instead of learning my lesson, I covered the white squares of the chessboard on my little table with pen-and-ink pictures of myself doing all kinds of courageous things. One day my father said, 'There was a man in Nelson's ship at the battle of Trafalgar, a ship's purser, whose hair turned white; what a sensitive temperament! That man should have achieved something!' I was vexed and bewildered, and am still bewildered and still vexed, finding it a poor and crazy thing that we who have imagined so many noble persons cannot bring our flesh to heel.

When I arrived at the Clarence Basin, Liverpool (the dock Clarence Mangan had his first name from), on my way to Sligo for my holidays I was among Sligo people. When I was a little boy, an old woman who had come to

Liverpool with crates of fowl made me miserable by throwing her arms around me, the moment I had alighted from my cab, and telling the sailor who carried my luggage that she had held me in her arms when I was a baby. The sailor may have known me almost as well, for I was often at Sligo quay to sail my boat; and I came and went once or twice in every year upon the s.s. *Sligo* or the s.s. *Liverpool* which belonged to a company that had for directors my grandfather and his partner William Middleton. I was always pleased if it was the *Liverpool*, for she had been built to run the blockade during the war of North and South.

I waited for this voyage always with excitement and boasted to other boys about it, and when I was a little boy had walked with my feet apart as I had seen sailors walk. I used to be sea-sick, but I must have hidden this from the other boys and partly even from myself; for, as I look back, I remember very little about it, while I remember stories I was told by the captain or by his first mate, and the look of the great cliffs of Donegal, and Tory Island men coming alongside with lobsters, talking Irish and, if it was night, blowing on a burning sod to draw our attention. The captain, an old man with square shoulders and a fringe of grey hair round his face, would tell his first mate, a very admiring man, of fights he had had on shore at Liverpool; and perhaps it was of him I was thinking when I was very small and asked my grandmother if God was as strong as sailors. Once, at any rate, he had been nearly wrecked; the *Liverpool* had been all but blown upon the Mull of Galloway with her shaft broken, and the captain had said to his mate, 'Mind and jump when she strikes, for we don't want to be killed by the falling spars'; and when the mate answered, 'My God, I cannot swim', he had said, 'Who could keep afloat for five minutes in a sea like that?' He would often say his mate was the most timid of men and that 'a girl along the quays could laugh him out of anything'. My grandfather had more than once given him a ship of his own, but he had always thrown up his berth to sail with his old captain where he felt safe. Once he had been put in charge of a ship in a dry dock in Liverpool, but a boy was drowned in Sligo, and before the news could have reached him he wired to his wife, 'Ghost, come at once, or I will throw up berth'. He had been wrecked a number of times, and maybe that had broken his nerve or maybe he had a sensitiveness that would in another class have given him taste and culture. I once forgot a copy of *Count Robert of Paris* on a deck-seat, and when I found it again, it was all covered with the prints of his dirty thumb. He had once seen the coach-a-baur or death coach. It came along the road, he said, till it was hidden by a cottage and it never came out of the other side of the cottage.

Once I smelled new-mown hay when we were quite a long way from land, and once when I was watching the sea-parrots (as the sailors call the puffin) I noticed they had different ways of tucking their heads under their wings, or I fancied it, and said to the captain, 'They have different characters'. Sometimes my father came too, and the sailors when they saw him coming would say, 'There is John Yeats and we shall have a storm', for he was considered unlucky.

I no longer cared for little shut-in places, for a coppice against the stable-yard at Merville where my grandfather lived or against the gable at Seaview where Aunt Micky lived, and I began to climb the mountains, sometimes with the stable-boy for companion, and to look up their stories in the county history. I fished for trout with a worm in the mountain streams and went out herring-fishing at night; and because my grandfather had said the English were in the right to eat skate, I carried a large skate all the six miles or so from Rosses Point, but my grandfather did not eat it.

One night, just as the equinoctial gales were coming, when I was sailing home in the coastguard's boat, a boy told me a beetle of solid gold, strayed maybe from Poe's *Gold Bug*, had been seen by somebody in Scotland and I do not think that either of us doubted his news. Indeed, so many stories did I hear from sailors along the wharf, or round the fo'castle fire of the little steamer that ran between Sligo and Rosses, or from boys out fishing that the world seemed full of monsters and marvels. The foreign sailors wearing earrings did not tell me stories, but like the fishing-boys I gazed at them in wonder and admiration.

Sometimes I would ride to Castle Dargan, where lived a brawling squireen, married to one of my Middleton cousins, and once I went thither on a visit with my cousin, George Middleton. It was, I daresay, the last household where I could have found the reckless Ireland of a hundred years ago in final degradation. But I liked the place for the romance of its two ruined castles facing one another across a little lake, Castle Dargan and Castle Fury. The squireen lived in a small house his family had moved to from their castle some time in the eighteenth century, and two old Miss Furys, who let lodgings in Sligo, were the last remnants of the breed of the other ruin. Once in every year he drove to Sligo for the two old women, that they might look upon the ancestral stones and remember their gentility, and he would put his wildest horses into the shafts to enjoy their terror.

He himself, with a reeling imagination, knew not where to find a spur for the heavy hours. The first day I came there he gave my cousin a revolver (we were upon the high road), and to show it off, or his own shooting, he shot a passing chicken; and half an hour later, at the lake's edge under his castle, now but the broken corner of a tower with a winding stair, he fired at or over an old countryman walking on the far edge of the lake. The next day I heard him settling the matter with the old countryman over a bottle of whiskey, and both were in good humour. Once he had asked a timid aunt of mine if she would like to see his last new pet, and thereupon had marched a racehorse in through the hall door and round the dining-room table. And once she came down to a bare table because he had thought it a good joke to open the window and let his harriers eat the breakfast. There was a current story, too, of his shooting, in the pride of his marksmanship, at his own door with a Martini-Henry rifle till he had shot the knocker off. At last he quarrelled with my great-uncle, William Middleton, and to avenge himself gathered a rabble of wild country lads, mounted them and himself upon the most broken-down rascally horses he could lay hands on and marched them through Sligo under a Land League banner. After that, having neither friends nor money, he made off to Australia or to Canada.

I fished for pike at Castle Dargan and shot at birds with a muzzle-loading pistol until somebody shot a rabbit and I heard it squeal. From that on I would kill nothing but the dumb fish.

The great event of a boy's life is the awakening of sex. He will bathe many times a day, or get up at dawn and having stripped leap to and fro over a stick laid upon two chairs, and hardly know, and never admit, that he had begun to take pleasure in his own nakedness, nor will he understand the change until some dream discovers it. He may never understand at all the greater change in his mind.

It all came upon me when I was close upon seventeen like the bursting of a shell. Somnambulistic country girls, when it is upon them, throw plates about or pull them with long hairs in simulation of the poltergeist, or become mediums for some genuine spirit-mischief, surrendering to their desire of the marvellous. As I look backward, I seem to discover that my passions, my loves and my despairs, instead of being my enemies, a disturbance and an attack, became so beautiful that I had to be constantly alone to give them my whole attention. I notice that now, for the first time, what I saw when alone is more vivid in my memory than what I did or saw in company.

A herd had shown me a cave some hundred and fifty feet below the cliff path and a couple of hundred above the sea, and told me that an evicted tenant called Macrom, dead some fifteen years, had lived there many years, and shown me a rusty nail in the rock which had served perhaps to hold up some wooden protection from wind and weather. Here I stored a tin of cocoa and some biscuits, and instead of going to my bed, would slip out on warm nights and sleep in the cave on the excuse of catching moths. One had to pass over a rocky ledge, safe enough for any one with a fair head, yet seeming, if looked at from above, narrow and sloping; and a remonstrance from a stranger who had seen me climbing along it doubled my delight in the adventure. When, however, upon a bank holiday, I found lovers in my cave, I was not content with it again till I heard that the ghost of Macrom had been seen a little before the dawn, stooping over his fire in the cave-mouth. I had been trying to cook eggs, as I had read in some book, by burying them in the earth under a fire of sticks.

At other times, I would sleep among the rhododendrons and rocks in the wilder part of the grounds of Howth Castle. After a while my father said I must stay indoors half the night, meaning that I should get some sleep in my bed; but I, knowing that I would be too sleepy and comfortable to get up again, used to sit over the kitchen fire till half the night was gone. Exaggerated accounts spread through the school, and sometimes when I did not know a lesson some master would banter me about the way my nights were spent. My interest in science began to fade, and presently I said to myself, 'It has all been a misunderstanding'. I remembered how soon I tired of my specimens, and how little I knew after all my years of collecting, and I came to believe that I had gone through so much labour because of a text, heard for the first time in Saint John's Church in Sligo, and copied Solomon, who had knowledge of hyssop and of tree, that I might be certain of my own wisdom. I still carried my green net, but I began to play at being a sage, a magician or a poet. I had many idols, and as I climbed along the narrow ledge I was now Manfred on his glacier, and now Prince Athanase with his solitary lamp, but I soon chose Alastor for my chief of men and longed to share his melancholy, and maybe at last to disappear from everybody's sight as he disappeared drifting in a boat along some slow-moving river between great trees. When I thought of women they were modelled on those in my favourite poets and loved in brief tragedy, or like the girl in *The Revolt of Islam*, accompanied their lovers through all manner of wild places, lawless women without homes and without children.

My father's influence upon my thoughts was at its height. We went to Dublin by train every morning, breakfasting in his studio. He had taken a large room with a beautiful eighteenth-century mantelpiece in a York Street tenement-house, and at breakfast he read passages from the poets, and always from the play or poem at its most passionate moment. He never read me a passage because of its speculative interest, and indeed did not care at all for poetry where there was generalization or abstraction however impassioned. He would read out the first speeches of the *Prometheus Unbound*, but never the ecstatic lyricism of that famous fourth act; and another day the scene where

Coriolanus comes to the house of Aufidius and tells the impudent servants that his home is under the canopy. I have seen *Coriolanus* played a number of times since then, and read it more than once, but that scene is more vivid than the rest, and it is my father's voice that I hear and not Irving's or Benson's. He did not care even for a fine lyric passage unless he felt some actual man behind its elaboration of beauty, and he was always looking for the lineaments of some desirable, familiar life. When the spirits sang their scorn of Manfred, and Manfred answered, 'O sweet and melancholy voices', I was told that they could not, even in anger, put off their spiritual sweetness. He thought Keats a greater poet than Shelley, because less abstract, but did not read him, caring little, I think, for any of that most beautiful poetry which has come in modern times from the influence of painting. All must be an idealization of speech, and at some moment of passionate action or somnambulistic reverie. I remember his saying that all contemplative men were in a conspiracy to overrate their state of life, and that all writers were of them, excepting the great poets. Looking backwards, it seems to me that I saw his mind in fragments, which had always hidden connections I only now begin to discover. He disliked the Victorian poetry of ideas, and Wordsworth but for certain passages or whole poems. He said one morning over his breakfast that he had discovered in the shape of the head of a Wordsworthian scholar, an old and greatly respected clergyman whose portrait he was painting, all the animal instincts of a prize-fighter. He despised the formal beauty of Raphael, that calm which is not an ordered passion but an hypocrisy, and attacked Raphael's life for its love of pleasure and its self-indulgence. In literature he was always Pre-Raphaelite, and carried into literature principles that, while the Academy was still unbroken, had made the first attack upon academic form.

He no longer read me anything for its story, and all our discussion was of style.

I found a supporter at Sligo in my elderly uncle, a man of fifty-three or fifty-four, with the habits of a much older man. He had never left the West of Ireland, except for a few days to London every year, and a single fortnight's voyage to Spain on board a trading schooner, in his boyhood. He was in politics a Unionist and Tory of the most obstinate kind, and knew nothing of Irish literature or history. He was, however, strangely beset by the romance of Ireland, as he discovered it among the people who served him, sailing upon his ships or attending to his horses, and, though narrow and obstinate of opinion, and puritanical in his judgment of life, was perhaps the most tolerant man I have ever known. He never expected anybody to agree with him, and if you did not upset his habits by cheating him over a horse, or by offending his taste, he would think as well of you as he did of other men, and that was not very well; and help you out of any scrape whatever. I was accustomed to people much better read than he, much more liberal-minded, but they had no life but the intellectual life, and if they and I differed, they could not take it lightly, and were often angry, and so for years now I had gone to Sligo, sometimes because I could not afford my Dublin lodging, but most often for freedom and peace. He would receive me with, 'I have learned that your friend So-and-so has been seen at the Gresham Hotel talking to Mr William Redmond. What will not people do for notoriety?' He considered all Irish Nationalist Members of Parliament as outside the social pale, but after dinner, when conversation grew intimate, would talk sympathetically of the Fenians in Ballina, where he spent his early manhood, or of the Fenian privateer that landed the wounded man at Sligo in the 'sixties. When Parnell was contesting an election at Sligo a little before his death, other Unionist magistrates refused or made difficulties when asked for some assistance, what I do not remember, made necessary under election law; and so my uncle gave that assistance. He walked up and down some Town Hall assembly-room or some court-room with Parnell, but would tell me nothing of that conversation, except that Parnell spoke of Gladstone with extravagant hatred. He would not repeat words spoken by a great man in his bitterness, yet Parnell at the moment was too angry to care who listened. I knew one other man who kept as firm a silence; he had attended Parnell's last public meeting, and after it sat alone beside him, and heard him speak of the followers that had fallen away, or were showing their faint hearts; but Parnell was the chief devotion of his life.

When I first began my visits, he had lived in the town itself, and close to a disreputable neighbourhood called the Burrough, till one evening, while he sat over his dinner, he heard a man and woman quarrelling under his window. 'I mind the time,' shouted the man, 'when I slept with you and your daughter in the one bed.' My uncle was horrified, and moved to a little house about a quarter of a mile into the country, where he lived with an old second-sighted servant, and a man-servant to look after the racehorse that was browsing in the neighbouring field, with a donkey to keep it company. His furniture had not been changed since he set up house for himself as a very young man, and in a room opposite his dining-room were the saddles of his youth, and though he would soon give up riding, they would be oiled and the stirrups kept clean and bright till the day of his death. Some love affair had gone wrong when he was a very young man; he had now no interest in women; certainly never sought favour of a woman, and yet he took great care of his appearance. He did not let his beard grow, although he had, or believed that he had, for he was hypochondriacal, a sensitiveness of the skin that forced him to spend an hour in shaving, and he would take to club and dumb-bell if his waist thickened by a hair's breadth, and twenty years after, when a very old man, he had the erect shapely figure of his youth. I often wondered why he went through so much labour, for it was not pride, which had seemed histrionic in his eyes – and certainly he had no vanity; and now, looking back, I am convinced that it was from habit, mere habit, a habit formed when he was a young man, and the best rider of his district.

Probably through long association with Mary Battle, the second-sighted servant, he had come to believe much in the supernatural world, and would tell how several times, arriving home with an unexpected guest, he had found the table set for three, and that he himself had dreamed of his brother's illness in Liverpool before he had other news of it. He saw me using images learned from Mathers to start reverie, and, though I held out for a long time, thinking him too old and habit-bound, he persuaded me to tell him their use, and from that on we experimented continually, and after a time I began to keep careful record. In summer he always had the same little house at Rosses Point, and it was at Rosses Point that he first became sensitive to the cabbalistic symbols. There are some high sandhills and low cliffs, and I adopted the practice of walking by the seashore while he walked on cliff or sandhill; I, without speaking, would imagine the symbol, and he would notice what passed before his mind's eye, and in a short time he would practically never fail of the appropriate vision. In the symbols which are used certain colours are classified as 'actives', while certain other colours are 'passives', and I had soon discovered that if I used 'actives' George Pollexfen would see nothing. I therefore gave him exercises to make him sensitive to those colours, and gradually we found ourselves well fitted for this work, and he began to take as lively an interest as was possible to a nature given over to habit in my plans for the Castle on the Rock.

I worked with others, sworn to the scheme for the most part, and I made many curious observations. It was the symbol itself, or, at any rate, not my conscious intention that produced the effect, for if I made an error and told someone to gaze at the wrong symbol – they were painted upon cards – the vision would be suggested by the symbol, not by my thought, or two visions would appear side by side, one from the symbol and one from my thought. When two people, between whose minds there was even a casual sympathy, worked together under the same symbolic influence, the dream or reverie would divide itself between them, each half being the complement of the other; and now and again these complementary dreams, or reveries, would arise spontaneously. I find, for instance, in an old notebook: 'I saw quite suddenly a tent with a wooden badly-carved idol, painted dull red; a man looking like a Red Indian was prostrate before it. The idol was seated to the left. I asked X. what he saw. He saw a most august immense being, glowing with a ruddy opalescent colour, sitting on a throne to the left', or, to summarize from a later notebook, . . . I am meditating in one room and my fellow-student in another, when I see a boat full of tumult and movement on a still sea, and my friend sees a boat with motionless sails upon a tumultuous sea. There was nothing in the originating symbol to suggest a boat.

We never began our work until George's old servant was in her bed; and yet, when we went upstairs to our beds, we constantly heard her crying out with nightmare, and in the morning we would find that her dream echoed our vision. One night, started by what symbol I forget, we had seen an allegorical marriage of Heaven and Earth. When Mary Battle brought in the breakfast next morning, I said, 'Well, Mary, did you dream anything last night?' and she replied (I am quoting from an old notebook) 'indeed she had', and that it was 'a dream she would not have liked to have had twice in one night'. She had dreamed that her bishop, the Catholic bishop of Sligo, had gone away 'without telling anybody', and had married 'a very high-up lady, and she not too young, either'. She had thought in her dream, 'Now all the clergy will get married, and it will be no use going to confession'. There were 'layers upon layers of flowers, many roses, all round the church'.

Another time, when George Pollexfen had seen in answer to some evocation of mine a man with his head cut in two, she woke to find that she 'must have cut her face with a pin, as it was all over blood'. When three or four saw together, the dream or vision would divide itself into three or four parts, each seeming complete in itself, and all fitting together, so that each part was an adaptation of the general meaning to a particular personality. A visionary being would give, let us say, a lighted torch to one, an unlighted candle to another, an unripe fruit to a third, and to the fourth a ripe fruit. At times coherent stories were built up, as if a company of actors were to improvise, and play, not only without previous consultation, but without foreseeing at any moment what would be said or done the moment after. Who made the story? Was it the mind of one of the visionaries? Perhaps, for I have endless proof that, where two worked together, the symbolic influence commonly took upon itself, though no word was spoken, the quality of the mind that had first fixed a symbol in the mind's eye. But, if so, what part of the mind? One friend, in whom the symbolic impulse produced actual trance, described an elaborate and very strange story while the trance was upon him, but upon waking told a story that after a certain point was quite different. 'They gave me a cup of wine, and after that I remembered nothing.' While speaking out of trance he had said nothing of the cup of wine, which must have been offered to a portion of his mind quite early in the dream. Then, too, from whence come the images of the dream? Not always, I was soon persuaded, from the memory, perhaps never in trance or sleep. One man, who certainly thought that Eve's apple was the sort that you got from the greengrocer, and as certainly never doubted its story's literal truth, said, when I used some symbol to send him to Eden, that he saw a walled garden on the top of a high mountain, and in the middle of it a tree with great birds in the branches, and fruit out of which, if you held a fruit to your ear, came the sound of fighting. I had not at the time read Dante's *Purgatorio*, and it caused me some trouble to verify the mountain garden, and, from some passage in the *Zohar*, the great birds among the boughs. A young girl, on being sent to the same garden, heard 'the music of Heaven' from a tree, and on listening with her ear against the trunk, found that it was made by the 'continual clashing of swords'. Whence came that fine thought of music-making swords, that image of the garden, and many like images and thoughts? I had as yet no clear answer, but knew myself face to face with the Anima Mundi described by Platonic philosophers, and more especially in modern times by Henry More, which has a memory independent of embodied individual memories, though they constantly enrich it with their images and their thoughts.

VI

At Sligo we walked twice every day, once after lunch and once after dinner, to the same gate on the road to Knocknarea; and at Rosses Point, to the same rock upon the shore; and as we walked we exchanged those thoughts that never rise before me now without bringing some sight of mountain or of shore. Considering that Mary Battle received our thoughts in sleep, though coarsened or turned to caricature, do not the thoughts of the scholar or the hermit, though they speak no word, or something of their shape and impulse, pass into the general mind? Does not the emotion of some woman of fashion, caught in the subtle torture of self-analysing passion, pass down, although she speak no word, to Joan with her Pot, Jill with her Pail and, it may be, with one knows not what nightmare melancholy, to Tom the Fool?

The Celtic Twilight

A TELLER OF TALES

Many of the tales in this book were told me by one Paddy Flynn, a little bright-eyed old man, who lived in a leaky and one-roomed cabin in the village of Ballisodare, which is, he was wont to say, 'the most gentle' – whereby he meant faery – 'place in the whole of County Sligo.' Others hold it, however, but second to Drumcliff and Dromahair. The first time I saw him he was bent above the fire with a can of mushrooms at his side; the next time he was asleep under a hedge, smiling in his sleep. He was indeed always cheerful, though I thought I could see in his eyes (swift as the eyes of a rabbit, when they peered out of their wrinkled holes) a melancholy which was wellnigh a portion of their joy; the visionary melancholy of purely instinctive natures and of all animals.

And yet there was much in his life to depress him, for in the triple solitude of age, eccentricity, and deafness, he went about much pestered by children. It was for this very reason perhaps that he ever recommended mirth and hopefulness. He was fond, for instance, of telling how Columcille cheered up his mother. 'How are you to-day, mother?' said the saint. 'Worse,' replied the mother. 'May you be worse to-morrow,' said the saint. The next day Columcille came again, and exactly the same conversation took place, but the third day the mother said, 'Better, thank God.' And the saint replied, 'May you be better to-morrow.' He was fond too of telling how the Judge smiles at the Last Day alike when he rewards the good and condemns the lost to unceasing flames. He had many strange sights to keep him cheerful or to make him sad. I asked him had he ever seen the faeries, and got the reply, 'Am I not annoyed with them?' I asked too if he had ever seen the banshee. 'I have seen it,' he said, 'down there by the water, batting the river with its hands.'

WAR

When there was a rumour of war with France a while ago, I met a poor Sligo woman, a soldier's widow, that I know, and I read her a sentence out of a letter I had just had from London: 'The people here are mad for war, but France seems inclined to take things peacefully,' or some like sentence. Her mind ran a good deal on war, which she imagined partly from what she had heard from soldiers, and partly from tradition of the rebellion of '98, but the word London doubled her interest, for she knew there were a great many people in London, and she herself had once lived in 'a congested district.' 'There are too many over one another in London. They are getting tired of the world. It is killed they want to be. It will be no matter; but sure the French want nothing but peace and quietness. The people here don't mind the war coming. They could not be worse than they are. They may as well die soldierly before God. Sure they will get quarters in Heaven.' Then she began to say that it would be a hard thing to see children tossed about on bayonets, and I knew her mind was running on traditions of the great rebellion. She said presently, 'I never knew a man that was in a battle that liked to speak of it after. They'd sooner be throwing hay down from a hayrick.' She told me how she and her neighbours used to be sitting over the fire when she was a girl, talking of the war that was coming, and now she was afraid it was coming again, for she had dreamed that all the bay was 'stranded and covered with seaweed.' I asked her if it was in the Fenian times that she had been so much afraid of war coming. But she cried out, 'Never had I such fun and pleasure as in the Fenian times. I was in a house where some of the officers used to be staying, and in the daytime I would be walking after the soldiers' band, and at night I'd be going down to the end of the garden watching a soldier, with his red coat on him, drilling the Fenians in the field behind the house. One night the boys tied the liver of an old horse, that had been dead three weeks, to the knocker, and I found it when I opened the door in the morning.' And presently our talk of war shifted, as it had a way of doing, to the battle of the Black Pig, which seems to her a battle between Ireland and England, but to me an Armageddon which shall quench all things in the Ancestral Darkness again, and from this to sayings about war and vengeance. 'Do you know,' she said, 'what the curse of the Four Fathers is? They put the man-child on the spear, and somebody said to them, "You will be cursed in the fourth generation after you," and that is why disease or anything always comes in the fourth generation.'

'DUST HATH CLOSED HELEN'S EYE'

I

I have been lately to a little group of houses, not many enough to be called a village, in the barony of Kiltartan in County Galway, whose name, Ballylee, is known through all the west of Ireland. There is the old square castle, Ballylee, inhabited by a farmer and his wife, and a cottage where their daughter and their son-in-law live, and a little mill with an old miller, and old ash-trees throwing green shadows upon a little river and great stepping-stones. I went there two or three times last year to talk to the miller about Biddy Early, a wise woman that lived in Clare some years ago, and about her saying, 'There is a cure for all evil between the two mill-wheels of Ballylee,' and to find out from him or another whether she meant the moss between the running waters or some other herb. I have been there this summer, and I shall be there again before it is autumn, because Mary Hynes, a beautiful woman whose name is still a wonder by turf fires, died there sixty years ago; for our feet would linger where beauty has lived its life of sorrow to make us understand that it is not of the world. An old man brought me a little way from the mill and the castle, and down a long, narrow boreen that was nearly lost in brambles and sloe-bushes, and he said, 'That is the little old foundation of the house, but the most of it is taken for building walls, and the goats have ate those bushes that are growing over it till they've got cranky, and they won't grow any more. They say she was the handsomest girl in Ireland, her skin was like dribbled snow' – he meant driven snow, perhaps, – 'and she had blushes in her cheeks. She had five handsome brothers, but all are gone now!' I talked to him about a poem in Irish, Raftery, a famous poet, made about her, and how it said, 'There is a strong cellar in Ballylee.' He said the strong cellar was the great hole where the river sank underground, and he brought me to a deep pool, where an otter hurried away under a grey boulder, and told me that many fish came up out of the dark water at early morning 'to taste the fresh water coming down from the hills.'

I first heard of the poem from an old woman who lives about two miles farther up the river, and who remembers Raftery and Mary Hynes. She says, 'I never saw anybody so handsome as she was, and I never will till I die,' and that he was nearly blind, and had 'no way of living but to go round and to mark some house to go to, and then all the neighbours would gather to hear. If you treated him well he'd praise you, but if you did not, he'd fault you in Irish. He was the greatest poet in Ireland, and he'd make a song about that bush if he chanced to stand under it. There was a bush he stood under from the rain, and he made verses praising it, and then when the water came through he made verses dispraising it.' She sang the poem to a friend and to myself in Irish, and every word was audible and expressive, as the words in a song were always, as I think, before music grew too proud to be the garment of words, flowing and changing with the flowing and changing of their energies. The poem is not as natural as the best Irish poetry of the last century, for the thoughts are arranged in a too obviously traditional form, so the old poor half-blind man who made it has to speak as if he were a rich farmer offering the best of everything to the woman he loves, but it has naïve and tender phrases. The friend that was with me has made some of the translation, but some of it has been made by the countrypeople themselves. I think it has more of the simplicity of the Irish verses than one finds in most translations.

Going to Mass by the will of God,
The day came wet and the wind rose;
I met Mary Hynes at the cross of Kiltartan,
And I fell in love with her then and there.

I spoke to her kind and mannerly,
As by report was her own way;
And she said, 'Raftery, my mind is easy,
You may come to-day to Ballylee.'

When I heard her offer I did not linger,
When her talk went to my heart my heart rose.
We had only to go across the three fields,
We had daylight with us to Ballylee.

The table was laid with glasses and a quart measure,
She had fair hair, and she sitting beside me;
And she said, 'Drink, Raftery, and a hundred welcomes,
There is a strong cellar in Ballylee.'

O star of light and O sun in harvest,
O amber hair, O my share of the world,
Will you come with me upon Sunday
Till we agree together before all the people?

I would not grudge you a song every Sunday evening,
Punch on the table, or wine if you would drink it,
But, O King of Glory, dry the roads before me,
Till I find the way to Ballylee.

There is sweet air on the side of the hill
When you are looking down upon Ballylee;
When you are walking in the valley picking nuts and blackberries,
There is music of the birds in it and music of the Sidhe.

What is the worth of greatness till you have the light
Of the flower of the branch that is by your side?
There is no god to deny it or to try and hide it,
She is the sun in the heavens who wounded my heart.

There is no part of Ireland I did not travel,
From the rivers to the tops of the mountains,
To the edge of Lough Greine whose mouth is hidden,
And I saw no beauty but was behind hers.

Her hair was shining, and her brows were shining too;
Her face was like herself, her mouth pleasant and sweet.
She is the pride, and I give her the branch,
She is the shining flower of Ballylee.

It is Mary Hynes, the calm and easy woman,
Has beauty in her mind and in her face.
If a hundred clerks were gathered together,
They could not write down a half of her ways.

An old weaver, whose son is supposed to go away among the Sidhe (the faeries) at night, says, 'Mary Hynes was the most beautiful thing ever made. My mother used to tell me about her, for she'd be at every hurling, and wherever she was she was dressed in white. As many as eleven men asked her in marriage in one day, but she wouldn't have any of them. There was a lot of men up beyond Kilbecanty one night sitting together drinking, and talking of her, and one of them got up and set out to go to Ballylee and see her; but Cloone Bog was open then, and when he came to it he fell into the water, and they found him dead there in the morning. She died of the fever that was before the famine.' Another old man says he was only a child when he saw her, but he remembered that 'the strongest man that was among us, one John Madden, got his death of the head of her, cold he got crossing rivers in the night-time to get to Ballylee.' This is perhaps the man the other remembered, for tradition gives the one thing many shapes. There is an old woman who remembers her, at Derrybrien among the Echtge hills, a vast desolate place, which has changed little since the old poem said, 'the stag upon the cold summit of Echtge hears the cry of the wolves, but still mindful of many poems and of the dignity of ancient speech. She says, 'The sun and the moon never shone on anybody so handsome, and her skin was so white that it looked blue, and she had two little blushes on her cheeks.' And an old wrinkled woman who lives close by Ballylee, and has told me many tales of the Sidhe, says, 'I often saw Mary Hynes, she was handsome indeed. She had two bunches of curls beside her cheeks, and they were the colour of silver. I saw Mary Molloy that was drowned in the river beyond, and Mary Guthrie that was in Ardrahan, but she took the sway of them both, a very comely creature. I was at her wake too – she had seen too much of the world. She was a kind creature. One day I was coming home through that field beyond, and I was tired, and who should come out but the Poisin Glegeal (the shining flower), and she gave me a glass of new milk.' This old woman meant no more than some beautiful bright colour by the colour of silver, for though I knew an old man – he is dead now – who thought she might know 'the cure for all the evils in the world,' that the Sidhe knew, she has seen too little gold to know its colour. But a man by the shore at Kinvara, who is too young to remember Mary Hynes, says, 'Everybody says there is no one at all to be seen now so handsome; it is said she had beautiful hair, the colour of gold. She was poor, but her clothes every day were the same as Sunday, she had such neatness. And if she went to any kind of a meeting, they would all be killing one another for a sight of her, and there was a great many in love with her, but she died young. It is said that no one that has a song made about them will ever live long.'

Those who are much admired are, it is held, taken by the Sidhe, who can use ungoverned feeling for their own ends, so that a father, as an old herb-doctor told me once, may give his child into their hands, or a husband his wife. The admired and desired are only safe if one says 'God bless them' when one's eyes are upon them. The old woman that sang the song thinks, too, that Mary Hynes was 'taken,' as the phrase is, 'for they have taken many that are not handsome, and why would they not take her? And people came from all parts to look at her, and maybe there were some that did not say "God bless her."' An old man who lives by the sea at Duras has as little doubt that she was taken, 'for there are some living yet can remember her coming to the pattern there beyond, and she was said to be the handsomest girl in Ireland.' She died young because the gods loved her, for the Sidhe are the gods, and it may be that the old saying, which we forget to understand literally, meant her manner of death in old times. These poor countrymen and countrywomen in their beliefs, and in their emotions, are many years nearer to that old Greek world, that set beauty beside the fountain of things, than are our men of learning. She 'had seen too much of the world'; but these old men and women, when they tell of her, blame another and not her, and though they can be hard, they grow gentle as the old men of Troy grew gentle when Helen passed by on the walls.

The poet who helped her to so much fame has himself a great fame throughout the west of Ireland. Some think that Raftery was half blind, and say, 'I saw Raftery, a dark man, but he had sight enough to see her,' or the like, but some think he was wholly blind, as he may have been at the end of his life. Fable makes all things perfect in their kind, and her blind people must never look on the world and the sun. I asked a man I met one day, when I was looking for a pool *na mná Sidhe* where women of Faery have been seen, how Raftery could have admired Mary Hynes so much if he had been altogether blind. He said, 'I think Raftery was altogether blind, but those that are blind have a way of seeing things, and have the power to know more, and to feel more, and to do more, and to guess more than those that have their sight, and a certain wit and a certain wisdom is given to them.' Everybody, indeed, will tell you that he was very wise, for was he not only blind but a poet? The weaver, whose words about Mary Hynes I have already given, says, 'His poetry was the gift of the Almighty, for there are three things that are the gift of the Almighty – poetry and dancing and principles. That is why in the old times an ignorant man coming down from the hillside would be better behaved and have better learning than a man with education you'd meet now, for they got it from God'; and a man at Coole says, 'When he put his finger to one part of his head, everything would come to him as if it was written in a book'; and an old pensioner at Kiltartan says, 'He was standing under a bush one time, and he talked to it, and it answered him back in Irish. Some say it was the bush that spoke, but it must have been an enchanted voice in it, and it gave him the knowledge of all the things of the world. The bush withered up afterwards, and it is to be seen on the roadside now between this and Rahasine.' There is a poem of his about a bush, which I have never seen, and it may have come out of the cauldron of Fable in this shape.

A friend of mine met a man once who had been with him when he died, but the people say that he died alone, and one Maurteen Gillane told Dr. Hyde that all night long a light was seen streaming up to heaven from the roof of the house where he lay, and 'that was the angels who were with him'; and all night long there was a great light in the hovel, 'and that was the angels who were waking him. They gave that honour to him because he was so good a poet, and sang such religious songs.' It may be that in a few years Fable, who changes mortalities to immortalities in her cauldron, will have changed Mary Hynes and Raftery to perfect symbols of the sorrow of beauty and of the magnificence and penury of dreams.

When I was in a northern town a while ago I had a long talk with a man who had lived in a neighbouring country district when he was a boy. He told me that when a very beautiful girl was born in a family that had not been noted for good looks, her beauty was thought to have come from the Sidhe, and to bring misfortune with it. He went over the names of several beautiful girls that he had known, and said that beauty had never brought happiness to anybody. It was a thing, he said, to be proud of and afraid of. I wish I had written out his words at that time, for they were more picturesque than my memory of them.

ENCHANTED WOODS

I

Last summer, whenever I had finished my day's work, I used to go wandering in certain roomy woods, and there I would often meet an old countryman, and talk to him about his work and about the woods, and once or twice a friend came with me to whom he would open his heart more readily than to me. He had spent all his life lopping away the witch-elm and the hazel and the privet and the hornbeam from the paths, and had thought much about the natural and supernatural creatures of the wood. He has heard the hedgehog – 'grainne oge,' he calls him – 'grunting like a Christian,' and is certain that he steals apples by rolling about under an apple-tree until there is an apple sticking to every quill. He is certain too that the cats, of whom there are many in the woods, have a language of their own – some kind of old Irish. He says, 'Cats were serpents, and they were made into cats at the time of some great change in the world. That is why they are hard to kill, and why it is dangerous to meddle with them. If you annoy a cat it might claw or bite you in a way that would put poison in you, and that would be the serpent's tooth.' Sometimes he thinks they change into wild cats, and then a nail grows on the end of their tails; but these wild cats are not the same as the marten cats, who have been always in the woods. The foxes were once tame, as the cats are now, but they ran away and became wild. He talks of all wild creatures except squirrels – whom he hates – with what seems an affectionate interest, though at times his eyes will twinkle with pleasure as he remembers how he made hedgehogs unroll themselves when he was a boy, by putting a wisp of burning straw under them.

I am not certain that he distinguishes between the natural and supernatural very clearly. He told me the other day that foxes and cats like, above all, to be in the 'forths' and lisses after nightfall; and he will certainly pass from some story about a fox to a story about a spirit with less change of voice than when he is going to speak about a marten cat – a rare beast nowadays. Many years ago he used to work in the garden, and once they put him to sleep in a garden-house where there was a loft full of apples, and all night he could hear people rattling plates and knives and forks over his head in the loft. Once, at any rate, he has seen an unearthly sight in the woods. He says, 'One time I was out cutting timber over in Inchy, and about eight o'clock one morning when I got there I saw a girl picking nuts, with her hair hanging down over her shoulders, brown hair, and she had a good, clean face, and she was tall and nothing on her head, and her dress no way gaudy but simple, and when she felt me coming she gathered herself up and was gone as if the earth had swallowed her up. And I followed her and looked for her, but I never could see her again from that day to this, never again.' He used the word clean as we would use words like fresh or comely.

Others too have seen spirits in the Enchanted Woods. A labourer told us of what a friend of his had seen in a part of the woods that is called Shan-walla, from some old village that was before the wood. He said, 'One evening I parted from Lawrence Mangan in the yard, an' he went away through the path in Shan-walla, an' bid me good-night. And two hours after, there he was back again in the yard, an' bid me light a candle that was in the stable. An' he told me that when he got into Shan-walla, a little fellow about as high as his knee, but having a head as big as a man's body, came beside him and led him out of the path an' round about, and at last it brought him to the lime-kiln, and then it vanished and left him.'

A woman told me of a sight that she and others had seen by a certain deep pool in the river. She said, 'I came over the stile from the chapel, and others along with me; and a great blast of wind came and two trees were bent and broken and fell into the river, and the splash of water out of it went up to the skies. And those that were with me saw many figures, but myself I only saw one, sitting there by the bank where the trees fell. Dark clothes he had on, and he was headless.'

A man told me that one day, when he was a boy, he and another boy went to catch a horse in a certain field, full of boulders and bushes of hazel and creeping juniper and rock-roses, that is where the lake-side is for a little clear of the woods. He said to the boy that was with him, 'I bet a button that if I fling a pebble on to that bush it will stay on it,' meaning that the bush was so matted the pebble would not be able to go through it. So he took up 'a pebble of cow-dung, and as soon as it hit the bush there came out of it the most beautiful music that ever was heard.' They ran away, and when they had gone about two hundred yards they looked back and saw a woman dressed in white, walking round and round the bush. 'First it had the form of a woman, and then of a man, and it was going round the bush.'

II

I often entangle myself in arguments more complicated than even those paths of Inchy as to what is the true nature of apparitions. But at other times I say as Socrates said when they told him a learned opinion about a nymph of the Ilissus, 'The common opinion is enough for me'; and believe that all nature is full of invisible people, and that some of these are ugly or grotesque, some wicked or foolish, many beautiful beyond any one we have ever seen, and that the beautiful are not far away when we are walking in pleasant and quiet places. Even when I was a boy I could never walk in a wood without feeling that at any moment I might find before me somebody or something I had long looked for without knowing what I looked for. And now I will at times explore every little nook of some poor coppice with almost anxious footsteps, so deep a hold has this imagination upon me. You too meet with a like imagination, doubtless, somewhere, wherever your ruling stars will have it, Saturn driving you to the woods, or the Moon, it may be, to the edges of the sea. I will not of a certainty believe that there is nothing in the sunset, where our forefathers imagined the dead following their shepherd the sun, or nothing but some vague presence as little moving as nothing. If beauty is not a gateway out of the net we were taken in at our birth, it will not long be beauty, and we will find it better to sit at home by the fire and fatten a lazy body or to run hither and thither in some foolish sport than to look at the finest show that light and shadow ever made among green leaves.

I say to myself, when I am well out of that thicket of argument, that they are surely there, the divine people, for only we who have neither simplicity nor wisdom have denied them, and the simple of all times and the wise men of ancient times have seen them and even spoken to them. They live out their passionate lives not far off, as I think, and we shall be among them when we die if we but keep our natures simple and passionate. May it not even be that death shall unite us to all romance, and that some day we shall fight dragons among blue hills or come to that whereof all romance is but

> Foreshadowings mingled with the images
> Of man's misdeeds in greater days than these,

as the old men thought in *The Earthly Paradise* when they were in good spirits?

A VISIONARY

A young man came to see me at my lodgings the other night, and began to talk of the making of the earth and the heavens and much else. I questioned him about his life and his doings. He had written many poems and painted many mystical designs since we met last, but latterly had neither written nor painted, for his whole heart was set upon making his character vigorous and calm, and the emotional life of the artist was bad for him, he feared. He recited his poems readily, however. He had them all in his memory. Some indeed had never been written down. Suddenly it seemed to me that he was peering about him a little eagerly. 'Do you see anything, X——?' I said. 'A shining, winged woman, covered by her long hair, is standing near the doorway,' he answered, or some such words. 'Is it the influence of some living person who thinks of us, and whose thoughts appear to us in that symbolic form?' I said; for I am well instructed in the ways of the visionaries and in the fashion of their speech. 'No,' he replied; 'for if it were the thoughts of a person who is alive I should feel the living influence in my living body, and my heart would beat and my breath would fail. It is a spirit. It is some one who is dead or who has never lived.'

I asked what he was doing, and found he was clerk in a large shop. His pleasure, however, was to wander about upon the hills, talking to half-mad and visionary peasants, or to persuade queer and conscience-stricken persons to deliver up the keeping of their troubles into his care. Another night, when I was with him in his own lodging, more than one turned up to talk over their beliefs and disbeliefs, and sun them as it were in the subtle light of his mind. Sometimes visions come to him as he talks with them, and he is rumoured to have told divers people true matters of their past days and distant friends, and left them hushed with dread of their strange teacher, who seems scarce more than a boy, and is so much more subtle than the oldest among them.

The poetry he recited me was full of his nature and his visions. Sometimes it told of other lives he believes himself to have lived in other centuries, sometimes of people he had talked to, revealing them to their own minds. I told him I would write an article upon him and it, and was told in turn that I might do so if I did not mention his name, for he wished to be always 'unknown, obscure, impersonal.' Next day a bundle of his poems arrived, and with them a note in these words: 'Here are copies of verses you said you liked. I do not think I could ever write or paint any more. I prepare myself for a cycle of other activities in some other life. I will make rigid my roots and branches. It is not now my turn to burst into leaves and flowers.'

The poems were all endeavours to capture some high, impalpable mood in a net of obscure images. There were fine passages in all, but these were often embedded in thoughts which have evidently a special value to his mind, but are to other men the counters of an unknown coinage. At other times the beauty of the thought was obscured by careless writing as though he had suddenly doubted if writing was not a foolish labour. He had frequently illustrated his verses with drawings, in which an imperfect anatomy did not altogether smother a beauty of feeling. The faeries in whom he believes have given him many subjects, notably Thomas of Ercildoune sitting motionless in the twilight while a young and beautiful creature leans softly out of the shadow and whispers in his ear. He had delighted above all in strong effects of colour: spirits who have upon their heads instead of hair the feathers of peacocks; a phantom reaching from a swirl of flame towards a star; a spirit passing with a globe of iridescent crystal – symbol of the soul – half shut within his hand. But always under this largess of colour lay some appeal to human sympathy. This appeal draws to him all those who, like himself, seek for illumination or else mourn for a joy that has gone. One of these especially comes to mind. A winter or two ago he spent much of the night walking up and down upon the mountain talking to an old peasant who, dumb to most men, poured out his cares for him. Both were unhappy: X——because he had then first decided that art and poetry were not for him, and the old peasant because his life was ebbing out with no achievement remaining and no hope left him. The peasant was wandering in his mind with prolonged sorrow. Once he burst out with, 'God possesses the heavens – God possesses the heavens – but He covets the world'; and once he lamented that his old neighbours were gone, and that all had forgotten him: they used to draw a chair to the fire for him in every cabin, and now they said, 'Who is that old fellow there?' 'The fret' (Irish for doom) 'is over me,' he repeated, and then went on to talk once more of God and Heaven. More than once also he said, waving his arm towards the mountain. 'Only myself knows what happened under the thorn-tree forty years ago'; and as he said it the tears upon his face glistened in the moonlight.

BY THE ROADSIDE

Last night I went to a wide place on the Kiltartan road to listen to some Irish songs. While I waited for the singers an old man sang about that country beauty who died so many years ago, and spoke of a singer he had known who sang so beautifully that no horse would pass him, but must turn its head and cock its ears to listen. Presently a score of men and boys and girls, with shawls over their heads, gathered under the trees to listen. Somebody sang *Sa Muirnín Díles*, and then somebody else *Jimmy Mo Mílestór*, mournful songs of separation, of death, and of exile. Then some of the men stood up and began to dance, while another lilted the measure they danced to, and then somebody sang *Eiblín a Rúin*, that glad song of meeting which has always moved me more than other songs, because the lover who made it sang it to his sweetheart under the shadow of a mountain I looked at every day through my childhood. The voices melted into the twilight, and were mixed into the trees, and when I thought of the words they too melted away, and were mixed with the generations of men. Now it was a phrase, now it was an attitude of mind, an emotional form, that had carried my memory to older verses, or even to forgotten mythologies. I was carried so far that it was as though I came to one of the four rivers, and followed it under the wall of Paradise to the roots of the Trees of Knowledge and of Life. There is no song or story handed down among the cottages that has not words and thoughts to carry one as far, for though one can know but a little of their ascent, one knows that they ascend like mediaeval genealogies through unbroken dignities to the beginning of the world. Folk-art is, indeed, the oldest of the aristocracies of thought, and because it refuses what is passing and trivial, the merely clever and pretty, as certainly as the vulgar and insincere, and because it has gathered into itself the simplest and most unforgettable thoughts of the generations, it is the soil where all great art is rooted. Wherever it is spoken by the fireside, or sung by the roadside, or carved upon the lintel, appreciation of the arts that a single mind gives unity and design to, spreads quickly when its hour is come.

In a society that has cast out imaginative tradition, only a few people – three or four thousand out of millions – favoured by their own characters and by happy circumstance, and only then after much labour, have understanding of imaginative things, and yet 'the imagination is the man himself.' The Churches in the Middle Ages won all the arts into their service because men understood that when imagination is impoverished, a principal voice – some would say the only voice – for the awakening of wise hope and durable faith, and understanding charity, can speak but in broken words, if it does not fall silent. And so it has always seemed to me that we, who would re-awaken imaginative tradition by making old songs live again, or by gathering old stories into books, take part in the quarrel of Galilee. Those who are Irish and would spread foreign ways, which, for all but a few, are ways of spiritual poverty, take part also. Their part is with those who were of Jewry, and yet cried out, 'If thou let this man go thou art not Caesar's friend.'

Rosa Alchemica

This is the first of three tales, published in 1877 (*Ed.*)

I

It is now more than ten years since I met, for the last time, Michael Robartes, and for the first time and the last time his friends and fellow-students; and witnessed his and their tragic end, and passed through strange experiences, which have changed me so that my writings have grown less popular and less intelligible, and may compel me to take refuge in the habit of Saint Dominic. I had just published *Rosa Alchemica*, a little work on the Alchemists, somewhat in the manner of Sir Thomas Browne, and had received many letters from believers in the arcane sciences, upbraiding what they called my timidity, for they could not believe so evident sympathy but the sympathy of the artist, which is half pity, for everything which has moved men's hearts in any age. I had discovered, early in my researches, that their doctrine was no merely chemical fantasy, but a philosophy they applied to the world, to the elements and to man himself; and that they sought to fashion gold out of common metals merely as part of a universal transmutation of all things into some divine and imperishable substance; and this enabled me to make my little book a fanciful reverie over the transmutation of life into art, and a cry of measureless desire for a world made wholly of essences.

I was sitting dreaming of what I had written, in my house in one of the old parts of Dublin; a house my ancestors had made almost famous through their part in the politics of the city and their friendships with the famous men of their generations; and was feeling an unwonted happiness at having at last accomplished a long-cherished design, and changed my rooms into an expression of this favourite doctrine. The portraits, of more historical than artistic interest, had gone; and tapestry, full of the blue and bronze of peacocks, fell over the doors, and shut out all history and activity untouched with beauty and peace; and now when I looked at my Crivelli and pondered on the rose in the hand of the Virgin, wherein the form was so delicate and precise that it seemed more like a thought than a flower, or my Francesca, so full of ghostly astonishment, I knew a Christian's ecstasy without his slavery to rule and custom. When I pondered over the antique bronze gods and goddesses, which I had mortgaged my house to buy, I had all a pagan's delight in various beauty and without his terror at sleepless destiny and his labour with many sacrifices; and I had but to go to my bookshelf, where every book was bound in leather, stamped with intricate ornament, and of a carefully chosen colour: Shakespeare in the orange of the glory of the world, Dante in the dull red of his anger, Milton in the blue-grey of his formal calm; to know what I would of human passions without their bitterness and without satiety. I had gathered about me all gods because I believed in none, and experienced every pleasure because I gave myself to none, but held myself apart, individual, indissoluble, a mirror of polished steel. I looked in the triumph of this imagination at the birds of Hera, glittering in the light of the fire as though of Byzantine mosaic; and to my mind, for which symbolism was a necessity, they seemed the doorkeepers of my world, shutting out all that was not as affluent a beauty as their own; and for a moment I thought, as I had thought in so many other moments, that it was possible to rob life of every bitterness except the bitterness of death; and then a thought which had followed his thought, time after time, filled me with a passionate sorrow. All those forms: that Madonna with her brooding purity, those delighted ghostly faces under the morning light, those bronze divinities with their passionless dignity, those wild shapes rushing from despair to despair, belonged to a divine world wherein I had no part; and every experience, however profound, every perception, however exquisite, would bring me the bitter dream of a limitless energy I could never know, and even in my most perfect moment I would be two selves, the one watching with heavy eyes the other's moment of content. I had heaped about me the gold born in the crucibles of others; but the supreme dream of the alchemist, the transmutation of the weary heart into a weariless spirit, was as far from me as, I doubted not, it had been from him also. I turned to my last purchase, a set of alchemical apparatus which, the dealer in the Rue Le Peletier had assured me, once belonged to Raymond Lully, and as I joined the alembic to the athanor and laid the *lavacrum maris* at their side, I understood the alchemical doctrine, that all beings, divided from the great deep where spirits wander, one and yet a multitude, are weary; and sympathised, in the pride of my connoisseurship, with the consuminy thirst for destruction which made the alchemist veil under his symbols of lions and dragons, of eagles and ravens, of dew and of nitre, a search for an essence which would dissolve all mortal things. I repeated to myself the ninth key of

Basilius Valentinus, in which he compares the fire of the Last Day to the fire of the alchemist, and the world to the alchemist's furnace, and would have us know that all must be dissolved before the divine substance, material gold or immaterial ecstasy, awake. I had dissolved indeed the mortal world and lived amid immortal essences, but had obtained no miraculous ecstasy. As I thought of these things, I drew aside the curtains and looked out into the darkness, and it seemed to my troubled fancy that all those little points of light filling the sky were the furnaces of innumerable divine alchemists, who labour continually, turning lead into gold, weariness into ecstasy, bodies into souls, the darkness into God, and at their perfect labour my mortality grew heavy, and I cried out, as so many dreamers and men of letters in our age have cried, for the birth of that elaborate spiritual beauty which could alone uplift souls weighted with so many dreams.

II

My reverie was broken by a loud knocking at the door, and I wondered the more at this because I had no visitors, and had bid my servants do all things silently, lest they broke the dream of an all but secret life. Feeling a little curious, I resolved to go to the door myself, and, taking one of the silver candlesticks from the mantelpiece, began to descend the stairs. The servants appeared to be out, for though the sound poured through every corner and crevice of the house there was no stir in the lower rooms. I remembered that because my needs were so few, my part in life so little, they had begun to come and go as they would, often leaving me alone for hours. The emptiness and silence of a world from which I had driven everything but dreams suddenly overwhelmed me, and I shuddered as I drew the bolt. I found before me Michael Robartes, whom I had not seen for years, and whose wild red hair, fierce eyes, sensitive, tremulous lips and rough clothes, made him look now, just as they used to do fifteen years before, something between a debauchee, a saint, and a peasant. He had recently come to Ireland, he said, and wished to see me on a matter of importance: indeed, the only matter of importance for him and for me. His voice brought up before me our student years in Paris, and, remembering the magnetic power he had once possessed over me, a little fear mingled with much annoyance at this irrelevant intrusion, as I led the way up the wide staircase, where Swift had passed joking and railing, and Curran telling stories and quoting Greek, in simpler days, before men's minds, subtilised and complicated by the romantic movement in art and literature, began to tremble on the verge of some unimagined revelation. I felt that my hand shook, and saw that the light of the candle wavered more than it need have upon the gods and nymphs set upon the wall by some Italian plasterer of the eighteenth century, making them look like the first beings slowly shaping in the formless and void darkness. When the door had closed, and the peacock curtain fell between us and the world, I felt, in a way I could not understand, that some singular and unexpected thing was about to happen. I went over to the mantelpiece, and finding that a little chainless bronze censer, set, upon the outside, with pieces of painted china by Orazio Fontana, which I had filled with antique amulets, had fallen upon its side and poured out its contents, I began to gather the amulets into the bowl, partly to collect my thoughts and partly with that habitual reverence which seemed to me the due of things so long connected with secret hopes and fears. 'I see,' said Michael Robartes, 'that you are still fond of incense, and I can show you an incense more precious than any you have ever seen,' and as he spoke he took the censer out of my hand and put the amulets in a little heap between the athanor and the alembic. I sat down, and he sat down at the side of the fire, and sat there for a while looking into the fire, and holding the censer in his hand. 'I have come to ask you something,' he said, 'and the incense will fill the room, and our thoughts, with its sweet odour while we are talking. I got it from an old man in Syria, who said it was made from flowers, of one kind with the flowers that laid their heavy purple petals upon the hands and upon the hair and upon the feet of Christ in the Garden of Gethsemane, and folded Him in their heavy breath, until He cried against the cross and His destiny.' He shook some dust into the censer out of a small silk bag, and set the censer upon the floor and lit the dust, which sent up a blue stream of smoke, that spread out over the ceiling, and flowed downwards again until it was like Milton's banyan tree. It filled me, as incense often does, with a faint sleepiness, so that I started when he said, 'I have come to ask you that question which I asked you in Paris, and which you left Paris rather than answer.'

He had turned his eyes towards me, and I saw them glitter in the firelight, through the incense cloud, as I replied: 'You mean, will I become an initiate of your Order of the Alchemical Rose? I would not consent in Paris, when I was full of unsatisfied desire, and now that I have at last fashioned my life according to my desire, am I likely to consent?'

'You have changed greatly since then,' he answered. 'I have read your books, and now I see you among all these images, and I understand you better than you do yourself, for I have been with many and many dreamers at the same crossways. You have shut away the world and gathered the gods about you, and if you do not throw yourself at their feet, you will be always full of lassitude, and of wavering purpose, for a man must forget he is miserable in the bustle and noise of the multitude in this world and in time; or seek a mystical union with the multitude who govern this world and time.' And then he murmured something I could not hear, and as though to some one I could not see.

For a moment the room appeared to darken, as it used to do when he was about to perform some singular experiment, and in the darkness the peacocks upon the doors seemed to glow with a more intense colour. I cast off the illusion, which was, I believed, merely caused by memory, and by the twilight of incense, for I would not acknowledge that he could overcome my now mature intellect; and I said, 'Even if I grant that I need a spiritual belief and some form of worship, why should I go to Eleusis and not to Calvary?' He leaned forward and began speaking with a slightly rhythmical intonation, and as he spoke I had to struggle again with the shadow, as of some older night than the night of the sun, which began to dim the light of the candles and to blot out the little gleams upon the corner of picture-frames and on the bronze divinities, and to turn the blue of the incense to a heavy purple; while it left the peacocks to glimmer and glow as though each separate colour were a living spirit. I had fallen into a profound dream-like reverie in which I heard him speaking as at a distance. 'And yet there is no one who communes with only one god,' he was saying, 'and the more a man lives in imagination and in a refined understanding, the more gods does he meet with and talk with, and the more does he come under the power of Roland, who sounded in the Valley of Roncesvalles the last trumpet of the body's will and pleasure; and of Hamlet, who saw them perishing away, and sighed; and of Faust, who looked for them up and down the world and could not find them; and under the power of all those countless divinities who have taken upon themselves spiritual bodies in the minds of the modern poets and romance-writers, and under the power of the old divinities, who since the Renaissance have won everything of their ancient worship except the sacrifice of birds and fishes, the fragrance of garlands and the smoke of incense. The many think humanity made these divinities, and that it can unmake them again; but we who have seen them pass in rattling harness, and in soft robes, and heard them speak with articulate voices while we lay in deathlike trance, know that they are always making and unmaking humanity, which is indeed but the trembling of their lips.'

He had stood up and begun to walk to and fro, and had become in my waking dream a shuttle weaving an immense purple web whose folds had begun to fill the room. The room seemed to have become inexplicably silent, as though all but the web and the weaving were at an end in the world. 'They have come to us; they have come to us,' the voice began again; 'all that have ever been in your reverie, all that you have met with in books. There is Lear, his head still wet with the thunderstorm, and he laughs because you thought yourself an existence who are but a shadow, and him a shadow who is an eternal god; and there is Beatrice, with her lips half parted in a smile, as though all the stars were about to pass away in a sigh of love; and there is the mother of the God of humility, He who has cast so great a spell over men that they have tried to unpeople their hearts that He might reign alone, but she holds in her hand the rose whose every petal is a god; and there, O, swiftly she comes! is Aphrodite under a twilight falling from the wings of numberless sparrows, and about her feet are the grey and white doves.' In the midst of my dream I saw him hold out his left arm and pass his right hand over it as though he stroked the wings of doves. I made a violent effort which seemed almost to tear me in two, and said with forced determination, 'You would sweep me away into an indefinite world which fills me with terror; and yet a man is a great man just in so far as he can make his mind reflect everything with indifferent precision like a mirror.' I seemed to be perfectly master of myself, and went on, but more rapidly, 'I command you to leave me at once, for your ideas and fantasies are but the illusions that creep like maggots into civilisations when they begin to decline, and into minds when they begin to decay.' I had grown suddenly angry, and seizing the alembic from the table, was about to rise and strike him with it, when the peacocks on the door behind him appeared to grow immense; and then the alembic fell from my fingers and I was drowned in a tide of green and blue and bronze feathers, and as I struggled hopelessly I heard a distant voice saying, 'Our master Avicenna has written that all life proceeds out of corruption.' The glittering feathers had now covered me completely, and I knew that I had struggled for hundreds of years, and was conquered at last. I was sinking into the depth when the green and blue and bronze that seemed to fill the world became a sea of flame and swept me away, and as I was swirled along I heard a voice over my head cry, 'The mirror is broken in two pieces,' and another voice answer, 'The mirror is broken in four pieces,' and a more distant voice cry with an exultant cry, 'The mirror is broken into numberless pieces'; and then a multitude of pale hands were reaching towards me, and strange gentle faces bending above me, and half-wailing and half-caressing voices uttering words that were forgotten the moment they were spoken. I was being lifted out of the tide of flame, and felt my memories, my hopes, my thoughts, my will, everything I held to be myself, melting away; then I seemed to rise through numberless companies of beings who were, I understood, in some way more certain than thought, each wrapped in his eternal moment, in the perfect lifting of an arm, in a little circlet of rhythmical words, in dreaming with dim eyes and half-closed eyelids. And then I passed beyond these forms, which were so beautiful they had almost ceased to be, and, having endured strange moods, melancholy, as it seemed, with the weight of many worlds, I passed into the Death which is Beauty itself, and into that Loneliness which all the multitudes desire without ceasing. All things that had ever lived seemed to come and dwell in my heart, and I in theirs; and I had never again known mortality or tears, had I not suddenly fallen from the certainty of vision into the uncertainty of dream, and become a drop of molten gold falling with immense rapidity, through a night elaborate with stars, and all about me a melancholy exultant wailing. I fell and fell and fell, and then the wailing was but the wailing of the wind in the chimney, and I awoke to find myself leaning upon the table and supporting my head with my hands. I saw the alembic swaying from side to side in the distant corner it had rolled to, and Michael Robartes watching me and waiting. 'I will go wherever you will,' I said, 'and do whatever you bid me, for I have been with eternal things.' 'I knew,' he replied, 'you must needs answer as you have answered, when I heard the storm begin. You must come to a great distance, for we were commanded to build our temple between the pure multitude by the waves and the impure multitude of men.'

I did not speak as we drove through the deserted streets, for my mind was curiously empty of familiar thoughts and experiences; it seemed to have been plucked out of the definite world and cast naked upon a shoreless sea. There were moments when the vision appeared on the point of returning, and I would half remember, with an ecstasy of joy or sorrow, crimes and heroisms, fortunes and misfortunes; or begin to contemplate, with a sudden leaping of the heart, hopes and terrors, desires and ambitions, alien to my orderly and careful life; and then I would awake shuddering at the thought that some great imponderable being had swept through my mind. It was indeed days before this feeling passed perfectly away, and even now, when I have sought refuge in the only definite faith, I feel a great tolerance for those people with incoherent personalities, who gather in the chapels and meeting-places of certain obscure sects, because I also have felt fixed habits and principles dissolving before a power, which was *hysterica passio* or sheer madness, if you will, but was so powerful in its melancholy exultation that I tremble lest it wake again and drive me from my new-found peace.

When we came in the grey light to the great half-empty terminus, it seemed to me I was so changed that I was no more, as man is, a moment shuddering at eternity, but eternity weeping and laughing over a moment; and when we had started and Michael Robartes had fallen asleep, as he soon did, his sleeping face, in which there was no sign of all that had so shaken me and that now kept me wakeful, was to my excited mind more like a mask than a face. The fancy possessed me that the man behind it had dissolved away like salt in water, and that it laughed and sighed, appealed and denounced at the bidding of beings greater or less than man. 'This is not Michael Robartes at all: Michael Robartes is dead; dead for ten, for twenty years perhaps,' I kept repeating to myself. I fell at last into a feverish sleep, waking up from time to time when we rushed past some little town, its slated roofs shining with wet, or still lake gleaming in the cold morning light. I had been too preoccupied to ask where we were going, or to notice what tickets Michael Robartes had taken, but I knew now from the direction of the sun that we were going westward; and presently I knew also, by the way in which the trees had grown into the semblance of tattered beggars flying with bent heads towards the east, that we were approaching the western coast. Then immediately I saw the sea between the low hills upon the left, its dull grey broken into white patches and lines.

When we left the train we had still, I found, some way to go, and set out, buttoning our coats about us, for the wind was bitter and violent. Michael Robartes was silent, seeming anxious to leave me to my thoughts; and as we walked between the sea and the rocky side of a great promontory, I realized with a new perfection what a shock had been given to all my habits of thought and of feeling, if indeed some mysterious change had not taken place in the substance of my mind, for the grey waves, plumed with scudding foam, had grown part of a teeming, fantastic inner life; and when Michael Robartes pointed to a square ancient-looking house, with a much smaller and newer building under its lee, set out on the very end of a dilapidated and almost deserted pier, and said it was the Temple of the Alchemical Rose, I was possessed with the fantasy that the sea, which kept covering it with showers of white foam, was claiming it as part of some indefinite and passionate life, which had begun to war upon our orderly and careful days, and was about to plunge the world into a night as obscure as that which followed the downfall of the classical world. One part of my mind mocked this fantastic terror, but the other, the part that still lay half plunged in vision, listened to the clash of unknown armies, and shuddered at unimaginable fanaticisms, that hung in those grey leaping waves.

We had gone but a few paces along the pier when we came upon an old man, who was evidently a watchman, for he sat in an overset barrel, close to a place where masons had been lately working upon a break in the pier, and had in front of him a fire such as one sees slung under tinkers' carts. I saw that he was also a voteen, as the peasants say, for there was a rosary hanging from a nail on the rim of the barrel, and as I saw I shuddered, and I did not know why I shuddered. We had passed him a few yards when I heard him cry in

Gaelic, 'Idolaters, idolaters, go down to Hell with your witches and your devils; go down to Hell that the herrings may come again into the bay'; and for some moments I could hear him half screaming and half muttering behind us. 'Are you not afraid,' I said, 'that these wild fishing people may do some desperate thing against you?'

'I and mine,' he answered, 'are long past human hurt or help, being incorporate with immortal spirits, and when we die it shall be the consummation of the supreme work. A time will come for these people also, and they will sacrifice a mullet to Artemis, or some other fish to some new divinity, unless indeed their own divinities set up once more their temples of grey stone. Their reign has never ceased, but only waned in power a little, for the Sidhe still pass in every wind, and dance and play at hurley, but they cannot build their temples again till there have been martyrdoms and victories, and perhaps even that long-foretold battle in the Valley of the Black Pig.'

Keeping close to the wall that went about the pier on the seaward side, to escape the driving foam and the wind, which threatened every moment to lift us off our feet, we made our way in silence to the door of the square building. Michael Robartes opened it with a key, on which I saw the rust of many salt winds, and led me along a bare passage and up an uncarpeted stair to a little room surrounded with bookshelves. A meal would be brought, but only of fruit, for I must submit to a tempered fast before the ceremony, he explained, and with it a book on the doctrine and method of the Order, over which I was to spend what remained of the winter daylight. He then left me, promising to return an hour before the ceremony. I began searching among the bookshelves, and found one of the most exhaustive alchemical libraries I have ever seen. There were the works of Morienus, who hid his immortal body under a shirt of hair-cloth; of Avicenna, who was a drunkard and yet controlled numberless legions of spirits; of Alfarabi, who put so many spirits into his lute that he could make men laugh, or weep, or fall in deadly trance as he would; of Lully, who transformed himself into the likeness of a red cock; of Flamel, who with his wife Pernella achieved the elixir many hundreds of years ago, and is fabled to live still in Arabia among the Dervishes; and of many of less fame. There were very few mystics but alchemical mystics, and because, I had little doubt, of the devotion to one god of the greater number and of the limited sense of beauty, which Robartes would hold an inevitable consequence; but I did notice a complete set of facsimiles of the prophetical writings of William Blake, and probably because of the multitudes that thronged his illumination and were 'like the gay fishes on the wave when the moon sucks up the dew.' I noted also many poets and prose writers of every age, but only those who were a little weary of life, as indeed the greatest have been everywhere, and who cast their imagination to us, as a something they needed no longer now that they were going up in their fiery chariots.

Presently I heard a tap at the door, and a woman came in and laid a little fruit upon the table. I judged that she had once been handsome, but her cheeks were hollowed by what I would have held, had I seen her anywhere else, an excitement of the flesh and a thirst for pleasure, instead of which it doubtless was an excitement of the imagination and a thirst for beauty. I asked her some question concerning the ceremony, but getting no answer except a shake of the head, saw that I must await initiation in silence. When I had eaten, she came again, and having laid a curiously wrought bronze box on the table, lighted the candles, and took away the plates and the remnants. So soon as I was alone, I turned to the box, and found that the peacocks of Hera spread out their tails over the sides and lid, against a background on which were wrought great stars, as though to affirm that the heavens were a part of their glory. In the box was a book bound in vellum, and having upon the vellum and in very delicate colours, and in gold, the Alchemical Rose with many spears thrusting against it, but in vain, as was shown by the shattered points of those nearest to the petals. The book was written upon vellum, and in beautiful clear letters, interspersed with symbolical pictures and illuminations, after the manner of the *Splendor Solis*.

The first chapter described how six students, of Celtic descent, gave themselves separately to the study of alchemy, and solved, one the mystery of the Pelican, another the mystery of the Green Dragon, another the mystery of the Eagle, another that of Salt and Mercury. What seemed a succession of accidents, but was, the book declared, the contrivance of preternatural powers, brought them together in the garden of an inn in the South of France, and while they talked together the thought came to them that alchemy was the gradual distillation of the contents of the soul, until they were ready to put off the mortal and put on the immortal. An owl passed, rustling among the vine-leaves overhead, and then an old woman came, leaning upon a stick, and, sitting close to them, took up the thought where they had dropped it. Having expounded the whole principle of spiritual alchemy, and bid them found the Order of the Alchemical Rose, she passed from among them, and when they would have followed was nowhere to be seen. They formed themselves into an Order, holding their goods and making their researches in common, and, as they became perfect in the alchemical doctrine, apparitions came and went among them, and taught them more and more marvellous mysteries. The book then went on to expound so much of these as the neophyte was permitted to know, dealing at the outset and at considerable length with the independent reality of our thoughts, which was, it declared, the doctrine from which all true doctrines rose. If you imagine, it said, the semblance of a living being, it is at once possessed by a wandering soul, and goes hither and thither working good or evil, until the moment of its death has come; and gave many examples, received, it said, from many gods. Eros had taught them how to fashion forms in which a divine soul could dwell and whisper what it would into sleeping minds; and Ate, forms from which demonic beings could pour madness, or unquiet dreams, into sleeping blood; and Hermes, that if you powerfully imagined a hound at your bedside it would keep watch there until you woke, and drive away all but the mightiest demons, but that if your imagination was weakly, the hound would be weakly also, and the demons prevail, and the hound soon die; and Aphrodite, that if you made, by a strong imagining, a dove crowned with silver and bade it flutter over your head, its soft cooing would make sweet dreams of immortal love gather and brood over mortal sleep; and all divinities alike had revealed with many warnings and lamentations that all minds are continually giving birth to such beings, and sending them forth to work health or disease, joy or madness. If you would give forms to the evil powers, it went on, you were to make them ugly, thrusting out a lip with the thirsts of life, or breaking the proportions of a body with the burdens of life; but the divine powers would only appear in beautiful shapes, which are but, as it were, shapes trembling out of existence, folding up into a timeless ecstasy, drifting with half-shut eyes into a sleepy stillness. The bodiless souls who descended into these forms were what men called the moods; and worked all great changes in the world; for just as the magician or the artist could call them when he would, so they could call out of the mind of the magician or the artist, or if they were demons, out of the mind of the mad or the ignoble, what shape they would, and through its voice and its gestures pour themselves out upon the world. In this way all great events were accomplished; a mood, a divinity, or a demon, first descending like a faint sigh into men's minds and then changing their thoughts and their actions until hair that was yellow had grown black, or hair that was black had grown yellow, and empires moved their border, as though they were but drifts of leaves. The rest of the book contained symbols of form, and sound, and colour, and their attribution to divinities and demons, so that the initiate might fashion a shape for any divinity or any demon, and be as powerful as Avicenna among those who live under the roots of tears and of laughter.

A couple of hours after sunset Michael Robartes returned and told me that I would have to learn the steps of an exceedingly antique dance, because before my initiation could be perfected I had to join three times in a magical dance, for rhythm was the wheel of Eternity, on which alone the transient and accidental could be broken, and the spirit set free. I found that the steps, which were simple enough, resembled certain antique Greek dances, and having been a good dancer in my youth and the master of many curious Gaelic steps, I soon had them in my memory. He then robed me and himself in a costume which suggested by its shape both Greece and Egypt, but by its crimson colour a more passionate life than theirs; and having put into my hands a little chainless censer of bronze, wrought into the likeness of a rose, by some modern craftsman, he told me to open a small door opposite to the door by which I had entered. I put my hand to the handle, but the moment I did so the fumes of the incense, helped perhaps by his mysterious glamour, made me fall again into a dream, in which I seemed to be a mask, lying on the counter of a little Eastern shop. Many persons, with eyes so bright and still that I knew them for more than human, came in and tried me on their faces, but at last flung me into a corner laughing; but all this passed in a moment, for when I awoke my hand was still upon the handle. I opened the door, and found myself in a marvellous passage, along whose sides were many divinities wrought in a mosaic, not less beautiful than the mosaic in the Baptistery at Ravenna, but of a less severe beauty; the predominant colour of each divinity, which was surely a symbolic colour, being repeated in the lamps that hung from the ceiling, a curiously scented lamp before every divinity. I passed on, marvelling exceedingly how these enthusiasts could have created all this beauty in so remote a place, and half persuaded to believe in a material alchemy, by the sight of so much hidden wealth; the censer filling the air, as I passed, with smoke of ever-changing colour.

I stopped before a door, on whose bronze panels were wrought great waves in whose shadow were faint suggestions of terrible faces. Those beyond it seemed to have heard our steps, for a voice cried, 'Is the work of the Incorruptible Fire at an end?' and immediately Michael Robartes answered, 'The perfect gold has come from the athanor.' The door swung open, and we were in a great circular room, and among men and women who were dancing slowly in crimson robes. Upon the ceiling was an immense rose wrought in mosaic; and about the walls, also in mosaic, was a battle of gods and angels, the gods glimmering like rubies and sapphires, and the angels of the one greyness, because, as Michael Robartes whispered, they had renounced their divinity, and turned from the unfolding of their separate hearts, out of love for a God of humility and sorrow. Pillars supported the roof and made a kind of circular cloister, each pillar being a column of confused shapes, divinities, it seemed, of the wind, who, in a whirling dance of more than human vehemence, rose playing upon pipes and cymbals; and from among these shapes were thrust out hands, and in these hands were censers. I was bid place my censer also in a hand and take my place and dance, and as I turned from the pillars towards the dancers, I saw that the floor was of a green stone, and that a pale Christ on a pale cross was wrought in the midst. I asked Robartes the meaning of this, and was told that they desired 'to trouble His unity with their multitudinous feet.' The dance wound in and out, tracing upon the floor the shapes of petals that copied the petals in the rose overhead, and to the sound of hidden instruments which were perhaps of an antique pattern, for I have never heard the like; and every moment the dance was more passionate, until all the winds of the world seemed to have awakened under our feet. After a little I had grown weary, and stood under a pillar watching the coming and going of those flame-like figures; until gradually I sank into a half-dream, from which I was awakened by seeing the petals of the great rose, which had no longer the look of mosaic, falling slowly through the incense-heavy air, and, as they fell, shaping into the likeness of living beings of an extraordinary beauty. Still faint and cloud-like, they began to dance, and as they danced took a more and more definite shape, so that I was able to distinguish beautiful Grecian faces and august Egyptian faces, and now and again to name a divinity by the staff in his hand or by a bird fluttering over his head; and soon every mortal foot danced by the white foot of an immortal; and in the troubled eyes that looked into untroubled shadowy eyes, I saw the brightness of uttermost desire as though they had found at length, after unreckonable wandering, the lost love of their youth. Sometimes, but only for a moment, I saw a faint solitary figure with a veiled face, and carrying a faint torch, flit among the dancers, but like a dream within a dream, like a shadow of a shadow, and I knew by an understanding born from a deeper fountain than thought, that it was Eros himself, and that his face was veiled because no man or woman from the beginning of the world has ever known what Love is, or looked into his eyes, for Eros alone of divinities is altogether a spirit, and hides in passions not of his essence if he would commune with a mortal heart. So that if a man love nobly he knows Love through infinite pity, unspeakable trust, unending sympathy; and if ignobly through vehement jealousy, sudden hatred, and unappeasable desire; but unveiled Love he never knows. While I thought these things, a voice cried to me from the crimson figures, 'Into the dance! there is none that can be spared out of the dance; into the dance! into the dance! that the gods may make them bodies out of the substance of our hearts'; and before I could answer, a mysterious wave of passion, that seemed like the soul of the dance moving within our souls, took hold of me, and I was swept, neither consenting nor refusing, into the midst. I was dancing with an immortal august woman, who had black lilies in her hair, and her dreamy gesture seemed laden with a wisdom more profound than the darkness that is between star and star, and with a love like the love that breathed upon the waters; and as we danced on and on, the incense drifted over us and round us, covering us away as in the heart of the world, and ages seemed to pass, and tempests to awake and perish in the folds of our robes and in her heavy hair.

Suddenly I remembered that her eyelids had never quivered, and that her lilies had not dropped a black petal, nor shaken from their places, and understood with a great horror that I danced with one who was more or less than human, and who was drinking up my soul as an ox drinks up a wayside pool; and I fell, and darkness passed over me.

V

I awoke suddenly as though something had awakened me, and saw that I was lying on a roughly painted floor, and that on the ceiling, which was at no great distance, was a roughly painted rose, and about me on the walls half-finished paintings. The pillars and the censers had gone; and near me a score of sleepers lay wrapped in disordered robes, their upturned faces looking to my imagination like hollow masks; and a chill dawn was shining down upon them from a long window I had not noticed before; and outside the sea roared. I saw Michael Robartes lying at a little distance and beside him an overset bowl of wrought bronze which looked as though it had once held incense. As I sat thus, I heard a sudden tumult of angry men's and women's voices mix with the roaring of the sea; and leaping to my feet, I went quickly to Michael Robartes, and tried to shake him out of his sleep. I then seized him by the shoulder and tried to lift him, but he fell backwards, and sighed faintly; and the voices became louder and angrier; and there was a sound of heavy blows upon the door, which opened on to the pier. Suddenly I heard a sound of rending wood, and I knew it had begun to give, and I ran to the door of the room. I pushed it open and came out upon a passage whose bare boards clattered under my feet, and found in the passage another door which led into an empty kitchen; and as I passed through the door I heard two crashes in quick succession, and knew by the sudden noise of feet and the shouts that the door which opened on to the pier had fallen inwards. I ran from the kitchen and out into a small yard, and from this down some steps which descended the seaward and sloping side of the pier, and from the steps clambered along the water's edge, with the angry voices ringing in my ears. This part of the pier had been but lately refaced with blocks of granite, so that it was almost clear of seaweed; but when I came to the old part, I found it so slippery with green weed that I had to climb up on to the roadway. I looked towards the

Temple of the Alchemical Rose, where the fishermen and the women were still shouting, but somewhat more faintly, and saw that there was no one about the door or upon the pier; but as I looked, a little crowd hurried out of the door and began gathering large stones from where they were heaped up in readiness for the next time a storm shattered the pier, when they would be laid under blocks of granite. While I stood watching the crowd, an old man, who was, I think, the voteen, pointed to me, and screamed out something, and the crowd whitened, for all the faces had turned towards me. I ran, and it was well for me that pullers of the oar are poorer men with their feet than with their arms and their bodies; and yet while I ran I scarcely heard the following feet or the angry voices, for many voices of exultation and lamentation, which were forgotten as a dream is forgotten the moment they were heard, seemed to be ringing in the air over my head.

There are moments even now when I seem to hear those voices of exultation and lamentation, and when the indefinite world, which has but half lost its mastery over my heart and my intellect, seems about to claim a perfect mastery; but I carry the rosary about my neck, and when I hear, or seem to hear them, I press it to my heart and say, 'He whose name is Legion is at our doors deceiving our intellects with subtlety and flattering our hearts with beauty, and we have no trust but in Thee'; and then the war that rages within me at other times is still, and I am at peace.

Poetry

By now a new serenity had come into Yeats's life through his friendship with Lady Gregory and the refuge she gave him at her lovely country house, Coole, where he could do his work. In Olivia Shakespear he had found a lover and friend who had helped him to bear the torture that Maud Gonne's rejection had caused him. In the Abbey Theatre he had found a wonderful outlet to bring his imaginative ideas and philosophies before the people and bring about the marriage he always desired between the artist and the public.

The first poem, 'In the Seven Woods', is as near as possible to what can be called a perfect poem. The three lines with which it commences

> I have heard the pigeons of the Seven Woods
> Make their faint thunder, and the garden bees
> Hum in the lime-tree flowers;

throb with woods and summer. Then, in 'Never Give All the Heart', in which Yeats is clearly writing out of his own experience, the dilemma between man and woman in the joust of love has never been better caught.

Yet in 'No Second Troy' he will excuse all in the name of beauty, even if 'All Things Can Tempt Me' is almost a hymn of despair.

IN THE SEVEN WOODS

> I have heard the pigeons of the Seven Woods
> Make their faint thunder, and the garden bees
> Hum in the lime-tree flowers; and put away

The unavailing outcries and the old bitterness
That empty the heart. I have forgot awhile
Tara uprooted, and new commonness
Upon the throne and crying about the streets
And hanging its paper flowers from post to post,
Because it is alone of all things happy.
I am contented, for I know that Quiet
Wanders laughing and eating her wild heart
Among pigeons and bees, while that Great Archer,
Who but awaits His hour to shoot, still hangs
A cloudy quiver over Pairc-na-lee.

NEVER GIVE ALL THE HEART

Never give all the heart, for love
Will hardly seem worth thinking of
To passionate women if it seem
Certain, and they never dream
That it fades out from kiss to kiss;
For everything that's lovely is
But a brief, dreamy, kind delight.
O never give the heart outright,
For they, for all smooth lips can say,
Have given their hearts up to the play.
And who could play it well enough
If deaf and dumb and blind with love?
He that made this knows all the cost,
For he gave all his heart and lost.

NO SECOND TROY

Why should I blame her that she filled my days
With misery, or that she would of late
Have taught to ignorant men most violent ways,
Or hurled the little streets upon the great,
Had they but courage equal to desire?
What could have made her peaceful with a mind
That nobleness made simple as a fire,

With beauty like a tightened bow, a kind
That is not natural in an age like this,
Being high and solitary and most stern?
Why, what could she have done, being what she is?
Was there another Troy for her to burn?

ALL THINGS CAN TEMPT ME

All things can tempt me from this craft of verse:
One time it was a woman's face, or worse –
The seeming needs of my fool-driven land;
Now nothing but comes readier to the hand
Than this accustomed toil. When I was young,
I had not given a penny for a song
Did not the poet sing it with such airs
That one believed he had a sword upstairs;
Yet would be now, could I but have my wish,
Colder and dumber and deafer than a fish.

Dramatis Personae

In the first decade of the century Yeats was much occupied with the Irish Literary Theatre, whose founder members had been Edward Martyn, Lady Gregory, Yeats himself and George Moore. After the production of *Diarmuid and Grainne* in 1901, the Irish Literary Theatre broke up with the departure from the company of Moore and Martyn. Then Yeats linked up with the Irish National Dramatic Company run by the Fay brothers, Frank and Willie. The Fays were a remarkable pair who pioneered in the English language many of the naturalistic techniques of acting that were later to be used in the Moscow Arts Theatre and the Actors Studio in New York.

By now Synge had joined the Abbey Company with Yeats and Lady Gregory and had become a member of the board of the Irish National Theatre Society. Another breakaway occurred when the Abbey opened in 1904, with the Fays running the repertory company. In *Dramatis Personae* Yeats, writing in 1932, recalls the leading figures of these years. Perhaps one of those who has had the least credit is Edward Martyn, who lived at Tulira Castle, about four miles from Lady Gregory's house at Coole. Edward came from a wealthy County Galway family who had settled in the West in the eleventh century. They traced their descent from an Oliver Martyn who had come to Ireland with the Norman Baron Strongbow. The Martyns were in the unique position of having had an Act of Parliament passed to enable them to retain their land. As Catholics they would have been subject to the savage Penal Laws enacted in the reign of Queen Anne to restrict the right of their co-religionists to own land, but because of some ancestor who had been merciful to Protestants during the Jacobite Wars, an Act had been passed exempting them from these laws. The result was that at the end of the nineteenth century the Martyns owned extensive estates in two counties as well as house property in Galway city. Thus, on the death of Edward's father, when the boy was eight, he was left a considerable fortune. It was Martyn's energy and stubbornness and private wealth which kept the theatre company going in the first years. Despite his fanatical Catholicism he worshipped Ibsen as a playwright and used to describe how he had come back to his rooms transfigured after seeing *Little Eyolf*, with 'its exquisite music trembling in my heart and wishing to be alone so the exultation should not be interrupted.'

It would be wrong to regard Edward as a pious dolt. He was intelligent and sensitive and, when he could emancipate himself from religious prejudice, capable of good writing, as he would later demonstrate. He had an excellent eye for painting and a natural ear for music, and was to found a school for stained glass as well as a famous polyphonic choir.

In *Dramatis Personae* Yeats also gives a good portrait of Douglas Hyde, the scholar-poet-linguist, regarded by some as the father of the Literary Renaissance. Hyde's wonderful gift for rendering the difficult rhythms and assonances of the Gaelic into beautiful English had a powerful effect in bringing Yeats, Lady Gregory and Synge towards the culture that was at their doorstep. He was also responsible for the founding of the Gaelic League, which was described by Michael Collins, the Sinn Féin leader, as 'one of the most important events in the two hundred years of Irish history'.

But the two principal figures dealt with in *Dramatis Personae* are Lady Gregory and George Moore, and it is largely from the material dealing with them that I have made my selections. Yeats's portrait of Lady Gregory is a tribute to one who had helped to change his life. But his account of George Moore hovers between satire and caricature. It is absurd to deny Moore a major literary gift, or to jeer at him as 'Milton's lion rising up, pawing out of the earth, but, unlike that lion, stuck half-way', or to describe Manet's picture of Moore, which hangs today in the Metropolitan Museum in New York, as 'a caricature'. On Moore, Yeats is at his most Irish – malicious, irresponsible, unreliable, but always hilariously funny.

One has to keep in mind, as one enjoys the sheer brilliance of Yeats's attack, Moore's record as a literary innovator. He had introduced the realism of the French school to England with his novel *The Mummer's Wife*, and had popularized the works of the Impressionist painters with his brilliant essays on Manet, Degas and others who had been his friends in Paris. His essay on Verlaine in the *Contemporary Review* had introduced that poet to English readers. What is more, Joyce had certainly borrowed from Moore's novel *Vain Fortune* for 'The Dead', one of the short stories in *Dubliners*, and more than likely conceived the form that collection took after reading Moore's *The Untilled Field*. But, while keeping Moore's achievement before the mind, it is impossible at times not to roar out with laughter at some of Yeats's outrageous yarns. An extract from one of these, *Dramatis Personae*, follows.

It was now that George Moore came into our affairs, brought by Edward Martyn, who invited him to find a cast for *The Heather Field*. They were cousins and inseparable friends, bound one to the other by mutual contempt. When I told Martyn that Moore had good points, he replied: 'I know Moore a great deal longer than you do. He has no good points.' And a week or two later Moore said: 'That man Martyn is the most selfish man alive. He thinks that I am damned and he doesn't care.'

Moore and Martyn were indeed in certain characteristics typical peasants, the peasant sinner, the peasant saint. Moore's grandfather or great-grandfather had been a convert, but there were Catholic marriages. Catholic families, beaten down by the Penal Laws, despised by Irish Protestants, by the few English Catholics they met, had but little choice as to where they picked their brides; boys, on one side of old family, grew up squireens, half-sirs, peasants who had lost their tradition, gentlemen who had lost theirs. Lady Gregory once told me what marriage coarsened the Moore blood, but I have forgotten.

George Moore had a ceaseless preoccupation with painting and the theatre, within certain limits a technical understanding of both; whatever idea possessed him, courage and explosive power; but sacrificed all that seemed to other men good breeding, honour, friendship, in pursuit of what he considered the root facts of life. I had seen him once in the Cheshire Cheese. I had with me some proof-sheets of the Ellis and Yeats study of Blake's philosophy, and the drooping tree on the second page of *The Book of Thel* stirred him to eloquence. His 'How beautiful, how beautiful!' is all I can remember. Then one evening, in a narrow empty street between Fleet Street and the river, I heard a voice resounding as if in a funnel, someone in a hansom cab was denouncing its driver, and Moore drove by. Then I met him in Arthur Symons' flat in the Temple. He threw himself into a chair with the remark: 'I wish that woman would wash'. He had just returned from an assignation with his mistress, a woman known to Symons personally, to me by repute, an accomplished, witty, somewhat fashionable woman. All his friends suffered in some way; good behaviour was no protection, for it was all chance whether the facts he pursued were in actual life or in some story that amused him. Had 'that woman' prided herself upon her cleanliness, he would, had he decided upon a quarrel, have said with greater publicity: 'I wish that woman would wash'. His pursuit had now and then unfortunate results. 'What has depressed you, Moore?' said an acquaintance. 'I have been paying attention to a certain woman. I had every reason to think she liked me. I came to the point to-day and was turned down completely.' 'You must have said something wrong.' 'No, what I said was all right.' 'What was it?' 'I said I was clean and healthy and she could not do better.' Upon occasion it made him brutal and witty. He and I went to the town of Galway for a Gaelic festival that coincided with some assembly of priests. When we lunched at the Railway Hotel the room was full of priests. A Father Moloney, supposed to know all about Greek Art, caught sight of Moore and introduced himself. He probably knew nothing about Moore, except that he was some kind of critic, for he set out upon his favourite topic with: 'I have always considered it a proof of Greek purity that though they left the male form uncovered, they invariably draped the female'. 'Do you consider, Father Moloney,' said Moore in a voice that rang through the whole room, 'that the female form is inherently more indecent than the male?' Every priest turned a stern and horrified eye upon Father Moloney, who sat hunched up and quivering.

I have twice known Moore alarmed and conscience-struck, when told that he had injured somebody's financial prospects – a financial prospect is a root fact – but he attacked with indifference so long as nothing suffered but his victim's dignity or feelings. To injure a famous scholar in a quarrel not his he had printed all the scandalous stories he could rake together, or invent, in a frenzy of political hatred. I had remonstrated in vain, except that he cut out a passage describing his victim as 'a long pink pig', yet when he thought he might have deprived that scholar of a post he was miserable.

He had gone to Paris straight from his father's racing stables, from a house where there was no culture, as Symons and I understood that word, acquired copious inaccurate French, sat among art students, young writers about to become famous, in some café; a man carved out of a turnip, looking out of astonished eyes. I see him as that circle saw him, for I have in memory Manet's caricature. He spoke badly and much in a foreign tongue, read nothing, and was never to attain the discipline of style. 'I wrote a play in French,' he said, 'before I had seen dialogue on paper.' I doubt if he had read a play of Shakespeare's even at the end of his life. He did not know that style existed until he returned to Ireland in middle life; what he learned, he learned from conversation, from acted plays, from pictures. A revolutionary in revolt against the ignorant Catholicism of Mayo, he chose for master Zola as another might have chosen Karl Marx. Even to conversation and acted plays, he gave an inattentive ear, instincts incapable of clear expression deafened him and blinded him; he was Milton's lion rising up, pawing out of the earth, but, unlike that lion, stuck half-way.

On a visit to Coole, during some revising of *The Bending of the Bough*, or to begin *Diarmuid and Grania*, its successor, he behaved well till there came a long pause in the conversation one night after dinner. 'I wonder,' said Moore, 'why

Mrs.———threw me over; was it because she wanted to marry———' – he named a famous woman and a famous peer – 'or was it conscience?' I followed Moore to his room and said, 'You have broken the understanding?' 'What understanding?' 'That your conversation would be fit for Robert.' Robert, Lady Gregory's son, was on holiday there from Harrow. 'The word conscience can have only one meaning.' 'But it's true.' 'There is a social rule that bars such indiscretions.' 'It has gone out.' 'Not here.' 'But it is the only thing I can say about her that she would mind.' Mrs.——— had been much taken with Moore, I had heard her talk of him all evening, but was of strict morals: I knew from the friend who had listened to Moore's daily complaints and later to his contradictory inventions, that he had courted her in vain. Two or three years after his Coole transgression, he was accustomed to say: 'Once she and I were walking in the Green Park. "There is nothing more cruel than lust," she said. "There is," I said. "What is that?" "Vanity", and I let her go a step or two ahead and gave her a kick behind.'

Moore had inherited a large Mayo estate, and no Mayo country gentleman had ever dressed the part so well. He lacked manners, but had manner; he could enter a room so as to draw your attention without seeming to, his French, his knowledge of painting, suggested travel and leisure. Yet nature had denied to him the final touch: he had a coarse palate. Edward Martyn alone suspected it. When Moore abused the waiter or the cook, he had thought, 'I know what he is hiding'. In a London restaurant on a night when the soup was particularly good, just when Moore had the spoon at his lip, he said: 'Do you mean to say you are going to drink that?' Moore tasted the soup, then called the waiter, and ran through the usual performance. Martyn did not undeceive him, content to chuckle in solitude. Moore had taken a house in Upper Ely Place; he spent a week at our principal hotel while his furniture was moving in: he denounced the food to the waiter, to the manager, went down to the kitchen and denounced it to the cook. 'He has written to the proprietress,' said the manager, 'that the steak is like brown paper. How can you believe a word such a man would say, a steak cannot be like brown paper.' He had his own bread sent in from the baker and said on the day he left: 'How can these people endure it?' 'Because,' said the admiring head-waiter, 'they are not *comme il faut*.' A little later I stayed with him and wrote to Lady Gregory: 'He is boisterously enduring the sixth cook.' Then from Sligo a few days later: 'Moore dismissed the sixth cook the day I left – six in three weeks. One brought in a policeman, Moore had made so much noise. He dragged the policeman into the dining-room and said: "Is there a law in this country to compel me to eat this abominable omelette?"'

Sometimes Moore, instead of asking us to accept for true some monstrous invention, would press a spontaneous action into deliberate comedy; starting in bad blood or blind passion, he would all in a moment see himself as others saw him. When he arrived in Dublin, all the doors in Upper Ely Place had been painted white by an agreement between the landlord and the tenants. Moore had his door painted green, and three Miss Beams – no, I have not got the name quite right – who lived next door protested to the landlord. Then began a correspondence between Moore and the landlord wherein Moore insisted on his position as an art critic, that the whole decoration of his house required a green door – I imagine that he had but wrapped the green flag around him – then the indignant young women bought a copy of *Esther Waters*, tore it up, put the fragments into a large envelope, wrote thereon: 'Too filthy to keep in the house', dropped it into his letter-box. I was staying with Moore, I let myself in with a latch-key some night after twelve, and found a note on the hall table asking me to put the door on the chain. As I was undressing, I heard Moore trying to get in; when I had opened the door and pointed to the note he said: 'Oh, I forgot. Every night I go out at eleven, at twelve, at one, and rattle my stick on the railing to make the Miss Beams' dogs bark.' Then I saw in the newspapers that the Miss Beams had hired organ-grinders to play under Moore's window when he was writing, that he had prosecuted the organ-grinders. Moore had a large garden on the other side of the street, a blackbird sang there; he received his friends upon Saturday evening and made a moving speech upon the bird. 'I enjoy its song. If I were the bad man people say I am, could I enjoy its song?' He wrote every morning at an open window on the ground floor, and one morning saw the Miss Beams' cat cross the street, and thought, 'That cat will get my bird'. He went out and filled his pocket with stones, and whenever he saw the cat, threw a stone. Somebody, perhaps the typist, must have laughed, for the rest of the tale fills me with doubt. I was passing through Dublin just on my way to Coole; he came to my hotel. 'I remembered how early that cat got up. I thought it might get the blackbird if I was not there to protect it, so I set a trap. The Miss Beams wrote to the Society for the Prevention of Cruelty to Animals, and I am carrying on a correspondence with its secretary, cat versus bird.' (Perhaps after all, the archives of the society do contain that correspondence. The tale is not yet incredible.) I passed through Dublin again, perhaps on my way back. Moore came to see me in seeming great depression. 'Remember that trap?' 'Yes.' 'Remember that bird?' 'Yes.' 'I have caught the bird.'

Moore gave a garden party during the annual festival of the Gaelic League; there was a Gaelic play by Douglas Hyde based upon a scenario of Moore's, and to this garden party he invited the Catholic Archbishop, beginning the letter with: 'Cher confrère'. The Archbishop did not answer. He had already in a letter to the Press invited the Archbishop to institute a stage censorship. 'But, my dear Yeats, Archbishops are educated men. If there is some difficulty about a play, I will call upon him. I will explain. He will approve the play. No more mob rule. No more such trouble as we had about *The Countess Cathleen*. No more letters to the Press signed "Father of a Family".'

It was Moore's own fault that everybody hated him except a few London painters. In one of Dostoievsky's novels there is a man who proposes that everybody present should tell his worst action. Nobody takes the proposal seriously; everybody is witty or amusing until his turn comes. He confesses that he once stole half-a-crown and left a servant-girl to bear the blame. Moore might have so confessed, but his confession would have been a plagiarism or a whole lie. I met a man who hated Moore because Moore told some audience that he had selected a Parisian street-boy, for one day dressed him in good clothes, housed him in an expensive hotel, gave him all that he wanted, then put him back into rags and turned him out to discover what would happen: a plagiarism from a well-known French author. 'Yeats,' he said to me once, 'I was sitting here in my room the other night when there was a ring. My servant was out; when I opened the door a woman ran in and threw her arms round my neck. "At last I have found you. There were thirteen George Moores in the *London Directory*. You're the ninth I have called on. What? Not recollect me – not recollect the woman you raped in Paris twenty years ago?"' She had called about her daughter's musical education, he said. Had I been more sympathetic I would have heard of a new Evelyn Innes. He was jealous of his own Sir Owen Asher. He was all self and yet had so little self that he would destroy his reputation, or that of some friend, to make his audience believe that the story running in his head at the moment had happened, had only just happened.

In the early autumn Zola died, asphyxiated by a charcoal stove. Innumerable paragraphs and leading articles made Moore jealous and angry; he hated his own past in Zola. He talked much to his friends on Saturday nights. 'Anybody can get himself asphyxiated.' Then after some six weeks announced that he himself had awakened that very morning to smell gas, a few minutes more and he would have been dead; the obsession was over. But there had been another torture earlier in the year. A brother of his, Augustus Moore, a London journalist, had taken an action about a scenario, whether against an actor, a writer or a manager, I cannot remember; he would appear in the witness-box, be examined, cross-examined, re-examined, and would not, could not, rise to the occasion, whereas he, George Moore, could have been amusing, profound, all the world looking on. When it seemed likely that Benson, or some company brought together by Martyn, would continue the Irish Literary Theatre, I had told Moore a fantastic plot for a play, suggested collaboration, and for twenty minutes or half an hour walked up and down a path in his garden discussing it. He proposed that my hero's brother should seduce the housemaid. When I had decided to work with Fay, Moore had withdrawn from the movement. I had written him regretting that I must write that play without his help. He did not answer, the letter required no answer. Weeks or months passed, then at some Gaelic festival in the town of Galway we met. I saw that he had something on his mind, he was gloomy and silent. I pointed out the number of young women with Douglas Hyde's pseudonym in gilt letters round their hats: 'No woman, Moore, has ever done that for you,' I said. He took my banter well, threw off his gloom; had I not started his favourite theme? But on his return to Dublin he telegraphed: 'I have written a novel on that scenario we composed together. Will get an injunction if you use it.' Had I known about his brother's law-case I would have known that Moore had not written a line and that his telegram was drama; knowing nothing, I wrote or telegraphed that I would use nothing of his but would certainly use my own plot. I went to Coole, asked the assistance of Lady Gregory and of a certain cautious friend, whose name must be left out of this narrative, and in a fortnight they and I dictated or wrote a five-act tragedy. I called it *Where there is Nothing* and published it as a supplement to *United Ireland*, afterwards the organ of the Sinn Fein movement. Moore had been talking and his talk had reached me, he was expecting a London trial, and this was checkmate. Boys were shouting the supplement in the streets as he came out of the Antient Concert Rooms, where he had seen Fay's company. He bought a copy, spoke to nobody about it, always declared that he never read it, nor any other edition of the play. 'Has Yeats' hero got a brother?' he said to somebody. 'Yes.' 'Then Yeats has stolen the spoons.'

Douglas Hyde was at Coole in the summer of 1899. Lady Gregory, who had learnt Gaelic to satisfy her son's passing desire for a teacher, had founded a branch of the Gaelic League; men began to know the name of the poet whose songs they had sung for years. Lady Gregory and I wanted a Gaelic drama, and I made a scenario for a one-act play founded upon an episode in my *Stories of Red Hanrahan*; I had some hope that my invention, if Hyde would but accept it, might pass into legend as though he were a historical character. In later years Lady Gregory and I gave Hyde other scenarios and I always watched him with astonishment. His ordinary English style is without charm; he explores facts without explaining them, and in the language of the newspapers – Moore compared one of his speeches to frothing porter. His Gaelic, like the dialect of his *Love Songs of Connacht*, written a couple of years earlier, had charm, seemed all spontaneous, all joyous, every speech born out of itself. Had he shared our modern preoccupation with the mystery of life, learnt our modern construction, he might have grown into another and happier Synge. But emotion and imagery came as they would, not as he would; somebody else had to put them together. He had the folk mind as no modern man has had it, its qualities and its defects, and for a few days in the year Lady Gregory and I shared his absorption in that mind. When I wrote verse, five or six lines in two or three laborious hours were a day's work, and I longed for somebody to interrupt me; but he wrote all day, whether in verse or prose, and without apparent effort. Effort was there, but in the unconscious. He had given up verse writing because it affected his lungs or his heart. Lady Gregory kept watch, to draw him from his table after so many hours; the gamekeeper had the boat and the guns ready; there were ducks upon the lake. He wrote in joy and at great speed because emotion brought the appropriate word. Nothing in that language of his was abstract, nothing worn-out; he need not, as must the writer of some language exhausted by modern civilization, reject word after word, cadence after cadence; he had escaped our perpetual, painful, purification. I read him, translated by Lady Gregory or by himself into that dialect which gets from Gaelic its syntax and keeps its still partly Tudor vocabulary; little was, I think, lost.

> I was myself one time a poor barnacle goose;
> The night was not plain to me more than the day
> Till I got sight of her.

That does not impress me to-day; it is too easy to copy, too many have copied it:

Lady Gregory, as I first knew her, was a plainly dressed woman of forty-five, without obvious good looks, except the charm that comes from strength, intelligence and kindness. One who knew her at an earlier date speaks of dark skin, of an extreme vitality, and a portrait by Mrs Jopling that may have flattered shows considerable beauty. When her husband died, she had given up her London house, had devoted herself to the estate and to her son, spending little that mortgages might be paid off. The house had become her passion. That passion grew greater still when the house took its place in the public life of Ireland. She was a type that only the superficial observer could identify with Victorian earnestness, for her point of view was founded, not on any narrow modern habit, but upon her sense of great literature, upon her own strange feudal, almost mediaeval youth.

Born in 1852, she had passed her formative years in comparative peace, Fenianism a far-off threat; and her marriage with Sir William Gregory in her twenty-ninth year, visits to Ceylon, India, London, Rome, set her beyond the reach of the bitter struggle between landlord and tenant of the late 'seventies and early 'eighties. She knew Ireland always in its permanent relationships, associations – violence but a brief interruption –, never lost her sense of feudal responsibility, not of duty as the word is generally understood, but of burdens laid upon her by her station and her character, a choice constantly renewed in solitude. 'She has been,' said an old man to me, 'like a serving-maid among us. She is plain and simple, like the Mother of God, and that was the greatest lady that ever lived.' When in later years her literary style became in my ears the best written by woman, she had made the people a part of her soul; a phrase of Aristotle's had become her motto: 'To think like a wise man, but to express oneself like the common people'.

During these first years Lady Gregory was friend and hostess, a centre of peace, an adviser who never overestimated or underestimated trouble, but neither she nor we thought her a possible creator. And now all in a moment, as it seemed, she became the founder of modern Irish dialect literature. When her husband died she had sold her London house, hiring instead a small flat in Queen Anne's Mansions, lived most of the year at Coole, cutting down expenses that her son might inherit an unencumbered estate. In early life she had written two or three articles, such as many clever fashionable women write, more recently had edited her husband, Sir William Gregory's, *Autobiography* and *Mr. Gregory's Letter-Box*, a volume of letters to Richard Gregory, Irish Under-Secretary at the beginning of the nineteenth century, from Palmerston, Wellesley, many famous men, drawn from the Coole archives. Some slight desire to create had been put aside until her son reached manhood; but now he had left the university and she was fifty. I told her that Alfred Nutt had offered to supply me with translations of the Irish heroic cycles if I would pick the best versions and put my English upon them, attempting what Malory had done for the old French narratives. I told her that I was too busy with my own work. Some days later she asked if I would object to her attempting it, making or finding the translations herself. An eminent Trinity College professor had described ancient Irish literature as 'silly, religious, or indecent', and she thought such work necessary for the dignity of Ireland. 'We work to add dignity to Ireland' was a favourite phrase of hers. I hesitated, I saw nothing in her past to fit her for that work; but in a week or two she brought a translation of some heroic tale, what tale I cannot now remember, in the dialect of the neighbourhood, where one discovers the unemphatic cadence, the occasional poignancy of Tudor English. Looking back, *Cuchulain of Muirthemne* and *Gods and Fighting Men* at my side, I can see that they were made possible by her past; semi-feudal Roxborough, her inherited sense of caste, her knowledge of that top of the world where men and women are valued for their manhood and their charm, not for their opinions, her long study of Scottish Ballads, of Percy's *Reliques*, of the *Morte d'Arthur*. If she had not found those tales, or finding them had not found the dialect of Kiltartan, that past could not, as it were, have drawn itself together, come to birth as present personality. Sometimes in her letters, in her books when she wrote ordinary English, she was the late-Victorian woman turning aside from reality to what seems pleasing, or to a slightly sentimental persiflage as a form of politeness – in society, to discover 'eternity glaring', as Carlyle did when he met Charles Lamb for the first time, is scarcely in good taste – but in her last years, when speaking in her own character, she seemed always her greater self. A writer must die every day he lives, be reborn, as it is said in the Burial Service, an incorruptible self, that self opposite of all that he has named 'himself'. George Moore, dreading the annihilation of an impersonal bleak realism, used life like a mediaeval ghost making a body for itself out of drifting dust and vapour; and have I not sung in describing guests at Coole – 'There one that ruffled in a manly pose, For all his timid heart' – that one myself? Synge was a sick man picturing energy, a doomed man picturing gaiety; Lady Gregory, in her life much artifice, in her nature much pride, was born to see the glory of the world in a peasant mirror. 'I saw the household of Finn; it was not the household of a soft race; I had a vision of that man yesterday.... A King of heavy blows; my law; my adviser, my sense and my wisdom, prince and poet, braver than kings, King of the Fianna, brave in all countries; golden salmon of the sea, clean hawk of the air ... a high messenger in bravery and in music. His skin lime-white, his hair golden; ready to work, gentle to women. His great green vessels full of rough sharp wine, it is rich the king was, the head of his people.' And then Grania's song over the sleeping Diarmuid:

'"Sleep a little, sleep a little, for there is nothing at all to fear, Diarmuid, grandson of Duibhne; sleep here soundly, soundly, Diarmuid, to whom I have given my love. It is I will keep watch for you, grandchild of shapely Duibhne; sleep a little, a blessing on you, beside the well of the strong field; my lamb from above the lake, from the banks of the strong streams. Let your sleep be like the sleep in the North of fair comely Fionnchadh of Ess Ruadh, the time he took Slaine with bravery as we think, in spite of Failbhe of the Hard Head.

"Let your sleep be like the sleep in the West of Aine, daughter of Gailian, the time she went on a journey in the night with Dubhthach from Dorinis, by the light of torches.

"Let your sleep be like the sleep in the East of Deaghadh the proud, the brave fighter, the time he took Coincheann, daughter of Binn, in spite of fierce Decheall of Duibhreann.

"O heart of the valour of the world to the west of Greece, my heart will go near to breaking if I do not see you every day. The parting of us two will be the parting of two children of the one house; it will be the parting of life from the body."

'And then to rouse him she would make another song, and it is what she would say: "Caoinche will be loosed on your track; it is not slow the running of Caoilte will be; do not let death reach to you, do not give yourself to sleep forever.

"The stag to the East is not asleep, he does not cease from bellowing; the bog lark is not asleep to-night on the high stormy bogs; the sound of her clear voice is sweet; she is not sleeping between the streams."'

The Death of Synge

Yeats's closest friend in the world of writing was John Millington Synge, who died of Hodgkins Disease at the height of his powers in March 1901. It was a fearful blow to Yeats, and he expressed his despair in a strange journal kept that year, *The Death of Synge*.

I

Why does the struggle to come at truth take away our pity, and the struggle to overcome our passions restore it again?

II

National feeling could be roused again if some man of good education – if a Catholic, he should have been educated outside Ireland – gathered about him a few men like himself, and founded a new *Nation* newspaper, forbidding it all personal attacks, all arguments that assume a base motive in an opponent, and choosing for its national policy, not what seems most desirable in the abstract, but such policy as may stir the imagination and yet gather to its support the greatest possible number of educated men. Ireland is ruined by abstractions, and should prefer what may seem a worse policy if it gathers better men. So long as all is ordered for attack, and that alone, leaders will instinctively increase the number of enemies that they may give their followers something to do, and Irish enemies rather than English because they are the more easily injured. The greater the enemy, the greater the hatred, and therefore the greater seems the power. They would give a nation the frenzy of a sect. A sign that this method, powerful in the time of Parnell, no longer satisfies the nation is that parties are drifting into the hands of feebler and more ignorant men.

IV

March 17

As I go to and from my bedroom, here at Coole, I pass a wall covered with Augustus John's etchings and drawings. I notice a woman with strongly marked shoulder-blades and a big nose, and a pencil drawing called *Epithalamium*. In the *Epithalamium* an ungainly, ill-grown boy holds out his arms to a tall woman with thin shoulders and a large stomach. Near them is a vivid etching of a woman with the same large stomach and thin shoulders. There is not one of these fifty or sixty clerks and seamstresses and students that has not been broken by labour or wasted by sedentary life. A gymnast would find in all something to amend; and the better he mended the more would those bodies, as with the voice of Dürer, declare that ancient canon discovered in the Greek gymnasium, which, whenever present in painting or sculpture, shows a compact between the artist and society. John is not interested in the social need, in the perpetual thirst for greater health, but in character, in the revolt from all that makes one man like another. The old art, if carried to its logical conclusion, would have led to the creation of one single type of man, one single type of woman; gathering up by a kind of deification a capacity for all energy and all passion, into a Krishna, a Christ, a Dionysus; and at all times a poetical painter, a Botticelli, a Rossetti, creates as his supreme achievement one type of face, known afterwards by his name. The new art can create innumerable personalities, but in each of these the capacity for passion has been sacrificed to some habit of body or of mind. That woman with the big shoulder-blades has, for instance, a nature too keen, too clever for any passion, with the clevernesss of people who cannot rest, and that young lad with his arms spread out will sink back into disillusionment and exhaustion after the brief pleasure of a passion which is in part curiosity. Some limiting environment or idiosyncrasy is displayed; man is studied as an individual fact, and not as that energy which seems measureless and hates all that is not itself. It is a powerful but prosaic art, celebrating the 'fall into division' not the 'resurrection into unity'. Did not even Balzac, who looked at the world so often with similar eyes, find it necessary to deny character to his great ladies and young lovers that he might give them passion? What beautiful woman delights us by her look of character? That shows itself when beauty is gone, being the creation of habit, the bare stalk when the flower of spring has withered. Beauty consumes character with what Patmore calls 'the integrity of fire'.

It is this lack of the capacity for passion which makes women dislike the schools of characterization, and makes the modern artist despise woman's judgment. Women, for the same reason, dislike pure comedy. How few women like Molière!

Here at Coole my room is hung with Arundel prints from Botticelli, Benozzo Gozzoli, Giorgione, Mantegna and the Van Eycks. Here everywhere is the expression of desire, though in the Van Eycks the new interest has begun. All display bodies to please an amorous woman's eyes or the eyes of a great King. The martyrs and saints even must show the capacity for all they have renounced.

v

These notes are morbid, but I heard a man of science say that all progress is at the outset pathological, and I write for my own good.

The pain others give passes away in their later kindness, but that of our own blunders, especially when they hurt our vanity, never passes away. Our own acts are isolated and one act does not buy absolution for another. They are always present before a strangely abstract judgment. We are never a unity, a personality to ourselves. Small acts of years ago are so painful in the memory that often we start at the presence a little below 'the threshold of consciousness' of a thought that remains unknown. It sheds a vague light like that of the moon before it rises, or after its setting. Vanity is so intimately associated with our spiritual identity that whatever hurts it, above all if it came from it, is more painful in the memory than serious sin, and yet I do not think it follows that we are very vain. The harm we do to others is lost in changing events and passes away and so is healed by time, unless it was very great. Looking back, I find only one offence which is as painful to me as a hurt to vanity. It was done to a man who died shortly after. Because of his death, it has not been touched by the transforming hand – tolerant Nature has not rescued it from Justice.

VI

I think that all happiness depends on the energy to assume the mask of some other self; that all joyous or creative life is a rebirth as something not oneself, something which has no memory and is created in a moment and perpetually renewed. We put on a grotesque or solemn painted face to hide us from the terrors of judgment, invent an imaginative Saturnalia where one forgets reality, a game like that of a child, where one loses the infinite pain of self-realization. Perhaps all the sins and energies of the world are but its flight from an infinite blinding beam.

VII

F——is learning Gaelic. I would sooner see her in the Gaelic movement than
in any Irish movement I can think of. I fear some new absorption in political
opinion. Women, because the main event of their lives has been a giving
themselves and giving birth, give all to an opinion as if it were some terrible
stone doll. Men take up an opinion lightly and are easily false to it, and when
faithful keep the habit of many interests. We still see the world, if we are of
strong mind and body, with considerate eyes, but to women opinions become
as their children or their sweethearts, and the greater their emotional capacity
the more do they forget all other things. They grow cruel, as if in defence of
lover or child, and all this is done for 'something other than human life'. At
last the opinion is so much identified with their nature that it seems a part of
their flesh becomes stone and passes out of life. It was a part of F——'s
power in the past that though she made this surrender with her mind, she
kept the sweetness of her voice and much humour, and yet I am afraid.
Women should have their play with dolls finished in childish happiness, for if
they play with them again it is amid hatred and malice.

VIII

Women should find in the mask enough joy to forget the doll without regret.
There is always a living face behind the mask.

IX

Last night at 'The Theatre of Ireland' I talked to the man next to me. 'I have
been to your theatre also,' he said. 'I like your popular plays, *The Suburban
Groove* and those plays by the Frenchman, I do not remember his name'
(evidently Molière), 'but I don't like your mysteries.' I thought he meant
something of mine, as the word 'mystery' is a popular reproach since *The
Shadowy Waters*, but I found he meant *Kincora*. I said, 'Why do you find that
mysterious?' He said, 'O, I know nothing about all that history.' I replied,
'When I was young every Irish Nationalist young man knew as much about
King Brian as about Saint Patrick.' He thought I was talking of the peasants
and said he was afraid that sort of knowledge was dying out amongst them. He
evidently thought it their business alone, like the rath and the blessed well.

X

March 23

MacDonagh called to-day. Very sad about Ireland. Says that he finds a barrier between himself and the Irish-speaking peasantry, who are 'cold, dark and reticent' and 'too polite'. He watches the Irish-speaking boys at his school, and when nobody is looking, or when they are alone with the Irish-speaking gardener, they are merry, clever and talkative. When they meet an English speaker or one who has learned Gaelic, they are stupid. They are in a different world. Presently he spoke of his nine years in a monastery and I asked what it was like. 'O,' he said, 'everybody is very simple and happy enough. There is a little jealousy sometimes. If one brother goes into a town with a Superior, another brother is jealous.' He then told me that the Bishop of Raphoe had forbidden anybody in his See to contribute to the Gaelic League because its Secretary 'has blasphemed against the holy Adamnan'. The Secretary had said, 'The Bishop is an enemy, like the founder of his See, Saint Adamnan, who tried to injure the Gaelic language by writing in Latin.' MacDonagh says, 'Two old countrymen fell out and one said, "I have a brother who will make you behave", meaning the Bishop of Raphoe, and the other said, "I have a son who will put sense into you", meaning Cardinal Logue.'

XI

Molly Allgood came to-day to ask where I would be to-morrow, as Synge wishes to send for me if strong enough. He wants 'to make arrangements'. He is dying. They have ceased to give him food. Should we close the Abbey or keep it open while he still lives? Poor Molly is going through her work as always. Perhaps that is best for her. I feel Synge's coming death less now than when he first became ill. I am used to the thought of it and I do not find that I pity him. I pity her. He is fading out of life. I felt the same when I saw M——— in the madhouse. I pitied his wife. He seemed already dead. One does not feel that death is evil when one meets it, – evil, I mean, for the one who dies. Our Daimon is silent as was that other before the death of Socrates. The wildest sorrow that comes at the thought of death is, I think, 'Ages will pass over and no one ever again look on that nobleness or that beauty'. What is this but to pity the living and to praise the dead?

XII

March 24

Synge is dead. In the early morning he said to the nurse, 'It is no use fighting death any longer' and he turned over and died. I called at the hospital this afternoon and asked the assistant matron if he knew he was dying. She answered, 'He may have known it for weeks, but he would not have said so to anyone. He would have no fuss. He was like that.' She added, with emotion in her voice, 'We were devoted to him'.

XIV

I have been looking through his poems and have read once more that on page 21, 'I asked if I got sick and died'. Certainly they were there at the funeral, his 'idiot' enemies: A—— who against all regulations rushed up to the dressing-rooms during the *Playboy* riot to tell the actors they should not have played in so disgraceful a play; B—— who has always used his considerable influence with the company against Synge, and has spoken against him in public; there, too, were the feeble friends who pretended to believe but gave no help. And there was C—— whose obituary notice speaks of Synge's work as only important in promise, of the exaggeration of those who praise it, and then claims that its writer spent many hours a day with Synge in Paris (getting the date wrong by two years, however), with Synge who was proud and lonely, almost as proud of his old blood as of his genius, and had few friends. There was D——, the Secretary of the Society – it had sent a wreath – whose animosity had much to do with the attacks in *Sinn Fein*. It was, to quote E——, a funeral 'small but select'. A good friend of Synge's quoted to me:

> How shall the ritual then be read,
> The requiem how be sung
> By you, by yours the evil eye,
> By yours the slanderous tongue,
> That did to death the innocence
> That died, and died so young?

Yet these men came, though but in remorse; they saw his plays, though but to dislike; they spoke his name, though but to slander. Well-to-do Ireland never saw his plays nor spoke his name. Was he ever asked to any country house but

Coole? Was he ever asked to a dinner-party? How often I have wished that he might live long enough to enjoy that communion with idle, charming and cultivated women which Balzac in one of his dedications calls 'the chief consolation of genius'!

XV

In Paris Synge once said to me, 'We should unite stoicism, asceticism and ecstasy. Two of them have often come together, but the three never.'

XVI

I believe that some thing I said may have suggested 'I asked if I got sick and died'. S—— had frequently attacked his work while admitting him a man of genius. He attacked it that he might remain on good terms with the people about him. When Synge was in hospital to be operated upon, S—— was there too as a patient, and I told Synge that whenever I spoke of his illness to any man that man said, 'And isn't it sad about S——?' until I could stand it no longer and burst out with 'I hope he will die', and now, as someone said, I was 'being abused all over the town as without heart'. I had learned that people were calling continually to inquire how S—— was, but hardly anybody called to ask for Synge. Two or three weeks later Synge wrote this poem. Had my words set his mind running on the thought that fools flourish, more especially as I had prophesied that S—— would flourish, and in my mood at the moment it seemed that for S—— to be operated on at the same time with Synge was a kind of insolence? S——'s illness did, indeed, win for him so much sympathy that he came out to lucrative and honourable employment, and now when playing golf he says with the English accent he has acquired of late, to some player who needs a great man's favour, 'I know him well, I will say a word in that quarter'.

The Irish weekly papers notice Synge's death with short and for the most part grudging notices. There was an obscure Gaelic League singer who was a leader of the demonstration against the *Playboy*. He died on the same day. *Sinn Fein* notices both deaths in the same article and gives three-fourths of it to the rioter. For Synge it has but grudging words, as was to be expected.

Molly tells me that Synge went to see Stephen MacKenna and his wife before going into hospital and said good-bye with 'You will never see me again'.

XVII

CELEBRATIONS

1. He was one of those unmoved souls in whom there is a perpetual 'Last Day', a perpetual trumpeting and coming up for judgment.

2. He did not speak to men and women, asking judgment, as lesser writers do; but knowing himself part of judgment he was silent.

3. We pity the living and not such dead as he. He has gone upward out of his ailing body into the heroical fountains. We are parched by time.

4. He had the knowledge of his coming death and was cheerful to the end, even joking a little when that end had all but come. He had no need of our sympathies. It was as though we and the things about us died away from him and not he from us.

XVIII

DETRACTIONS

He had that egotism of the man of genius which Nietzsche compares to the egotism of a woman with child. Neither I nor Lady Gregory had ever a compliment from him. After *Hyacinth* Lady Gregory went home the moment the curtain fell, not waiting for the congratulation of friends, to get his supper ready. He was always ailing and weakly. All he said of the triumphant *Hyacinth* was, 'I expected to like it better'. He had under charming and modest manners, in almost all things of life, a complete absorption in his own dream. I have never heard him praise any writer, living or dead, but some old French farce-writer. For him nothing existed but his thought. He claimed nothing for it aloud. He never said any of those self-confident things I am enraged into saying, but one knew that he valued nothing else. He was too confident for self-assertion. I once said to George Moore, 'Synge has always the better of you, for you have brief but ghastly moments during which you admit the existence of other writers; Synge never has.' I do not think he disliked other writers – they did not exist. One did not think of him as an egotist. He was too sympathetic in the ordinary affairs of life and too simple. In the arts he knew no language but his own.

I have often envied him his absorption as I have envied Verlaine his vice. Can a man of genius make that complete renunciation of the world necessary to the full expression of himself without some vice or some deficiency? You were happy or at least blessed, 'blind old man of Scio's rocky isle'.

XX

To-day Molly told me that Synge often spoke of his coming death, indeed constantly for a year past, and tried hard to finish *Deirdre*. Sometimes he would get very despondent, thinking he could not finish it, and then she would act it for him and he would write a little more, and then he would despond again, and so the acting would begin again.

My sister Lily says that the ship Lolly saw on the night of Synge's death was not like a real ship, but like the *Shadowy Waters* ship on the Abbey stage, a sort of allegorical thing. There was also a girl in a bright dress, but she seemed to vanish as the ship ran ashore; all about the girl, and indeed everything, was broken and confused until the bow touched the shore in bright sunlight.

XXII

April 5

Walked home from Gurteen Dhas with D—— and walked through the brick-kilns of Egypt. He states everything in a slightly argumentative form and the soul is starved by the absence of self-evident truth. Good conversation unrolls itself like the spring or like the dawn; whereas effective argument, mere logical statement, founds itself on the set of facts or of experiences common to two or more. Each hides what is new or rich.

XXIII

The element which in men of action corresponds to style in literature is the moral element. Books live almost entirely because of their style, and the men of action who inspire movements after they are dead and those whose hold upon impersonal emotion and law lifts them out of immediate circumstance. Mitchel wrote better prose than Davis, Mangan better poetry, D'Arcy Magee better popular verse. Fintan Lalor saw deeper into a political event. O'Connell had more power and Meagher more eloquence, but Davis alone has influenced generations of young men, though Mitchel's narrower and more faulty nature has now and again competed with him. Davis showed this moral element not merely in his verse – I doubt if that could have had great effect along – but in his action, in his defence, for instance, of the rights of his political opponents of the Royal Irish Academy. His verses were but an illustration of principles shown in action. Men are dominated by self-conquest; thought that is a little obvious or platitudinous if merely written, becomes persuasive, immortal even, if held to amid the hurry of events. The self-conquest of the writer who is not a man of action is style.

Mitchel's influence comes mainly, though not altogether, from style, that also a form of power, an energy of life. It is curious that Mitchel's long martyred life, supported by style, has had less force than that of a man who died at thirty, was never in the hulks, did not write very well, and achieved no change of the law.

The act of appreciation of any great thing is an act of self-conquest. This is one reason why we distrust the serene moralist who has not approved his principles in some crisis. He would be troubled, broken even, if he had made that conquest. Yet the man who has proved himself in a crisis may be serene in words, for his battle was not in contemplation where words are combatants.

XXIV

Last night my sister told me that this book of Synge's (his poems) was the only book they began to print on a Friday. They tried to avoid this but could not, and it is not at all well printed. Do all they could, it would not come right.

XXV

Molly Allgood has just told me of three pre-visions. Some years ago, when the company were in England on that six weeks' tour, she, Synge and D—— were sitting in a tea-shop, she was looking at Synge, and suddenly the flesh seemed to fall from his face and she saw but a skull. She told him this and it gave him a great shock, and since then she has not allowed images to form before her eyes of themselves, as they often used to do. Synge was well at the time. Again last year, but before the operation and at a time when she had no fear, she dreamed that she saw him in a coffin being lowered into a grave, and a 'strange sort of cross' was laid over the coffin. (The company sent a cross of flowers to his funeral and it was laid upon the grave.) She told this also to Synge and he was troubled by it. Then some time after the operation she dreamed that she saw him in a boat. She was on the shore, and he waved his hand to her and the boat went away. She longed to go to him but could not.

XXVI

March 11
Stratford-on-Avon

Some weeks ago C—— wrote to me that it was a phase of M——'s madness to believe himself in heaven. All the great poets of other times were there, and he was helping to prepare for the reception of Swinburne. The angels were to stand in groups of three. And now I have just heard that Swinburne is dead.

XXVII

Dined with Ricketts and Shannon. Ricketts spoke of the grief Synge's death gave him – the ending of all that work. We talked of the disordered and broken lives of modern men of genius and the so different lives of the Italian painters. He said in those days men of genius were cared for, but now the strain of life is too heavy, no one thinks of them till some misfortune comes – madness or death. He then spoke, as he often does, of the lack of any necessary place for the arts in modern life and said, 'After all, the ceiling of the Sistine Chapel was the Pope's ceiling'. Later he said in comment upon some irascible act of Hugh Lane's, 'Everybody who is doing anything for the world is very disagreeable, the agreeable people are those for whom the world is doing something'.

XXVIII

Our modern public arts, architecture, plays, large decorations, have too many different tastes to please. Some taste is sure to dislike and to speak its dislike everywhere, and then because of the silence of the rest – partly from apathy, partly from dislike of controversy, partly from the difficulty of defence, as compared with the ease of attack – there is general timidity. All creation requires one mind to make and one mind of enjoyment. The theatre can at rare moments create this one mind of enjoyment, and once created, it is like the mind of an individual in solitude, immeasurably bold – all is possible to it. The only building received with enthusiasm during my time has been the Catholic Cathedral of Westminster – religion or the politics of religion created that one mind.

XXIX

I asked Molly if any words of hers made Synge write 'I asked if I got sick and died' and she said, 'He used often to joke about death with me and one day he said, "Will you go to my funeral?" and I said, "No, for I could not bear to see you dead and the others living".'

XXX

Went to S——'s the other night – everybody either too tall or too short, crooked or lop-sided. One woman had an excited voice, an intellect without self-possession, and there was a man with a look of a wood-kern, who kept bringing the conversation back and back to Synge's wrongdoing in having made a girl in the *Playboy* admire a man who had hamstrung 'mountain ewes'. He saw nothing else to object to but that one thing. He declared that the English would not give Home Rule because they thought Ireland cruel, and no Irishman should write a sentence to make them go on thinking that. There arose before my mind an image of this man arguing about Ireland with an endless procession of second-rate men. At last I said, 'When a country produces a man of genius he never is what it wants or believes it wants; he is always unlike its idea of itself. In the eighteenth century Scotland believed itself religious, moral and gloomy, and its national poet Burns came not to speak of these things but to speak of lust and drink and drunken gaiety. Ireland, since the Young Irelanders, has given itself up to apologetics. Every impression of life or impulse of imagination has been examined to see if it helped or hurt the glory of Ireland or the political claim of Ireland. A sincere impression of life became at last impossible, all was apologetics. There was no longer an impartial imagination, delighting in whatever is naturally exciting. Synge was the rushing up of the buried fire, an explosion of all that had been denied or refused, a furious impartiality, an indifferent turbulent sorrow. His work, like that of Burns, was to say all the people did not want to have said. He was able to do this because Nature had made him incapable of a political idea.' The wood-kern made no answer, did not understand a word I said, perhaps; but for the rest of the evening he kept saying to this person or to that person that he objected to nothing but the passage about the 'mountain ewes'.

XXXI

July 8

I dreamed this thought two nights ago: 'Why should we complain if men ill-treat our Muses, when all that they gave to Helen while she still lived was a song and a jest?'

131

XXXII

September 20

An idle man has no thought, a man's work thinks through him. On the other hand a woman gets her thought through the influence of a man. A man is to her what work is to a man. Man is a woman to his work and it begets his thoughts.

XXXIII

The old playwrights took old subjects, did not even arrange the subject in a new way. They were absorbed in expression, that is to say in what is most near and delicate. The new playwrights invent their subjects and dislike anything customary in the arrangement of the fable, but their expression is as common as the newspapers where they first learned to write.

XXXIV

October

I saw *Hamlet* on Saturday night, except for the chief 'Ophelia' scenes, and missed these (for I had to be in the Abbey) without regret. Their pathos, as they are played, has always left me cold. I came back for Hamlet at the graveside: there my delight always begins anew. I feel in *Hamlet*, as so often in Shakespeare, that I am in the presence of a soul lingering on the storm-beaten threshold of sanctity. Has not that threshold always been terrible, even crime-haunted? Surely Shakespeare, in those last seeming idle years, was no quiet country gentleman, enjoying, as men like Dowden think, the temporal reward of an unvalued toil. Perhaps he sought for wisdom in itself at last, and not in its passionate shadows. Maybe he had passed the threshold, and none the less for Jonson's drinking bout. Certainly one finds here and there in his work praise of country leisure sweetened by wisdom.

XXXV

Am I going against nature in my constant attempt to fill my life with work? Is my mind as rich as in idle days? Is not perhaps the poet's labour a mere rejection? If he seek purity – the ridding of his life of all but poetry – will not inspiration come? Can one reach God by toil? He gives Himself to the pure in heart. He asks nothing but attention.

XXXVI

I have been looking at Venetian costumes of the sixteenth century as pictured in *The Mask* – all fantastic; bodily form hidden or disguised; the women with long bodices, the men in stuffed doublets. Life had become so learned and courtly that men and women dressed with no thought of bodily activity. If they still fought and hunted, their imagination was not with these things. Does not the same happen to our passions when we grow contemplative and so liberate them from use? They also become fantastic and create the strange lives of poets and artists.

XXXVIII

December 16

Last night Molly had so much improved that I thought she may have tragic power. The lack of power and of clarity which I still find amid great charm and distinction, comes more from lack of construction, through lack of reflection and experience, than from mere lack of emotion. There are passages where she attempts nothing, or where she allows herself little external comedy impulses, more, I now think, because they are habitual than because she could not bring emotion out of herself. The chief failure is towards the end. She does not show immediately after the death of Naoise enough sense of what has happened, enough normal despair to permit of a gradual development into the wild unearthly feeling of the last speeches, though these last speeches are exquisitely spoken. My unfavourable impression of Friday came in part from the audience, which was heavy and, I thought, bored. Yesterday the audience – the pit entirely full – was enthusiastic and moved, raising once again my hope for the theatre and for the movement.

XXXIX

May 25

At Stratford-on-Avon the *Playboy* shocked a good many people, because it was a self-improving, self-educating audience, and that means a perverted and commonplace audience. If you set out to educate yourself you are compelled to have an ideal, a model of what you would be; and if you are not a man of genius, your model will be commonplace and prevent the natural impulses of the mind, its natural reverence, desire, hope, admiration, always half unconscious, almost bodily. That is why a simple round of religious duties, things that escape the intellect, is often so much better than its substitute, self-improvement.

XL

September 18
S. S. 'Zeeland'

I noticed in the train, as I came to Queenstown, a silent, fairly well-dressed man, who struck me as vulgar. It was not his face, which was quite normal, but his movements. He moved from his head only. His arm and hand, let us say, moved in direct obedience to the head, had not the instinctive motion that comes from a feeling of weight, of the shape of an object to be touched or grasped. There were too many straight lines in gesture and in pose. The result was an impression of vulgar smartness, a defiance of what is profound and old and simple. I have noticed that beginners sometimes move this way on the stage. They, if told to pick up something, show by the movement of their body that their idea of doing it is more vivid than the doing of it. One gets an impression of thinness in the nature. I am watching Miss V—— to find out if her inanimate movements when on the stage come from lack of experience or if she has them in life. I watched her sinking into a chair the other day to see if her body felt the size and shape of the chair before she reached it. If her body does not so feel she will never be able to act, just as she will never have grace of movement in ordinary life. As I write I see through the cabin door a woman feeding a child with a spoon. She thinks of nothing but the child, and every movement is full of expression. It would be beautiful acting. Upon the other hand her talk – she is talking to someone next her – in which she is not interested, is monotonous and thin in cadence. It is a mere purpose in the brain, made necessary by politeness.

XLI

October

A good writer should be so simple that he has no faults, only sins.

Poetry

1914–1919

*U*nderlying the poems of this period is the strain of poetic discontent. The artist is repelled by the stance of the self-seekers who control the society he wishes to turn towards the mind.

The controversy over Synge's *Playboy of the Western World* had set the stage for Yeats's position in relation to the public. Then, in 1909, Hugh Lane, Lady Gregory's nephew, had made his offer to the Municipal Gallery of Dublin of the finest collection of Impressionist paintings in the world outside the Luxembourg, but internal jealousies had aborted the project. Just before the outbreak of war Yeats wondered, in his poem 'September 1913', if the Ireland that he had been led to believe in by O'Leary would ever come to be.

'To a Shade', perhaps one of his greatest poems, takes up the theme, as he wonders at Parnell's grave if even the great hero of his life had died for something that had no reality.

> You had enough of sorrow before death –
> Away, away! You are safer in the tomb.

Maud Gonne again hovers in the background in 'Fallen Majesty' and in 'Friends', his eulogy to the three women who shaped his life.

The insurrection against England in Easter week 1916 changed Yeats's attitude completely. He felt the fires within him renewed. All his wonder about the power of the imagination to influence the course of people's lives is contained in 'Easter 1916'. Though it was written shortly after the Rebellion, Yeats did not publish it until 1928, but I have put it in this section because of the time of its composition. I have done the same with 'The Rose Tree'. Both poems show how much he took his inspiration from the evolution of his countrymen and how much his poetry was bound up with the affairs of Ireland.

. Lord Ardilaun, a rich brewer, had offered to subscribe to a gallery to house the Lane pictures, but this never came about and Ireland lost the paintings. The return of the Lane collection to Ireland was to be a lifelong obsession of Yeats and Lady Gregory, who believed the paintings were wrongfully withheld in the National Gallery in England. The history of the affair is well summed up in Yeats's Senate speech, so there is no need for the reader to know more here than Yeats's opinion of Lane as a great man whose genius as a collector had not been recognized by his countrymen.

TO A WEALTHY MAN WHO PROMISED A SECOND SUBSCRIPTION TO THE DUBLIN MUNICIPAL GALLERY IF IT WERE PROVED THE PEOPLE WANTED PICTURES

You gave, but will not give again
Until enough of Paudeen's pence
By Biddy's halfpennies have lain
To be 'some sort of evidence',
Before you'll put your guineas down,
That things it were a pride to give
Are what the blind and ignorant town
Imagines best to make it thrive.
What cared Duke Ercole, that bid
His mummers to the market-place,
What th' onion-sellers thought or did
So that his Plautus set the pace
For the Italian comedies?
And Guidobaldo, when he made
That grammar school of courtesies
Where wit and beauty learned their trade
Upon Urbino's windy hill,
Had sent no runners to and fro
That he might learn the shepherds' will.
And when they drove out Cosimo,
Indifferent how the rancour ran,
He gave the hours they had set free
To Michelozzo's latest plan
For the San Marco Library,
Whence turbulent Italy should draw
Delight in Art whose end is peace,

In logic and in natural law
By sucking at the dugs of Greece.

Your open hand but shows our loss,
For he knew better how to live.
Let Paudeens play at pitch and toss,
Look up in the sun's eye and give
What the exultant heart calls good
That some new day may breed the best
Because you gave, not what they would,
But the right twigs for an eagle's nest!

SEPTEMBER 1913

Robert Emmet, Edward Fitzgerald and Wolfe Tone, referred to in this poem,
were Irish patriots who were executed in rebellions against England in 1798
and 1803. The Wild Geese was a term applied to those Irishmen who, after
the Battle of the Boyne in 1693, rather than serve under one whom they
regarded as a Dutch usurper, exiled themselves on the Continent, where they
sought service in the armies of France, Austria, Spain, Sweden and Russia. It is
estimated that by the middle of the eighteenth century there were 400,000
Irish serving in foreign armies at one time. Marshals of France, Austria and
Russia – Lord Clare, Count Ulick Brown and Peter Lally – were all of Irish
birth.

What need you, being come to sense,
But fumble in a greasy till
And add the halfpence to the pence
And prayer to shivering prayer, until
You have dried the marrow from the bone?
For men were born to pray and save:
Romantic Ireland's dead and gone,
It's with O'Leary in the grave.

Yet they were of a different kind,
The names that stilled your childish play,
They have gone about the world like wind,
But little time had they to pray
For whom the hangman's rope was spun,

And what, God help us, could they save?
Romantic Ireland's dead and gone,
It's with O'Leary in the grave.

Was it for this the wild geese spread
The grey wing upon every tide;
For this that all that blood was shed,
For this Edward Fitzgerald died,
And Robert Emmet and Wolfe Tone,
All that delirium of the brave?
Romantic Ireland's dead and gone,
It's with O'Leary in the grave.

Yet could we turn the years again,
And call those exiles as they were
In all their loneliness and pain,
You'd cry, 'Some woman's yellow hair
Has maddened every mother's son':
They weighed so lightly what they gave.
But let them be, they're dead and gone,
They're with O'Leary in the grave.

TO A SHADE

Yeats, feeling that the work of 'passionate serving' men would come to
nothing in his 'fool-driven' land, wrote this powerful denunciation at Parnell's
graveside in Glasnevin cemetery.

If you have revisited the town, thin Shade,
Whether to look upon your monument
(I wonder if the builder has been paid)
Or happier-thoughted when the day is spent
To drink of that salt breath out of the sea
When grey gulls flit about instead of men,
And the gaunt houses put on majesty:
Let these content you and be gone again;
For they are at their old tricks yet.
                                        A man
Of your own passionate serving kind who had brought

In his full hands what, had they only known,
Had given their children's children loftier thought,
Sweeter emotion, working in their veins
Like gentle blood, has been driven from the place,
And insult heaped upon him for his pains,
And for his open-handedness, disgrace;
Your enemy, an old foul mouth, had set
The pack upon him.
             Go, unquiet wanderer,
And gather the Glasnevin coverlet
About your head till the dust stops your ear,
The time for you to taste of that salt breath
And listen at the corners has not come:
You had enough of sorrow before death—
Away, away! You are safer in the tomb.

ON THOSE WHO HATED
'THE PLAYBOY OF THE WESTERN WORLD'

Once, when midnight smote the air,
Eunuchs ran through Hell and met
On every crowded street to stare
Upon great Juan riding by:
Even like these to rail and sweat
Staring upon his sinewy thigh.

TO A FRIEND WHOSE WORK HAS COME TO NOTHING

Now all the truth is out,
Be secret and take defeat
From any brazen throat,
For how can you compete,
Being honour bred, with one
Who, were it proved he lies,
Were neither shamed in his own
Nor in his neighbours' eyes?
Bred to a harder thing
Than Triumph, turn away

And like a laughing string
Whereon mad fingers play
Amid a place of stone,
Be secret and exult,
Because of all things known
That is most difficult.

TO A CHILD DANCING IN THE WIND

Dance there upon the shore;
What need have you to care
For wind or water's roar?
And tumble out your hair
That the salt drops have wet;
Being young you have not known
The fool's triumph, nor yet
Love lost as soon as won,
Nor the best labourer dead
And all the sheaves to bind.
What need have you to dread
The monstrous crying of wind?

THE COLD HEAVEN

Suddenly I saw the cold and rook-delighting heaven
That seemed as though ice burned and was but the
     more ice,
And thereupon imagination and heart were driven
So wild that every casual thought of that and this
Vanished, and left but memories, that should be out
     of season
With the hot blood of youth, of love crossed long ago;
And I took all the blame out of all sense and reason,
Until I cried and trembled and rocked to and fro,
Riddled with light. Ah! when the ghost begins to
     quicken,
Confusion of the death-bed over, is it sent
Out naked on the roads, as the books say, and stricken

By the injustice of the skies for punishment?

A COAT

I made my song a coat
Covered with embroideries
Out of old mythologies
From heel to throat;
But the fools caught it,
Wore it in the world's eyes
As though they'd wrought it.
Song, let them take it,
For there's more enterprise
In walking naked.

EASTER 1916

In this poem, it is necessary to identify some of the characters. The 'young and beautiful' girl who 'rode to harriers' is Constance Gore-Booth, whom Yeats had known as a girl at Lissadell House in Sligo. She had been a Commandant in the Rebellion and had, through marriage, become Countess Markiewicz. She was condemned to death (but reprieved) for her part in the Rebellion. The man who 'kept a school And rode our wingèd horse' is Patrick Pearse, leader with James Connolly of the Rebellion, and executed after it. The 'helper and friend' is Thomas MacDonagh, poet and university lecturer, also executed. The 'drunken, vainglorious lout' who 'has been changed in his turn, Transformed utterly' is Major John MacBride, husband of Maud Gonne. The 'Connolly' referred to in the last five lines of the poem is General James Connolly of the Citizen Army, who was executed sitting on a chair as he was wounded and could not stand up.

I have met them at close of day
Coming with vivid faces
From counter or desk among grey
Eighteenth-century houses.
I have passed with a nod of the head
Or polite meaningless words,
Or have lingered awhile and said

Polite meaningless words,
And thought before I had done
Of a mocking tale or a gibe
To please a companion
Around the fire at the club,
Being certain that they and I
But lived where motley is worn:
All changed, changed utterly:
A terrible beauty is born.

That woman's days were spent
In ignorant good-will,
Her nights in argument
Until her voice grew shrill.
What voice more sweet than hers
When, young and beautiful,
She rode to harriers?
This man had kept a school
And rode our wingèd horse;
This other his helper and friend
Was coming into his force;
He might have won fame in the end,
So sensitive his nature seemed,
So daring and sweet his thought.
This other man I had dreamed
A drunken, vainglorious lout.
He had done most bitter wrong
To some who are near my heart,
Yet I number him in the song;
He, too, has resigned his part
In the casual comedy;
He, too, has been changed in his turn,
Transformed utterly:
A terrible beauty is born.

Hearts with one purpose alone
Through summer and winter seem
Enchanted to a stone
To trouble the living stream.
The horse that comes from the road,

The rider, the birds that range
From cloud to tumbling cloud,
Minute by minute they change;
A shadow of cloud on the stream
Changes minute by minute;
A horse-hoof slides on the brim,
And a horse plashes within it;
The long-legged moor-hens dive,
And hens to moor-cocks call;
Minute by minute they live:
The stone's in the midst of all.

Too long a sacrifice
Can make a stone of the heart.
O when may it suffice?
That is Heaven's part, our part
To murmur name upon name,
As a mother names her child
When sleep at last has come
On limbs that had run wild.
What is it but nightfall?
No, no, not night but death;
Was it needless death after all?
For England may keep faith
For all that is done and said.
We know their dream; enough
To know they dreamed and are dead;
And what if excess of love
Bewildered them till they died?
I write it out in a verse –
MacDonagh and MacBride
And Connolly and Pearse
Now and in time to be,
Wherever green is worn,
Are changed, changed utterly:
A terrible beauty is born.

FALLEN MAJESTY

Although crowds gathered once if she but showed
    her face,
And even old men's eyes grew dim, this hand alone,
Like some last courtier at a gypsy camping-place
Babbling of fallen majesty, records what's gone.

The lineaments, a heart that laughter has made sweet,
These, these remain, but I record what's gone. A crowd
Will gather, and not know it walks the very street
Whereon a thing once walked that seemed a burning
    cloud.

FRIENDS

(The three friends are Lady Gregory, Olivia Shakespear and Maud Gonne. *Ed.*)

Now must I these three praise –
Three women that have wrought
What joy is in my days:
One because no thought,
Nor those unpassing cares,
No, not in these fifteen
Many-times-troubled years,
Could ever come between
Mind and delighted mind;
And one because her hand
Had strength that could unbind
What none can understand,
What none can have and thrive,
Youth's dreamy load, till she
So changed me that I live
Labouring in ecstasy.
And what of her that took
All till my youth was gone
With scarce a pitying look?
How could I praise that one?
When day begins to break

I count my good and bad,
Being wakeful for her sake,
Remembering what she had,
What eagle look still shows,
While up from my heart's root
So great a sweetness flows
I shake from head to foot.

THE ROSE TREE

'O words are lightly spoken,'
Said Pearse to Connolly,
'Maybe a breath of politic words
Has withered our Rose Tree;
Or maybe but a wind that blows
Across the bitter sea.'

'It needs to be but watered,'
James Connolly replied,
'To make the green come out again
And spread on every side,
And shake the blossom from the bud
To be the garden's pride.'

'But where can we draw water,'
Said Pearse to Connolly,
'When all the wells are parched away?
O plain as plain can be
There's nothing but our own red blood
Can make a right Rose Tree.'

Poetry

1919–1921

*F*rom 1919 to 1921 the Anglo-Irish war was in full spate. Yeats was on the side of those who wished the English to leave Ireland. But his volume *The Wild Swans at Coole* (1919) has little political content. It was not until his next volume, *Michael Robartes and the Dance* (1921) that he published 'Easter 1916' and 'The Rose Tree', written shortly after the Rising in 1916. There are, however, other political poems in this volume, 'To a Political Prisoner' and 'Sixteen Dead Men'. *The Wild Swans at Coole* also contained the elegiac 'In Memory of Major Robert Gregory', which recalls Lady Gregory's son, who was killed flying in the RFC in 1918. He is placed side by side in the poem with Lionel Johnson and 'that enquiring man John Synge'.

Yeats saw Robert Gregory, boxer, painter and huntsman, as a Renaissance man. Robert had designed numerous side sets for Yeats's own plays. His painting, created with a pallette that even today has a modern glow, has been underestimated so far. In the poem 'An Irish Airman Foresees his Death', Yeats seemed to sense a fatalism in Robert Gregory which perhaps would have prevented the imaginative drive of the artist from forging its way to the surface in later life. But there can seldom have been a better summing-up of the sense of elation which the freedom to roam the unchartered skies brought to the young men of Gregory's pre-1914 generation:

> A lonely impulse of delight,
> Drove to this tumult in the clouds.

'The Second Coming' is Yeats's Tiresian prophesy of an impending apocalypse seen against the background of the Viconian cycle; Anarchy, Religion, Democracy and Anarchy once more, as an inevitable stage in society.

Surely the Second Coming is at hand . . .
And what rough beast, its hour come round at last,
Slouches towards Bethlehem to be born?

In the title poem in the book Yeats shows how much he is in touch with the
spirit of Modernism, paring his words like a sculptor with a chisel, the lyricism
subdued with the cold light of the mind.

Unwearied still, lover by lover,
They paddle in the cold
Companionable streams or climb the air.

Again only he could use words that no longer seem to have a place in verse –
'mysterious', 'beautiful' – and give them once more the quality of beauty.

By now they drift on the still water,
Mysterious, beautiful;
Among what rushes will they build,
By what lake's edge or pool
Delight men's eyes when I awake some day
To find they have flown away?

'The People' is one of his most public poems, in which he wishes that he could
have lived in some civilized community like Urbino in the time of Castiglione,
where the poet and courtier had a special place in society, instead of having to
endure at home 'the daily spite of this unmannerly town'.

THE WILD SWANS AT COOLE

The trees are in their autumn beauty,
The woodland paths are dry,
Under the October twilight the water
Mirrors a still sky;
Upon the brimming water among the stones
Are nine-and-fifty swans.

The nineteenth autumn has come upon me
Since I first made my count;

I saw, before I had well finished,
All suddenly mount
And scatter wheeling in great broken rings
Upon their clamorous wings.

I have looked upon those brilliant creatures,
And now my heart is sore.
All's changed since I, hearing at twilight,
The first time on this shore,
The bell-beat of their wings above my head,
Trod with a lighter tread.

Unwearied still, lover by lover,
They paddle in the cold
Companionable streams or climb the air;
Their hearts have not grown old;
Passion or conquest, wander where they will,
Attend upon them still.

But now they drift on the still water,
Mysterious, beautiful;
Among what rushes will they build,
By what lake's edge or pool
Delight men's eyes when I awake some day
To find they have flown away?

IN MEMORY OF MAJOR ROBERT GREGORY

I

Now that we're almost settled in our house
I'll name the friends that cannot sup with us
Beside a fire of turf in th' ancient tower,
And having talked to some late hour
Climb up the narrow winding stair to bed:
Discoverers of forgotten truth
Or mere companions of my youth,
All, all are in my thoughts to-night being dead.

II

Always we'd have the new friend meet the old
And we are hurt if either friend seem cold,
And there is salt to lengthen out the smart
In the affections of our heart,
And quarrels are blown up upon that head;
But not a friend that I would bring
This night can set us quarrelling,
For all that come into my mind are dead.

III

Lionel Johnson comes the first to mind,
That loved his learning better than mankind.
Though courteous to the worst; much falling he
Brooded upon sanctity
Till all his Greek and Latin learning seemed
A long blast upon the horn that brought
A little nearer to his thought
A measureless consummation that he dreamed.

IV

And that enquiring man John Synge comes next,
That dying chose the living world for text
And never could have rested in the tomb
But that, long travelling, he had come
Towards nightfall upon certain set apart
In a most desolate stony place,
Towards nightfall upon a race
Passionate and simple like his heart.

V

And then I think of old George Pollexfen,
In muscular youth well known to Mayo men
For horsemanship at meets or at racecourses,
That could have shown how pure-bred horses
And solid men, for all their passion, live

But as the outrageous stars incline
By opposition, square and trine;
Having grown sluggish and contemplative.

VI

They were my close companions many a year,
A portion of my mind and life, as it were,
And now their breathless faces seem to look
Out of some old picture-book;
I am accustomed to their lack of breath,
But not that my dear friend's dear son,
Our Sidney and our perfect man,
Could share in that discourtesy of death.

VII

For all things the delighted eye now sees
Were loved by him: the old storm-broken trees
That cast their shadows upon road and bridge;
The tower set on the stream's edge;
The ford where drinking cattle make a stir
Nightly, and startled by that sound
The water-hen must change her ground;
He might have been your heartiest welcomer.

VIII

When with the Galway foxhounds he would ride
From Castle Taylor to the Roxborough side
Or Esserkelly plain, few kept his pace;
At Mooneen he had leaped a place
So perilous that half the astonished meet
Had shut their eyes; and where was it
He rode a race without a bit?
And yet his mind outran the horses' feet.

IX

We dreamed that a great painter had been born

To cold Clare rock and Galway rock and thorn,
To that stern colour and that delicate line
That are our secret discipline
Wherein the gazing heart doubles her might.
Soldier, scholar, horseman, he,
And yet he had the intensity
To have published all to be a world's delight.

X

What other could so well have counselled us
In all lovely intricacies of a house
As he that practised or that understood
All work in metal or in wood,
In moulded plaster or in carven stone?
Soldier, scholar, horseman, he,
And all he did done perfectly
As though he had but that one trade alone.

XI

Some burn damp faggots, others may consume
The entire combustible world in one small room
As though dried straw, and if we turn about
The bare chimney is gone black out
Because the work had finished in that flare.
Soldier, scholar, horseman, he,
As 'twere all life's epitome.
What made us dream that he could comb grey hair?

XII

I had thought, seeing how bitter is that wind
That shakes the shutter, to have brought to mind
All those that manhood tried, or childhood loved
Or boyish intellect approved,
With some appropriate commentary on each;
Until imagination brought
A fitter welcome; but a thought
Of that late death took all my heart for speech.

AN IRISH AIRMAN FORESEES HIS DEATH

I know that I shall meet my fate
Somewhere among the clouds above;
Those that I fight I do not hate,
Those that I guard I do not love;
My country is Kiltartan Cross,
My countrymen Kiltartan's poor,
No likely end could bring them loss
Or leave them happier than before.
Nor law, nor duty bade me fight,
Nor public men, nor cheering crowds,
A lonely impulse of delight
Drove to this tumult in the clouds;
I balanced all, brought all to mind,
The years to come seemed waste of breath,
A waste of breath the years behind
In balance with this life, this death.

THE PEOPLE

'What have I earned for all that work,' I said,
'For all that I have done at my own charge?
The daily spite of this unmannerly town,
Where who has served the most is most defamed,
The reputation of his lifetime lost
Between the night and morning. I might have lived,
And you know well how great the longing has been,
Where every day my footfall should have lit
In the green shadow of Ferrara wall;
Or climbed among the images of the past –
The unperturbed and courtly images –
Evening and morning, the steep street of Urbino
To where the Duchess and her people talked
The stately midnight through until they stood
In their great window looking at the dawn;
I might have had no friend that could not mix
Courtesy and passion into one like those
That saw the wicks grow yellow in the dawn;

I might have used the one substantial right
My trade allows: chosen my company,
And chosen what scenery had pleased me best.
Thereon my phoenix answered in reproof,
'The drunkards, pilferers of public funds,
All the dishonest crowd I had driven away,
When my luck changed and they dared meet my face,
Crawled from obscurity, and set upon me
Those I had served and some that I had fed;
Yet never have I, now nor any time,
Complained of the people.'
                       All I could reply
Was: 'You, that have not lived in thought but deed,
Can have the purity of a natural force,
But I, whose virtues are the definitions
Of the analytic mind, can neither close
The eye of the mind nor keep my tongue from speech.'
And yet, because my heart leaped at her words,
I was abashed, and now they come to mind
After nine years, I sink my head abashed.

THE FISHERMAN

Although I can see him still,
The freckled man who goes
To a grey place on a hill
In grey Connemara clothes
At dawn to cast his flies,
It's long since I began
To call up to the eyes
This wise and simple man.
All day I'd looked in the face
What I had hoped 'twould be
To write for my own race
And the reality;
The living men that I hate,
The dead man that I loved,
The craven man in his seat,
The insolent unreproved,

And no knave brought to book
Who has won a drunken cheer,
The witty man and his joke
Aimed at the commonest ear,
The clever man who cries
The catch-cries of the clown,
The beating down of the wise
And great Art beaten down.

Maybe a twelvemonth since
Suddenly I began,
In scorn of this audience,
Imagining a man,
And his sun-freckled face,
And grey Connemara cloth,
Climbing up to a place
Where stone is dark under froth,
And the down-turn of his wrist
When the flies drop in the stream;
A man who does not exist,
A man who is but a dream;
And cried, 'Before I am old
I shall have written him one
Poem maybe as cold
And passionate as the dawn.'

LINES WRITTEN IN DEJECTION

When have I last looked on
The round green eyes and the long wavering bodies
Of the dark leopards of the moon?
All the wild witches, those most noble ladies,
For all their broom-sticks and their tears,
Their angry tears, are gone.
The holy centaurs of the hills are vanished;
I have nothing but the embittered sun;
Banished heroic mother moon and vanished,
And now that I have gone to fifty years
I must endure the timid sun.

HER PRAISE

She is foremost of those that I would hear praised.
I have gone about the house, gone up and down
As a man does who has published a new book,
Or a young girl dressed out in her new gown,
And though I have turned the talk by hook or crook
Until her praise should be the uppermost theme,
A woman spoke of some new tale she had read,
A man confusedly in a half dream
As though some other name ran in his head.
She is foremost of those that I would hear praised.
I will talk no more of books or the long war
But walk by the dry thorn until I have found
Some beggar sheltering from the wind, and there
Manage the talk until her name come round.
If there be rags enough he will know her name
And be well pleased remembering it, for in the old
    days,
Though she had young men's praise and old men's
    blame,
Among the poor both old and young gave her praise.

BROKEN DREAMS

There is grey in your hair.
Young men no longer suddenly catch their breath
When you are passing;
But maybe some old gaffer mutters a blessing
Because it was your prayer
Recovered him upon the bed of death.
For your sole sake – that all heart's ache have known,
And given to others all heart's ache,
From meagre girlhood's putting on
Burdensome beauty – for your sole sake
Heaven has put away the stroke of her doom,
So great her portion in that peace you make
By merely walking in a room.

Your beauty can but leave among us
Vague memories, nothing but memories.
A young man when the old men are done talking
Will say to an old man, 'Tell me of that lady
The poet stubborn with his passion sang us
When age might well have chilled his blood.'

Vague memories, nothing but memories,
But in the grave all, all, shall be renewed.
The certainty that I shall see that lady
Leaning or standing or walking
In the first loveliness of womanhood,
And with the fervour of my youthful eyes,
Has set me muttering like a fool.

You are more beautiful than any one,
And yet your body had a flaw:
Your small hands were not beautiful,
And I am afraid that you will run
And paddle to the wrist
In that mysterious, always brimming lake
Where those that have obeyed the holy law
Paddle and are perfect. Leave unchanged
The hands that I have kissed,
For old sake's sake.

The last stroke of midnight dies.
All day in the one chair
From dream to dream and rhyme to rhyme I have
    ranged
In rambling talk with an image of air:
Vague memories, nothing but memories.

A DEEP-SWORN VOW

Others because you did not keep
That deep-sworn vow have been friends of mine;
Yet always when I look death in the face,
When I clamber to the heights of sleep,

Or when I grow excited with wine,
Suddenly I meet your face.

AMONG SCHOOL CHILDREN

This poem was written after Yeats had become a friend of Joseph O'Connor, of the Department of Education, and on his advice visited a convent in Waterford where new ideas of teaching were being put into practice.

I

I walk through the long schoolroom questioning;
A kind old nun in a white hood replies;
The children learn to cipher and to sing,
To study reading-books and histories,
To cut and sew, be neat in everything
In the best modern way – the children's eyes
In momentary wonder stare upon
A sixty-year-old smiling public man.

II

I dream of a Ledaean body, bent
Above a sinking fire, a tale that she
Told of a harsh reproof, or trivial event
That changed some childish day to tragedy –
Told, and it seemed that our two natures blent
Into a sphere from youthful sympathy,
Or else, to alter Plato's parable,
Into the yolk and white of the one shell.

III

And thinking of that fit of grief or rage
I look upon one child or t'other there
And wonder if she stood so at that age –
For even daughters of the swan can share

Something of every paddler's heritage –
And had that colour upon cheek or hair,
And thereupon my heart is driven wild:
She stands before me as a living child.

IV

Her present image floats into the mind –
Did Quattrocento finger fashion it
Hollow of cheek as though it drank the wind
And took a mess of shadows for its meat?
And I though never of Ledaean kind
Had pretty plumage once – enough of that,
Better to smile on all that smile, and show
There is a comfortable kind of old scarecrow.

V

What youthful mother, a shape upon her lap
Honey of generation had betrayed,
And that must sleep, shriek, struggle to escape
As recollection or the drug decide,
Would think her son, did she but see that shape
With sixty or more winters on its head,
A compensation for the pang of his birth,
Or the uncertainty of his setting forth?

VI

Plato thought nature but a spume that plays
Upon a ghostly paradigm of things;
Solider Aristotle played the taws
Upon the bottom of a king of kings;
World-famous golden-thighed Pythagoras
Fingered upon a fiddle-stick or strings
What a star sang and careless Muses heard:
Old clothes upon old sticks to scare a bird.

VII

Both nuns and mothers worship images,
But those the candles light are not as those
That animate a mother's reveries,
But keep a marble or a bronze repose.
And yet they too break hearts – O Presences
That passion, piety or affection knows,
And that all heavenly glory symbolise –
A self-born mockers of man's enterprise;

VIII

Labour is blossoming or dancing where
The body is not bruised to pleasure soul,
Nor beauty born out of its own despair,
Nor blear-eyed wisdom out of midnight oil.
O chestnut-tree, great-rooted blossomer,
Are you the leaf, the blossom or the bole?
O body swayed to music, O brightening glance,
How can we know the dancer from the dance?

THE SECOND COMING

Turning and turning in the widening gyre
The falcon cannot hear the falconer;
Things fall apart; the centre cannot hold;
Mere anarchy is loosed upon the world,
The blood-dimmed tide is loosed, and everywhere
The ceremony of innocence is drowned;
The best lack all conviction, while the worst
Are full of passionate intensity.

Surely some revelation is at hand;
Surely the Second Coming is at hand.
The Second Coming! Hardly are those words out
When a vast image out of *Spiritus Mundi*
Troubles my sight: somewhere in sands of the desert
A shape with lion body and the head of a man,

A gaze blank and pitiless as the sun,
Is moving its slow thighs, while all about it
Reel shadows of the indignant desert birds.
The darkness drops again; but now I know
That twenty centuries of stony sleep
Were vexed to nightmare by a rocking cradle,
And what rough beast, its hour come round at last,
Slouches towards Bethlehem to be born?

TO A YOUNG GIRL

This was to Iseult, Maud Gonne's daughter.

My dear, my dear, I know
More than another
What makes your heart beat so;
Not even your own mother
Can know it as I know,
Who broke my heart for her
When the wild thought,
That she denies
And has forgot,
Set all her blood astir
And glittered in her eyes.

The Senate Speeches

After a Treaty had been signed with England and the ending of the Anglo-Irish war, the British administration and armed forces evacuated twenty-six counties of Ireland and a new self-governing Irish parliament was set up for that part of the country. This was called the Dáil. The second chamber was called the Seanad (Senate). Yeats was one of the thirty nominated members and for six years made many distinguished contributions to the assembly.

Perhaps his most important speech was on the issue of divorce. A bill had been introduced which would make divorce legally impossible, even for Irish citizens who were not members of the Church of the majority. Yeats believed that there were forces at work which would persuade the State into adopting a confessional stance, and he made his most famous public speech in the Debate on Divorce on 11 June 1925. He had prepared his address carefully, and as he delivered it he became carried away with the vehemence of the words and strode up and down the chamber, waving the notes he carried in his hands, to emphasize the rhetoric. A political opponent of his, Senator Jim Farrell, recalled to the author the effect of the speech on the Senate: 'He flayed us alive. It was magnificent.'

The key lines in the peroration were to be a stern reminder to Irishmen that their future inheritance was not confined to one section of the community only.

We against whom you have done this thing are no petty people. We are one of the great stocks of Europe. We are the people of Burke: we are the people of Grattan: we are the people of Swift, the people of Emmet, the people of Parnell. We have created the most of the modern literature of this country. We have created the best of its political intelligence.

He spoke on a variety of subjects (including Montessori methods for teaching at school), and made a major contribution as chairman of a committee for the design of the coinage.

Another important speech was on the subject of the Lane pictures. Though his passionate appeal did not have any immediate effect – the British Government remained adamant – a compromise was to be reached thirty years later when the National Gallery agreed to exchange every year with the Municipal Gallery in Dublin (now called the Hugh Lane Municipal Gallery) paintings from the Lane collection. These could now be estimated as being worth approximately £3 billion.

THE LANE PICTURES

MR. W. B. YEATS: I have the following motion to move:

> 'That the Seanad ask the Government to press upon the British Government the return to Dublin of the pictures mentioned in the unwitnessed codicil to Sir Hugh Lane's will.'

This is an old question. We have been agitating now for some years, and I have some reason for saying that the opposition against the return of these pictures is dying away. I think the justice of our case has been generally admitted. It is simply a question of the inertia of Government and of giving them the necessary impulse towards arriving at some definite decision. It is necessary, however, I think, to remind you of the circumstances under which that codicil was written. A good many years ago now Sir Hugh Lane established in Dublin a famous gallery of modern pictures. When he established it there was no modern gallery here in which students could study, and they had to go abroad to do so. Sir Hugh Lane was no mere picture dealer, but, in the words of an eminent authority, he lifted the trade of picture dealer into the realm of art. He sold pictures merely that he might buy other pictures, and he bought pictures in order that he might endow a great gallery. After he made the Dublin Municipal Gallery the most important collection of French pictures outside Luxembourg, he was somewhat discourteously treated by some of the Dublin newspapers and certain persons, and an acrimonious controversy arose.

In 1913, under the impulse of that controversy, he made a will leaving certain pictures, generally known as the Hugh Lane French pictures, to the National Gallery of London. These pictures had been given to the Municipal

Gallery conditional on certain requests being carried out. Those requests were not carried out, and he gave them to the English National Gallery. He felt the pictures were not valued here. He lent them to the English National Gallery to show that they were real pictures of worth. Then under irritation he made this will, by which he left all his property, with the exception of those French pictures, to the National Gallery of Ireland. He left certain pictures to the Municipal Gallery, but he left the French pictures to the London National Gallery. Two years later, in 1915, when he was going on a journey to America, which he knew to be dangerous, he made a codicil by which the National Gallery was to return the pictures known as the French Pictures back to Ireland. He wrote that codicil in ink. He signed it on each page. I have a photographic copy of it in my hand; when he made a slight correction in the date he initialled that correction. No document could be more formal except for one omission. He never had it witnessed. He spoke of this change of mind to various people. I have in this pamphlet three affidavits of how he spoke of changing his mind, and wishing that Ireland had his French pictures. Of his intention there can be no question whatever. From those various documents I think I may read you one affidavit made by his sister:

I, Ruth Shine, of Lindsey House, 100 Cheyne Walk, London, S.W., widow, do solemnly and sincerely declare as follows:

The late Sir Hugh Lane was a brother of mine, and he is hereinafter referred to as 'my brother.'

In January, 1915, my brother spoke to me of making another will. He went to Dublin, however, without having done so. It was there (on February 3rd) that he wrote and signed his codicil and locked it in his desk at the National Gallery in a sealed envelope addressed to me; it was very clearly and carefully written and I have no doubt whatever that he considered it legal.

My brother had no ordinary business habits in the ordinary sense of the word, and was ignorant of legal technicalities. He dictated both his wills to me, the first leaving all to the Modern Art Gallery in Dublin, and the second leaving all to the National Gallery of Dublin, with the exception of the French pictures left to London. But for my persistence, neither would have been witnessed; even when he dictated the second will he had forgotten all I had told him about that necessity. So little am I surprised at there being no witnesses to the codicil that my surprise is altogether that he should have written it so carefully. He must have made rough drafts, as he composed letters with great difficulty, and the codicil was so well written.

I think from my knowledge of him that if he thought of a witness at all he would perhaps have considered that a codicil to an already witnessed will needed no further formality. When he sealed up the envelope he was going on a dangerous journey to America, and was so much impressed by that danger that at first he had refused to go at all unless those who had invited him for business reasons would insure his life for £50,000 to clear his estate of certain liabilities, and he thought he was going not in seven or eight weeks, as it happened, but in two or three.

I have approached this subject without any bias in favour of Dublin, but as his sister, anxious that his intentions should be carried out, and I make this declaration conscientiously believing the same to be true and by virtue of the provisions of the statutory Declaration Act, 1835.

RUTH SHINE
Declared at Markham House, King's Road,
Chelsea, in the county of London, this 13th
day of February, 1917
    Before me,
    G.F. Wilkins
    A Commissioner for oaths.

That codicil would have been legal in Scotland. It seems to us that a request made to a great Gallery is something different from a request made to an individual; that a great Gallery like this cannot desire to retain property which was left to it by accident, and that it must desire, as we do, the return of these pictures if they are set free by Act of Parliament legalizing the codicil. We believe that that Act of Parliament can be obtained. One Irish Chief Secretary had prepared such a Bill, but it has been pushed aside by the pressure of Parliamentary business. It is very important for Ireland to recover these pictures. With the addition of the French pictures the Municipal Gallery is more than doubled in its importance, for those pictures are complementary to the pictures here in Dublin. He was not only a connoisseur; he had the gift of arranging pictures so as to display them to the best advantage. With those pictures there, we should have in the Municipal Gallery a possession which in future generations would draw people to Dublin, and help in enriching the city and the whole population by bringing those pilgrims. The actual money value of the pictures is hard to decide, because pictures constantly change their value, but about twelve years ago they were valued at about £75,000. It is quite probable they are worth more now. One picture, by Manet, might be bought at £20,000. They also have this further importance: they will never be in the market again. The great pictures of that period in French art are already finding their way into national collections. It is precisely for that reason that certain English critics have tried to keep the pictures in England. They know that if they cannot keep these French pictures in London they can never have a representative collection of French art. In fighting to recover these pictures you are fighting for a unique possession which will always remain unique and always give prestige to the Gallery that contains it.

DEBATE ON DIVORCE

Attempts had been made by certain political groups to prevent the introduction of a Bill of Divorce to the Oireachtas. On 11 June 1925 the Senate had before it the Committee of Standing Order's report which would limit the jurisdiction of the Senate in initiating a bill of this kind. Senator Douglas, like Yeats, a Protestant, had moved that a message be sent to the Dáil (the Lower House) which would make it possible at least for a bill proposing divorce legislation to be adequately debated there.

AN CATHAOIRLEACH: The next item on the Order Paper is 'Report of the Joint Committee on Standing Orders (Private Business) on the position in Saorstát Eireann of Bills relating to matrimonial matters (consideration resumed).' There is a motion in regard to this matter standing in the name of Senator Douglas.

DR. YEATS: Before Senator Douglas speaks, I would like to say that some of us desire to discuss this question on its merits, and I would like to know whether it would be in order to do so before he proposes his resolution.

AN CATHAOIRLEACH: I hope that every Senator will discuss the motion on its merits, but I think what you want to get an opinion from me on is whether you can discuss the main question as to whether there should be divorce *a vinculo matrimonii*.

DR. YEATS: Yes.

AN CATHAOIRLEACH: That undoubtedly does arise on the report and motion, and I shall not stop a general discussion upon it if that is the wish of the House.

DR YEATS: Owing to Senator Douglas's motion, I shall have to move its rejection in order to make the discussion germane to the matter.

AN CATHAOIRLEACH: That will give you an opportunity of enlarging on the matter.

DR. YEATS: It goes against my heart.

After a discussion by several Senators of certain technical matters, the Chairman returned to the topic of divorce legislation as follows:

AN CATHAOIRLEACH: The House might like to spend the rest of the day over this divorce business and if that is the universal wish of the House, the debate might be resumed. I call upon Senator Yeats.

DR. YEATS: I speak on this question after long hesitation and with a good deal of anxiety, but it is sometimes one's duty to come down to absolute fundamentals for the sake of the education of the people. I have no doubt whatever that there will be no divorce in this country for some time. I do not expect to influence a vote in this House. I am not speaking to this House. It is the custom of those who do address the House to speak sometimes to the Reporters.

COLONEL MOORE: No, no.

AN CATHAOIRLEACH: Perhaps the Senator would please address me. I do not think that Senator Yeats intended to be uncomplimentary to the House, but his observation looked like it.

DR. YEATS: I did not intend to be uncomplimentary. I should have said I do not intend to speak merely to the House. I have no doubt whatever, if circumstances were a little different, a very easy solution would be found for this whole difficulty. I judge from conversations that I have had with various persons that many would welcome a very simple solution, namely, that the Catholic members should remain absent when a Bill of Divorce was brought before the House that concerned Protestants and non-Catholics only, and that it would be left to the Protestant members or some committee appointed by those Protestant members, to be dealt with. I think it would be the first instinct of the members of both Houses to adopt some such solution and it is obvious, I think, that from every point of view of national policy and national reputation that would be a wise policy.

It is perhaps the deepest political passion with this nation that North and South be united into one nation. If it ever comes that North and South unite, the North will not give up any liberty which she already possesses under her constitution. You will then have to grant to another people what you refuse to grant to those within your borders. If you show that this country, Southern Ireland, is going to be governed by Catholic ideas and by Catholic ideas alone, you will never get the North. You will create an impassable barrier between

South and North, and you will pass more and more Catholic laws, while the North will, gradually, assimilate its divorce and other laws to those of England. You will put a wedge into the midst of this nation. I do not think this House has ever made a more serious decision than the decision which, I believe, it is about to make on this question. You will not get the North if you impose on the minority what the minority consider to be oppressive legislation. I have no doubt whatever that in the next few years the minority will make it perfectly plain that it does consider it exceedingly oppressive legislation to deprive it of rights which it has held since the seventeenth century. These rights were won by the labours of John Milton and other great men, and won after strife, which is a famous part of the history of the Protestant people.

There is a reason why this country did not act upon what was its first impulse, and why this House and the Dáil did not act on their first impulse. Some of you may probably know that when the Committee was set up to draw up the Constitution of the Free State, it was urged to incorporate in the constitution the indissolubility of marriage and refused to do so. That was the expression of the political mind of Ireland. You are now urged to act on the advice of men who do not express the political mind, but who express the religious mind. I admit it must be exceedingly difficult for members of this House to resist the pressure that has been brought upon them. In the long warfare of this country with England the Catholic clergy took the side of the people, and owing to that they possess here an influence that they do not possess anywhere else in Europe. It is difficult for you, and I am sure it is difficult for Senator Mrs Wyse-Power, stalwart fighter as she is –

MRS. WYSE-POWER: I do not see why my name should be mentioned.

AN CATHAOIRLEACH: It is not in order to refer in this way to members of this House.

DR. YEATS: I am sure it is difficult for members of this House to resist the advice of Archbishop O'Donnell.

MR. FITZGERALD: I think this is becoming very heated.

DR. YEATS: We shall all be much bitterer before we are finished with this question.

AN CATHAOIRLEACH: Order, order; address the chair.

MR. FARREN: Is it in order for a Senator to be bringing in names?

AN CATHAOIRLEACH: I am not a judge of taste. I cannot rule on matters of taste and I cannot say it is out of order.

DR. YEATS: Addressing the Catholic Truth Society in October last he used these words:

'No power on earth can break the marriage bond until death . . . that is true of all baptised persons no matter what the denomination may be. To be sure we hear that a section of our fellow-countrymen favour divorces. Well, with nothing but respect and sympathy for all our neighbours, we have to say that we place the marriages of such people higher than they do themselves. Their marriages are unbreakable before God and we cannot disobey God by helping break them.'

That is to say that you are to legislate on purely theological grounds and you are to force your theology upon persons who are not of your religion. It is not a question of finding it legally difficult or impossible to grant to a minority what the majority does not wish for itself. You are to insist upon members of the Church of Ireland or members of no church taking a certain view of Biblical criticism, or of the authority of the text upon which that criticism is exercised, a view that they notoriously do not take. If you legislate upon such grounds there is no reason why you should stop there. There is no reason why you should not forbid civil marriages altogether seeing that civil marriage is not marriage in the eyes of the Church –

MR. IRWIN: Is it in order for a Senator to read his speech?

AN CATHAOIRLEACH: It is not in order precisely, but very great latitude has been allowed always in regard to that. In fact, when dealing with a complicated question of this kind personally I think sometimes an advantage is derived from Senators sticking to their text. They are more likely to do that if they are reading from documents. I am bound to say in defense of the particular Senator that he is only reading, now and then, when quoting.

MR. O'FARRELL: I think you, sir, might appeal to Senators to restrain their feelings even though they may not agree with what is said. We do not agree with it, but that is no reason why we should lose our heads.

AN CATHAOIRLEACH: Particularly so in the case of a distinguished Irishman like Senator Yeats.

DR. YEATS: These are topics on which it is desirable that the use of words should be carefully weighed beforehand. That must be my excuse. It is just as much adultery according to that view as the remarriage of divorced persons is. Nor do I see why you should stop at that, for we teach in our schools and universities and print in our books many things which the Catholic Church does not approve of. Once you attempt legislation on religious grounds you open the way for every kind of intolerance and for every kind of religious persecution. I am not certain that there are not people in this country who would not urge you on that course. I have nothing but respect for Most Rev. Dr. O'Donnell. I am told that he is a vigorous and able man, and I can say this

coin now and another years later, as old dies wear out or the public changes its taste, it seemed best to give the coins some relation to one another. The most beautiful Greek coins are those that represent some god or goddess, as a boy or girl, or those that represent animals or some simple object like a wheat-ear. Those beautiful forms, when they are re-named Hibernia or Liberty, would grow empty and academic, and the wheat-ear had been adopted by several modern nations. If we decided upon birds and beasts, the artist, the experience of centuries has shown, might achieve a masterpiece, and might, or so it seemed to us, please those that would look longer at each coin than anybody else, artists and children. Besides, what better symbols could we find for this horse-riding, salmon-fishing, cattle-raising country?

III

We might have chosen figures from the history of Ireland, saints or national leaders, but a decision of the Executive Council excluded modern men, and no portraits have come down to us of St. Brigid or King Brian. The artist, to escape academical convention, would have invented a characteristic but unrecognizable head. I have before me a Swedish silver coin and a Swedish bronze medal, both masterly, that display the head of their mediaeval King, Gustavus Vasa. But those marked features were as familiar to the people as the incidents of his life, the theme of two famous plays. But even had we such a figure a modern artist might prefer not to suggest some existing knowledge, but to create new beauty by an arrangement of lines.

IV

But how should the Government choose its artists? What advice should we give? It should reject a competition open to everybody. No good artist would spend day after day designing, and perhaps get nothing by it. There should be but a few competitors, and whether a man's work were chosen or not he should be paid something, and he should know, that he might have some guarantee of our intelligence, against whom he competed. We thought seven would be enough, and that of these three should be Irish. We had hoped to persuade Charles Shannon, a master of design, whose impressive caps and robes the Benchers of the King's Inn had rejected in favour of wig and gown, to make one of these, but he refused, and that left us two Dublin sculptors of repute, Albert Power and Oliver Sheppard, and Jerome Connor arrived lately from New York. Before choosing the other four we collected examples of modern coinage with the help of various Embassies or of our friends. When we found anything to admire – the Italian coin with the wheat-ear or that with the Fascist emblem; the silver Swedish coin with the head of Gustavus Vasa; the American bison coin – we found out the artist's name and asked for other specimens of his work, if we did not know it already. We also examined the work of various medallists, and, much as we admired the silver Gustavus Vasa, we preferred a bronze Gustavus Vasa by the great Swedish sculptor Carl Milles. Carl Milles and Ivan Mestrovic, sculptor and medallist, have expressed in their work a violent rhythmical energy unknown to past ages, and seem to many the foremost sculptors of our day. We wrote to both these and to James E. Fraser, designer of the bison and of some beautiful architectural sculpture, and to Publio Morbiducci, designer of the coin with the Fascist emblem, but Fraser refused, and Mestrovic did not reply until it was too late.* We substituted for Fraser the American sculptor Manship, the creator of a Diana and her dogs, stylized and noble. But as yet we had no Englishman, and could think of no one among the well-known names that we admired both as sculptor and medallist. After some hesitation, for Charles Ricketts had recommended S. W. Carline, designer of a powerful Zeebrugge medal, and of a charming medal struck to the honour of Flinders Petrie, we selected, on the recommendation of the Secretary of the British School at Rome, Percy Metcalfe, a young sculptor as yet but little known.

*We had written to a wrong address and our letter took some time reaching him. He made one magnificent design and, on discovering that the date had passed, gave it to the Irish Free State with great generosity – W.B.Y.

v

Because when an artist takes up a task for the first time he must sometimes experiment before he has mastered the new technique, we advised that the artist himself should make every alteration necessary, and that, if he had to go to London or elsewhere for the purpose, his expenses should be paid. An Irish artist had made an excellent design for the seal of the Dublin National Gallery, and that design, founded upon the seal of an Irish abbey, had been altered by the Mint, round academic contours substituted for the planes and straight lines of a mediaeval design. One remembers the rage of Blake when his designs came smooth and lifeless from the hands of an engraver whose work had been substituted for his. The Deputy Master of the Mint has commended and recommended to other nations a precaution which protects the artist, set to a new task and not as yet a craftsman, from the craftsman who can never be an artist.

VI

We refused to see the designs until we saw them all together. The name of each artist, if the model had been signed, was covered with stamp paper. The models were laid upon tables, when the exception of one set, fastened to a board, which stood upright on the mantelpiece. We had expected to recognize the work of the different artists by its style, but we recognized only the powerful handling of Milles on the board over the mantelpiece. One set of designs seemed far to exceed the others as decorations filling each its circular space, and this set, the work of Percy Metcalfe, had so marked a style, and was so excellent throughout, that it seemed undesirable to mix its designs with those of any other artist. Though we voted coin by coin, I think we were all convinced of this. I was distressed by my conviction. I had been certain that we could mix the work of three or four different artists, and that this would make our coinage more interesting, and had written to Milles, or to some friend of his, that it was unthinkable that we should not take at least one coin from so great an artist. Nobody could lay aside without a pang so much fine work, and our Government, had it invited designs, without competition, from either Morbiducci or Manship, would have been lucky to get such work as theirs. Manship's Ram and Morbiducci's Bull are magnificent; Manship's an entirely new creation, Morbiducci's a re-creation of the Bull on the Greek coin we had sent him as an example. That I may understand the energy and imagination of the designs of Milles I tell myself that they had been dug out of Sicilian earth, that they passed to and fro in the Mediterranean traffic two thousand years and more ago, and thereupon I discover that his strange bull, his two horses, that angry woodcock, have a supernatural energy. But all are cut in high relief, all suggest more primitive dies than we use to-day, and turned into coins would neither pitch nor pack.

What can I say of the Irish artists who had all done well in some department of their craft – Sheppard's 'O'Leary' at the Municipal Gallery, and Power's 'Kettle' at the Dublin National Gallery, are known, and Connor's 'Emmet' may become known – except that had some powerful master of design been brought to Dublin years ago, and set to teach there, Dublin would have made a better show? Sir William Orpen affected Dublin painting, not merely because he gave it technical knowledge, but because he brought into a Dublin Art School the contagion of his vigour. The work of Metcalfe, Milles, Morbiducci, Manship, displays the vigour of their minds, and the forms of their designs symbolize that vigour, and our own is renewed at the spectacle.

VII

As certain of the beasts represent our most important industry, they were submitted to the Minister for Agriculture and his experts, and we awaited the results with alarm. I have not been to Chartres Cathedral for years, but remember somewhere outside the great door figures of angels or saints, whose spiritual dignity and architectural effect depend upon bodies much longer in proportion to the length of their heads than a man's body ever was. The artist who must fill a given space and suggest some spiritual quality or rhythmical movement finds it necessary to suppress or exaggerate. Art, as some French critic has said, is appropriate exaggeration. The expert on horse-flesh, or bull-flesh, or swine-flesh, on the other hand, is bound to see his subject inanimate and isolated. The coins have suffered less than we feared. The horse, as first drawn, was more alive than the later version, for when the hind legs were brought more under the body and the head lowered, in obedience to technical opinion, it lost muscular tension; we passed from the open country to the show-ground.

But, on the other hand, it is something to know that we have upon our half-crown a representation of an Irish hunter, perfect in all its points, and can add the horseman's pleasure to that of the children and the artists. The first bull had to go, though one of the finest of all the designs, because it might have upset, considered as an ideal, the eugenics of the farmyard, but the new bull is as fine, in a different way. I sigh, however, over the pig, though I admit that the state of the market for pig's cheeks made the old design impossible. A design is like a musical composition, alter some detail and all has to be altered. With the round cheeks of the pig went the lifted head, the look of insolence and of wisdom, and the comfortable round bodies of the little pigs. We have instead querulous and harassed animals, better merchandise but less living.

VIII

I have given here my own opinions and impressions, and I have no doubt my Committee differs from some, but I know no other way of writing. We had all our points of view, though I can only remember one decision that was not unanimous. A member had to be out-voted because he wanted to substitute a harrier for a wolf-hound on the ground that on the only occasion known to him when hare and wolf-hound met the wolf-hound ran away. I am sorry that our meetings have come to an end, for we learned to like each other well.

What remains to be said is said in the name of the whole Committee. Our work could not have been done so quickly nor so well had not the Department of Finance chosen Mr McCauley for our Secretary. Courteous, able and patient he has a sense of order that fills me with wonder.

The Bounty of Sweden

Yeats was awarded the Nobel Prize for Literature in 1923. In Sweden he found himself in a country where they respected a regal presence but had little time for the authority which goes with the trappings of the part. He felt himself very much at home in Stockholm, and was particularly taken with the blend of modernism and classicism in the style of its new Town Hall. He kept a journal of his stay, which he published as *The Bounty of Sweden*. He was delighted with his reception and, with his mind always dwelling on Castiglione's *Book of the Courtier*, was touched when a Swede told Mrs Yeats: 'Our Royal Family like your husband better than other Nobel Prize winners. They said he has the manners of a Courtier.'

I

Thirty years ago I visited Paris for the first time. The Cabbalist MacGregor Mathers said, 'Write your impressions at once, for you will never see Paris clearly again.' I can remember that I had pleased him by certain deductions from the way a woman at the other end of the café moved her hands over the dominoes. I might have seen that woman in London or in Dublin, but it would not have occurred to me to discover in her every kind of rapacity, the substance of the legendary harpy. 'Is not style,' as Synge once said to me, 'born out of the shock of new material?'

I am about to write, as in a kind of diary, impressions of Stockholm which must get whatever value they have from excitement, from the presence before the eyes of what is strange, mobile and disconnected.

II

Early in November [1923] a journalist called to show me a printed paragraph saying that the Nobel Prize would probably be conferred upon Herr Mann, the distinguished novelist, or upon myself. I did not know that the Swedish Academy had ever heard my name; tried to escape an interview by talking of Rabindranath Tagore, of his gift to his School of the seven thousand pounds awarded him; almost succeeded in dismissing the whole Reuter paragraph from my memory. Herr Mann has many readers, is a famous novelist with his fixed place in the world, and, said I to myself, well fitted for such an honour; whereas I am but a writer of plays which are acted by players with a literary mind for a few evenings, and I have altered them so many times that I doubt the value of every passage. I am more confident of my lyrics, or of some few amongst them, but then I have got into the habit of recommending or commending myself to general company for anything rather than my gift of lyric writing, which concerns such a meagre troop.

Every now and then, when something has stirred my imagination, I begin talking to myself. I speak in my own person and dramatize myself, very much as I have seen a mad old woman do upon the Dublin quays, and sometimes detect myself speaking and moving as if I were still young, or walking perhaps like an old man with fumbling steps. Occasionally, I write out what I have said in verse, and generally for no better reason than because I remember that I have written no verse for a long time. I do not think of my soliloquies as having different literary qualities. They stir my interest, by their appropriateness to the men I imagine myself to be, or by their accurate description of some emotional circumstance, more than by any aesthetic value. When I begin to write I have no object but to find for them some natural speech, rhythm and syntax, and to see it out in some pattern, so seeming old that it may seem all men's speech, and though the labour is very great, I seem to have used no faculty peculiar to myself, certainly no special gift. I print the poem and never hear about it again, until I find the book years after with a page dog-eared by some young man, or marked by some young girl with a violet, and when I have seen that, I am a little ashamed, as though somebody were to attribute to me a delicacy of feeling I should but do not possess. What came so easily at first, and amidst so much drama, and was written so laboriously at the last, cannot be counted among my possessions.

On the other hand, if I give a successful lecture, or write a vigorous, critical essay, there is immediate effect; I am confident that on some one point, which seems to me of great importance, I know more than other men, and I covet honour.

III

Then some eight days later, between ten and eleven at night, comes a telephone message from the *Irish Times* saying that the prize has indeed been conferred upon me; and some ten minutes after that comes a telegram from the Swedish Ambassador; then journalists come for interviews. At half past twelve my wife and I are alone, and search the cellar for a bottle of wine, but it is empty, and as a celebration is necessary we cook sausages. A couple of days pass and a letter from the Ambassador invites me to receive the prize at Stockholm, but a letter from the Swedish Academy offers to send medal, money, and diploma to Dublin.

I question booksellers in vain for some history of Sweden, or of Swedish literature. Even Gosse's *Studies in the Literature of Northern Europe*, which I read twenty years ago, is out of print, and among my own books there is nothing but the Life of Swedenborg, which contains photographs of Swedenborg's garden and garden-house, and of the Stockholm House of Nobles, built in Dutch style, and beautiful, with an ornament that never insists upon itself, and a dignity that has no pomp. It had housed in Swedenborg's day that Upper Chamber of the Swedish Parliament where he had voted and spoken upon finance, after the ennoblement of his family.

IV

My wife and I leave Harwich for Esbjerg in Denmark, on the night of December 6, and find our alarms were needless, for the sea is still and the air warm. The Danish steamboat is about the size of the Dublin-Holyhead mail-boat, but the cabins are panelled in pale birchwood, and when we sit down to supper, the table is covered by an astonishing variety of cold food, most of which we refuse because we do not recognize it, and some, such as eels in jelly, because we do. Our companions are commercial travellers and presently we are recognized, for somebody has a newspaper with my portrait, and a man who has travelled in Ireland for an exporter of Danish agricultural machinery talks to us at dinner. He was in Munster for the first part of our Civil War, and when the trains were stopped had found himself in great difficulties, and during parts of his journey had moved at breakneck speed, that his motor might escape capture by the Insurgents, but our Civil War was no part of his business, and had not stirred his imagination. He had, however, discovered a defect in Irish agriculture that was very much a part. Through lack of warm winter sheds and proper winter food for cattle, the Irish farmers had no winter butter, and so Ireland must import butter from his country. Though, as he said, against Danish interests, he had pointed this out to Irish farmers. 'But you have a Government,' they said, 'which looks after these things,' and this time he became really excited – 'Put that idea out of your head,' I told them. 'It was we ourselves who looked after these things, our Government has nothing to do with it.'

He asks why the Irish have so little self-reliance, and want the Government to do everything, and I say, 'Were the Danes always self-reliant?' and after a moment's thought, he answers, 'Not till the Bishop established his Schools; we owe everything to his High Schools.' I know something of Bishop Grundtvig and his Schools, for I often hear A.E. or some other at Plunkett House tell how he educated Denmark, by making examinations almost nothing and the personality of the teacher almost everything, and rousing the imagination with Danish literature and history. 'What our peasants need,' he had said, 'is not technical training, but mental.'

As we draw near our journey's end, an elderly Swede comes to say 'good-bye', and kisses my wife's hand, bending very low, and the moment he is out of ear-shot, the Danish commercial traveller says with a disgusted voice, 'No Dane would do that. The Swedes are always imitating the French.'

I see that he does not like Swedes, and I ask what he thinks of Norwegians. 'Rough,' he says, 'and they want everything, they want Greenland now.'

v

At Esbjerg I find a young man, a distinguished Danish poet sent by a Copenhagen newspaper, and he and I and my wife dine together. At Copenhagen journalists meet us at the railway station, and others at the hotel, and when I am asked about Ireland I answer always that if the British Empire becomes a voluntary Federation of Free Nations, all will be well, but if it remains as in the past, a domination of one, the Irish question is not settled. That done with, I can talk of the work of my generation in Ireland, the creation of a literature to express national character and feeling but with no deliberate political aim. A journalist who has lived in Finland says, 'Finland has had to struggle with Russian influence to preserve its national culture.' I ask many questions and one journalist says, 'O – Denmark is well educated, and education can reach everybody, as education cannot in big nations like

England and America', and he goes on to say that in Denmark 'you may dine at some professor's house, and find that you are sitting next your housemaid, who is among his favourite pupils, and next morning she will be your housemaid again, and too well educated to presume, or step out of her place'. Another, however, a very distinguished man, will have it that it is 'all wrong, for people who should hardly know what a book is now read books, and even write them. The High Schools have made the intellect of Denmark sentimental.' A little later on he says, 'We may have a Socialist Government one of these days', and I begin to wonder what Denmark will make of that mechanical eighteenth-century dream; we know what half-mediaeval Russia has made of it. Another Dane speaks of the Danish Royal Family as 'bourgeois and sporting, like the English'; but says, when I ask about the Royal Family of Sweden, 'O – such educated and intelligent people'. It is he, I think, who first tells me of Prince Eugene, friend and patron of Swedish artists, and himself an accomplished painter who has helped to decorate the Stockholm Town Hall, 'beginning every day at nine o'clock, and working all day like the rest, and for two years', and how at the opening ceremony he had not stood among the Royal Family, 'but among the artists and workmen', and that it was he who saw to it 'that every artist was given freedom to create as he would'. Another spoke much of Strindberg, and though he called him the 'Shakespeare of Sweden', seemed to approve the Swedish Academy's refusal of recognition; 'they could not endure his quarrels with his friends nor the book about his first wife'.

A train-ferry brings us across some eighteen miles of sea, and so into Sweden, and while we are waiting for the train to start again, I see through a carriage window many faces, but it is only just as the train starts, when a Swedish interviewer says – for there are interviewers here also – 'Did you not see all those people gazing at the Nobel Prize winner?', that I connect those faces with myself.

Away from the lights of the station it is too dark to see anything, but when the dawn breaks, we are passing through a forest.

VI

At the Stockholm station a man introduces himself, and reminds me that I met him in Paris thirty years ago, and asks me to read a pamphlet which he has written in English upon Strindberg, and especially a chapter called 'Strindberg and the Wolves'. The pamphlet comes to the hotel a couple of hours later, and turns out to be an attack upon the Swedish Academy, and an ardent defence of Strindberg. That outrageous, powerful book about his first wife is excused on the ground that it was not written for publication, and was published by an accident. And somebody once met Strindberg in a museum, dressed up according to the taste of one or other of his wives, 'with cuffs upon his pantaloons', by which the pamphlet means, I imagine, that like 'Mr Prufrock' he wore 'the bottoms of his trousers rolled'. I had met its writer in the rooms of an American artist, who was of Strindberg's Paris circle, and it was probably there that I had heard for the first time of stage scenery that might decorate a stage and suggest a scene, while attempting nothing that an easel painting can do better. I am pleased to imagine that the news of it may have come from Strindberg, whom I seem to remember as big and silent. I have always felt a sympathy for that tortured, self-torturing man who offered himself to his own soul as Buddha offered himself to the famished tiger. He and his circle were preoccupied with the deepest problems of mankind. He himself, at the time I speak of, was seeking with furnace and athanor for the philosophers' stone.

At my hotel, I find a letter from another of that circle, whom I remember as a fair girl like a willow, beginning with this sentence – 'God's blessing be upon your wife and upon yourself through the many holy men and women of this land'.

VII

The diplomas and medals are to be given us by the King at five in the afternoon of December 10th.

The American Ambassador, who is to receive those for an American man of science, unable to be present, and half a dozen men of various nations sit upon the platform. In the body of the Hall every seat is full, and all there are in evening dress, and in the front row are the King, Princess Ingeborg, wife of the King's brother, Prince Wilhelm, Princess Margaretha, and I think another Royalty. The President of the Swedish Academy speaks in English, and I see from the way he stands, from his self-possession, and from his rhythmical utterance, that he is an experienced orator. I study the face of the old King, intelligent and friendly, like some country gentleman who can quote Horace and Catullus, and the face of the Princess Margaretha, full of subtle beauty, emotional and precise, and impassive with a still intensity suggesting that final consummate strength which rounds the spiral of a shell. One finds a similar beauty in wooden busts taken from Egyptian tombs of the Eighteenth Dynasty, and not again till Gainsborough paints. Is it very ancient and very modern alone or did painters and sculptors cease to notice it until our day?

The Ambassador goes towards the King, descends from the platform by some five or six steps, which end a yard from the King's feet, and having received the diploma and medal, ascends those five or six steps walking backward. He does not go completely backward, but sideways, and seems to show great practice. Then there is music, and a man of science repeats the movement, imitating the Ambassador exactly and easily, for he is young and agile, and then more music, and two men of science go down the steps, side by side, for they have made discoveries that are related to one another, and the prize is divided between them. As it would be impossible for two men to go up backward, side by side, without much practice, one repeats the slanting movement, and the other turns his back on Royalty. Then the British Ambassador receives diploma and medal for two Canadians, but as he came from the body of the hall he has no steps to go up and down. Then more music and my turn comes. When the King has given me my diploma and medal and said, 'I thank you for coming yourself', and I have bowed my thanks, I glance for a moment at the face of the Princess Margaretha, and move backward towards the stair. As I am about to step sideways like the others, I notice that the carpet is not nailed down, and this suddenly concentrates my attention upon the parallel lines made by the two edges of the carpet, and, as though I were hypnotized, I feel that I must move between them, and so straight up backward without any sidelong movement. It seems to me that I am a long time reaching the top, and as the cheering grows much louder when I get there, I must have roused the sympathy of the audience. All is over, and I am able to examine my medal, its charming, decorative, academic design, French in manner, a work of the 'nineties. It shows a young man listening to a Muse, who stands young and beautiful with a great lyre in her hand, and I think as I examine it, 'I was good-looking once like that young man, but my unpractised verse was full of infirmity, my Muse old as it were; and now I am old and rheumatic, and nothing to look at, but my Muse is young. I am even persuaded that she is like those Angels in Swedenborg's vision, and moves perpetually "towards the day-spring of her youth".' At night there is a banquet, and when my turn comes, I speak of Swedenborg, Strindberg, and Ibsen. Then a very beautiful, stately woman introduces herself with this sentence, spoken slowly as though English were unfamiliar, 'What is this new religion they are making up in Paris that is all about the dead?' I wonder who has told her that I know anything of psychical research, for it must be of that she speaks, and I tell her of my own studies. We are going to change the thought of the world, I say, to bring it back to all its old truths, but I dread the future. Think what the people have made of the political thought of the eighteenth century, and now we must offer them a new fanaticism.

Then I stop ashamed, for I am talking habitual thoughts, and not adapting them to her ear, forgetting beauty in the pursuit of truth, and I wonder if age has made my mind rigid and heavy. I deliberately falter as though I could think of nothing more to say, that she may pass upon her smiling road.

VIII

Next day is the entrance of the new Crown Princess, and my wife and I watch it, now from the hotel window, now from the quayside. Stockholm is almost as much channelled by the sea as Venice; and with an architecture as impressive as that of Paris, or of London, it has the better even of Paris in situation. It seems to shelter itself under the walls of a great Palace, begun at the end of the seventeenth century. We come very slowly to realize that this building may deserve its great architectural reputation. The windows, the details of the ornaments, are in a style that has spread everywhere, and I cannot escape from memories of houses at Queen's Gate, and even, it may be, from that of the Ulster Bank at Sligo, which I have hardly seen since my childhood. Was it not indeed a glory and shame of that architecture that we have been able to combine its elements in all sorts of ways and for all sorts of purposes, as if they had come out of a child's box of wooden bricks? Among all these irrelevant associations, however, I discover at last a vast, dominating, unconfused outline, a masterful simplicity. The Palace is at the other side of the river, and away towards our left runs the river bordered by tall buildings, and above the roofs of the houses, towards our right, rises the tower of the new Town Hall, the glittering pole upon its top sustaining the three crowns of the Swedish Arms. Copenhagen is an anarchy of commercial streets, with fine buildings here and there, but here all seems premeditated and arranged.

Everywhere there are poles with flags, and at the moment when the Crown Prince and Princess leave the railway station for the Palace, the salvoes of artillery begin. After every salvo there are echoes, and I feel a quickening of the pulse, an instinctive alarm. I remember firing in Dublin last winter, the sudden noise that drew like echoes from the streets. I have to remind myself that these cannon are fired out of gaiety and goodwill. There are great crowds, and I get the impression of a family surrounded by loyalty and affection.

IX

The next night there is a reception at the Palace, and the Nobel Prize winners are among the guests. We wait in a long gallery for our turn to enter the throne-room, and upon the black coats of the civilians, as upon the grey and silver of the Guards, lie the chains of the three Swedish Orders. Among the black-coated men are men of learning, men of letters, men of science, much of the intellect of Sweden. What model has made all this, one wonders: Goethe's Weimar, or Sweden's own eighteenth-century Courts? There may be, must be, faults of commission or omission, but where else could a like assembly be gathered? I who have never seen a Court, find myself before the evening is ended moved as if by some religious ceremony, though to a different end, for here it is Life herself that is praised. Presently we walk through lines of sentries, in the costume of Charles XII, the last of Sweden's great military Kings, and then bow as we pass rapidly before the tall seated figures of the Royal Family. They seem to be like stage royalties. Just such handsome men and women would have been chosen by a London manager staging, let us say, some dramatized version of *The Prisoner of Zenda*. One has a general impression of youthful distinction, even the tall, slight figure of the old King seems young. Then we pass from the throne-room into a vast hall hung with Gobelins tapestries, which seem in the distance to represent scenes like those in a Watteau or in a Fragonard. Their green colour by contrast turns the marble pillars above into a dusky silver. At the end of the hall musicians are sitting in a high marble gallery, and in the side galleries are women in white dresses, many very young and handsome. Others upon the level of the floor sit grouped together, making patches of white among the brilliant uniforms and the black coats. We are shepherded to our places, and the musicians play much Swedish music, which I cannot describe, for I know nothing of music. During our first long wait all kinds of pictures had passed before me in reverie and now my imagination renews its excitement. I had thought how we Irish had served famous men and famous families, and had been, so long as our nation had intellect enough to shape anything of itself, good lovers of women, but had never served any abstract cause, except the one, and that we personified by a woman, and I wondered if the service of woman could be so different from that of a Court. I had thought how, before the emigration of our poor began, our gentlemen had gone all over Europe, offering their swords at every Court, and that many had stood, just as I, but with an anxiety I could but imagine, for their future hung upon a frown or a smile. I had run through old family fables and histories, to find if any man of my blood had so stood, and had thought that there were men living, meant by nature for that vicissitude, who had served a woman through all folly, because they had found no Court to serve. Then my memory had gone back twenty years to that summer when a friend read out to me at the end of each day's work Castiglione's commendations and descriptions of that Court of Urbino where youth for certain brief years imposed upon drowsy learning the discipline of its joy, and I remembered a cry of Bembo's made years after, 'Would that I were a shepherd that I might look down daily upon Urbino'. I had repeated to myself what I could remember of Ben Jonson's address to the Court of his time, 'Thou art a beautiful and brave spring and waterest all the noble plants of this Island. In thee the whole Kingdom dresseth itself and is ambitious to use thee as her glass. Beware then thou render men's figures truly and teach them no less to hate their deformities, than to love their forms. . . . Thy servant but not slave, Ben Jonson.'

And now I begin to imagine some equivalent gathering to that about me, called together by the heads of some State where every democratic dream had been fulfilled, and where all men had started level and only merit, acknowledged by all the people, ruled. The majority so gathered, certainly all who had supreme authority, would have reached that age when an English novelist becomes eligible for the Order of Merit. Times of disturbance might indeed carry into power some man of comparative youth, of fifty or sixty years perhaps, but I think of normal times. Here and there one would notice sons and daughters, perhaps even the more dutiful grandsons and grand-daughters, but in the eyes of those, though not in their conversation, an acute observer might discover disquiet and a restless longing for the moment when they could slip away to some night-club's compensating anarchy. In the conversation of old and young there would be much sarcasm, great numbers of those tales which we all tell to one another's disadvantage. For all men would display to others' envy the trophies won in their life of struggle.

Then suddenly my thought runs off to that old Gaelic poem made by the nuns of Iona. A Swedish or Danish ship had been cast upon the rocks, and all royalties on board had perished, but one baby. The nuns mothered the baby, and their cradle-song, famous for generations after, repeated over and over, praising in symbol every great man's child – every tested long-enduring stock – 'Daughter of a Queen, grand-daughter of a Queen, great-grand-daughter of a Queen, great-great-grand-daughter of a Queen'. Nature, always extravagant, scattering much to find a little, has found no means but hereditary honour to sustain the courage of those who stand waiting for the signal, cowed by the honour and authority of those who lie wearily at the goal. Perhaps, indeed, she created the family with no other object, and may even now mock in her secret way our new ideals – the equality of man, equality of rights, – meditating some wholly different end. Certainly her old arrangements, in all pursuits that gain from youth's recurring sway, or from its training in earliest childhood, surpassed what begins to be a world of old men. The politic Tudor kings and the masterful descendants of Gustavus Vasa were as able as the American presidents, and better educated, and the artistic genius of old Japan continually renewed itself through dynasties of painters. The descendants of Kanoka made all that was greatest in the art of their country from the ninth to the eleventh century, and then it but passed to other dynasties, in whom, as Mr Binyon says, 'the flower of genius was being continually renewed and revived in the course of many generations'. How serene their art, no exasperation, no academic tyranny, its tradition as naturally observed as the laws of a game or dance. Nor has our individualistic age wholly triumphed in Japan even yet, for it is a few years since a famous player published in his programme his genealogy, running back through famous players to some player of the Middle Ages; and one day in the British Museum Print-Room, I saw a Japanese at a great table judging Chinese and Japanese pictures. 'He is one of the greatest living authorities,' I was told, 'the Mikado's hereditary connoisseur, the fourteenth of his family to hold the post.' May it not have been possible that the use of the mask in acting, and the omission from painting of the cast shadow, by making observation and experience of life less important, and imagination and tradition more, made the arts transmittable and teachable? But my thoughts have carried me far away.

x

Near me stands a man who is moved also by the spectacle of the Court, but to a Jacobin frenzy, Swede, Englishman, American, German, what does it matter, seeing that his frenzy is international. I had spoken to him earlier in the day and found him a friendly, even perhaps a cultivated man, and certainly not the kind of man who is deliberately rude; but now, he imagines that an attempt has been made to impose upon him. He speaks his thoughts aloud, silenced occasionally by the music, but persistent in the intervals. While waiting to enter the throne-room, he had been anxious to demonstrate that he was there by accident, drifting irresponsibly, no way implicated, as it were, and having accomplished this demonstration by singing a little catch, 'I'm here because I'm here', had commented abundantly upon all he saw: 'The smaller the nation the grander the uniform'. 'Well – they never got those decorations in war', and so on. He was certain that the breastplates of the sentries were made of tin, but added with a meditative voice, as though anxious to be fair, 'The breastplates of the English Horse Guards are also made of tin'.

   As we came through the throne-room, I had heard him say, 'One of the royalties smiled, they consider us as ridiculous', and I had commented, entangled in my dream, 'We are ridiculous, we are the learned at whom the little boys laugh in the streets'. And now when, at a pause in the music, the

Queen passes down the great hall, pages holding her train, he says in the same loud voice as before, 'Well, a man has not to suffer that indignity', and then upbraids all forms of ceremony, and repeats an incident of his school life to demonstrate his distaste for Bishops.

As I leave the Palace, a man wearing orders stops for a moment to say, 'I am the Headmaster of a big school, I was the Prince's tutor, and I am his friend'.

XI

For the next two or three days we visit picture galleries, the gallery of the National Museum, that of Prince Eugene, that of Baron Thiel. At the National Museum pictures have been taken down and lean against the wall, that they may be sent to London for an exhibition of Swedish art. Someone, exaggerating the influence in London of the Nobel Prize winner, asks me to write something to get people to go and see it, and I half promise, but feel that I have not the necessary knowledge. I know something of the French Impressionism that gave their painters their first impulse, but almost nothing of German or Austrian, and I have seen that of Sweden for the first time. At a first glance Impressionism seems everywhere the same, with differences of power but not of sight or mind, and one has to live with it and make many comparisons, I think, to write more than a few sentences. The great myth-makers and mask-makers, the men of aristocratic mind, Blake, Ingres in the *Perseus*, Puvis de Chavannes, Rossetti before 1870, Watts when least a moralist, Gustave Moreau at all times, Calvert in the woodcuts, the Charles Ricketts of *The Danaides*, and of the earlier illustrations of *The Sphinx*, have imitators, but create no universal language. Administrators of tradition, they seem to copy everything, but in reality copy nothing, and not one of them can be mistaken for another, but Impressionism's gift to the world was precisely that it gave, at a moment when all seemed sunk in convention, a method as adaptable as that box of architectural Renaissance bricks. It has suddenly taught us to see and feel, as everybody that wills can see and feel, all those things that are as wholesome as rain and sunlight, to take into our hearts with an almost mystical emotion whatsoever happens without forethought or premeditation. It is not, I think, any accident that their art has coincided everywhere with a new sympathy for crowds, for the poor and the unfortunate. Certainly it arrived in these Scandinavian countries just at the moment when an intellectual awaking of the whole people was beginning, for I always read, or am told, that whatever I inquire about began with the 'eighties, or was the outcome of some movement of that time.

When I try to define what separates Swedish Impressionism from French, I notice that it has a stronger feeling for particular places. Monet will paint a group of trees by a pond in every possible light, changing his canvas every twenty minutes, and only returning to a canvas when the next day's clock brings up the same light, but then it is precisely the light that interests him, and interests the buyers of those almost scientific studies. Nobody will buy because it is a pond under his window, or that he passed in his boyhood on his way to school. I noticed in some house where I lunched two pictures of the Stockholm river, painted in different lights by Eugene Janson, and in the National Museum yet another with a third effect of light, but much as the light pleased his imagination, one feels that he cared very much for the fact before him, that he was never able to forget for long that he painted a well-loved, familiar scene. I am constantly reminded of my brother, who continually paints from memory the people and houses of the village where he lived as a child; but the people of Rosses will never care about his pictures, and these painters paint for all educated Stockholm. They have found an emotion held in common, and are no longer, like the rest of us, solitary spectators. I get the impression that their work rouses a more general interest than that of other painters, is less confined to small groups of connoisseurs; I notice in the booksellers' shops that there seems to be some little paper-covered pamphlet, full of illustrations, for every notable painter of the school, dead or living, and the people I meet ask constantly what I think of this painter or that other, or somebody will say, 'This is the golden age of painting'. When I myself try to recall what I have seen, I remember most clearly a picture of a white horse on the seashore, with its tints separated by little lines, that give it a general effect of mosaic, and certain portraits by Ernst Josephson, which prove that their painter was entirely preoccupied with the personality of the sitter, light, colour, design, all subordinate to that. An English portrait-painter is sometimes so preoccupied with the light that one feels he would have had equal pleasure in painting a bottle and an apple. But a preference after so brief a visit may be capricious, having some accidental origin.

XII

On Thursday I give my official lecture to the Swedish Royal Academy. I have chosen 'The Irish Theatre' for my subject, that I may commend all those workers, obscure or well-known, to whom I owe much of whatever fame in the world I may possess. If I had been a lyric poet only, if I had not become through this Theatre the representative of a public movement, I doubt if the

English committees would have placed my name upon that list from which the Swedish Academy selects its prize-winner. They would not have acknowledged a thought so irrelevant, but those dog-eared pages, those pressed violets, upon which the fame of a lyric poet depends at the last, might without it have found no strong voice. I have seen so much beautiful lyric poetry pass unnoticed for years, and indeed at this very moment a little book of exquisite verses lies upon my table, by an author who died a few years ago, whom I knew slightly, and whose work I ignored, for chance had shown me only that part of it for which I could not care.

On my way to the lecture hall I ask an Academician what kind of audience I will have, and he replies, 'An audience of women, a fit audience for a poet'; but there are men as well as women. I had thought it would be difficult to speak to an audience in a language they had learnt at school, but it is exceedingly easy. All I say seems to be understood, and I am conscious of that sympathy which makes a speaker forget all but his own thoughts, and soliloquize aloud. I am speaking without notes and the image of old fellow-workers comes upon me as if they were present, above all of the embittered life and death of one, and of another's laborious, solitary age, and I say, 'When your King gave me medal and diploma, two forms should have stood, one at either side of me, an old woman sinking into the infirmity of age and a young man's ghost. I think when Lady Gregory's name and John Synge's name are spoken by future generations, my name, if remembered, will come up in the talk, and that if my name is spoken first their names will come in their turn because of the years we worked together. I think that both had been well pleased to have stood beside me at the great reception at your Palace, for their work and mine has delighted in history and tradition.' I think as I speak these words of how deep down we have gone, below all that is individual, modern and restless, seeking foundations for an Ireland that can only come into existence in a Europe that is still but a dream.

XIII

On Friday we visit the great Town Hall, which is the greatest work of Swedish art, a master-work of the Romantic movement. The Royal Palace had taken ninety years to build, and been the organizing centre of the art of its time, and this new magnificence, its narrow windows opening out upon a formal garden, its tall tower rising from the quayside, has taken ten years. It, too, has been an organizing centre, but for an art more imaginative and amazing. Here there is no important French influence, for all that has not come out of the necessities of site and material, no matter in what school the artist studied, carries the mind backward to Byzantium. I think of but two comparable buildings, the Pennsylvania terminus in New York, and the Catholic Cathedral at Westminster, but the Pennsylvania terminus, noble in austerity, is the work of a single mind, elaborating a suggestion from a Roman Bath, a mind that – supported by the American deference to authority – has been permitted to refuse everything not relevant to a single dominating idea. The starting-hours of the trains are upon specially designed boards, of a colour that makes them harmonize with the general design, and all other advertisements are forbidden, even in the stations that the trains pass immediately after leaving or before entering the terminus. The mood of severity must be prolonged or prepared for. The Catholic Cathedral is of a greater magnificence in general design, but being planted in a country where public opinion rules and the subscribers to every fund expect to have their way, is half ruined by ignoble decoration, the most ignoble of all planned and paid for by my countrymen. The Town Hall of Stockholm, upon the other hand, is decorated by many artists, working in harmony with one another and with the design of the building as a whole, and yet all in seeming perfect freedom. In England and Ireland public opinion compels the employment of the worst artists, while here the authority of a Prince and the wisdom of a Socialist Minister of culture, and the approval of the most educated of all nations, have made possible the employment of the best. These myth-makers and mask-makers worked as if they belonged to one family, and the great walls where the roughened surface of the bricks, their carefully varied size and tint, takes away all sense of mechanical finish; the mosaic-covered walls of the 'Golden Room'; the paintings hung upon the walls of the committee-rooms; the fresco paintings upon the greater surfaces with their subjects from Swedish mythology; the wrought iron and the furniture, where all suggests history, and yet is full of invention; the statuary in marble and in bronze, now mythological in subject, now representations of great Swedes, modelled naked as if they had come down from some Roman heaven; all that suggestion of novelty and of an immeasurable past; all that multitude and unity, could hardly have been possible, had not love of Stockholm and belief in its future so filled men of different minds, classes and occupations that they almost attained the supreme miracle, the dream that has haunted all religions, and loved one another. No work comparable in method or achievement has been accomplished since the Italian cities felt the excitement of the Renaissance, for in the midst of our individualistic anarchy, growing always, as it seemed, more violent, have arisen once more subordination, design, a sense of human need.

XIV

On Saturday I see at the Royal Theatre a performance of my *Cathleen ni Houlihan*. The old father and mother are excellent and each performance differs but little from an exceedingly good Abbey performance, except for certain details of scene, and for differences of interpretation, made necessary by the change of audience. Lines spoken by Cathleen ni Houlihan just before she leaves the cottage always move an Irish audience powerfully for historical reasons, and so the actress begins at much the same emotional level as those about her, and then works up to a climax upon these lines. But here they could have no special appeal, so she strikes a note of tragedy at once and does not try for a strong climax. The management had sent to the West of Ireland for photographs of scenery, and the landscape, seen through the open door, has an appropriateness and grandeur our poverty-stricken Abbey has never attained. Upon the other hand the cottage and costume of the peasants suggest a richer peasantry than ours. The management has, I think, been misled by that one-hundred-pound dowry, for in Sweden, where the standard of living is high, a farmer would probably have thought it more necessary to feed his family and himself, and to look after his daughter's education, than to save one hundred pounds for her dowry. This affects the acting. The peasants are permitted to wear a light buckle-shoe indoors, whereas they would in reality have gone barefooted, or worn heavy working boots. Almost the first thing a new actor in the Abbey has to learn is to walk as if he wore those heavy boots, and this gives awkwardness and slowness to his movements. I do not point this out as an error in the Swedish production, for a symbolic play like *Cathleen* should, in most cases, copy whatever environment is most familiar to the audience. It is followed by *She Stoops to Conquer*, and by comparison our Abbey performance of that play seems too slow. Goldsmith's play is not in Sweden, I should think, the established classic that it is with us, and so a Swedish producer is less reverent. He discovers quickly that there are dull places and unrealities, that it is technically inferior to Molière, and that we may not discover this also, prefers a rattling pace.

XV

Everybody has told us that we have not seen Stockholm at its best because we have not seen it with the trees all white and the streets deep in snow. When snow has fallen it has melted immediately, and there is central heating everywhere. While we are packing for our journey a young American poet comes to our room, and introduces himself. 'I was in the South of France,' he says, 'and I could not get a room warm enough to work in, and if I cannot get a warm room here I will go to Lapland.'

Poetry

1928–1933

*I*n 1928 Yeats published *The Tower*, which contains two of his finest poems, 'Sailing To Byzantium' and 'Leda'. The first poem is a magnificent trumpet blast against the onset of age:

> Soul clap its hands and sing, and louder sing

in which the poet sees himself achieving immortality as a singing bird among the lords and ladies of Byzantium.

'Leda' deals with the legend that has been touched on by many painters and poets, from Leonardo to Courbet and from Petrarch to Cocteau: the Greek tale of the god who, in the form of a swan, makes love to the beautiful girl by the riverside, a liaison which results in the birth of Helen of Troy. Its mingling of the sensual and the martial attracts the imaginative mind. The powerful beginning of the Yeats poem:

> A sudden blow: the great wings beating still
> Above the staggering girl, her thighs caressed
> By the dark webs, her nape caught in his bill,

catches the swoop of the god as it has never been done before in either painting or literature, and there has been no better summing-up of the Trojan adventure than:

> A shudder in the loins engenders there
> The broken wall, the burning roof and tower
> And Agamemnon dead.

The excerpt from Oedipus and Colonus is a chorus from Yeats's work on

Sophocles' plays, done with the help of his friend Gogarty, who chanted in his ear the Greek original as Yeats took down his verse in rhythm in English.

SAILING TO BYZANTIUM

I

That is no country for old men. The young
In one another's arms, birds in the trees,
– Those dying generations – at their song,
The salmon-falls, the mackerel-crowded seas,
Fish, flesh, or fowl, commend all summer long
Whatever is begotten, born, and dies.
Caught in that sensual music all neglect
Monuments of unageing intellect.

II

An aged man is but a paltry thing,
A tattered coat upon a stick, unless
Soul clap its hand and sing, and louder sing
For every tatter in its mortal dress,
Nor is there singing school but studying
Monuments of its own magnificence;
And therefore I have sailed the seas and come
To the holy city of Byzantium.

III

O sages standing in God's holy fire
As in the gold mosaic of a wall,
Come from the holy fire, perne in a gyre,
And be the singing-masters of my soul.
Consume my heart away; sick with desire
And fastened to a dying animal
It knows not what it is; and gather me
Into the artifice of eternity.

IV

Once out of nature I shall never take
My bodily form from any natural thing,
But such a form as Grecian goldsmiths make
Of hammered gold and gold enamelling
To keep a drowsy Emperor awake;
Or set upon a golden bough to sing
To lords and ladies of Byzantium
Of what is past, or passing, or to come.

LEDA AND THE SWAN

A sudden blow: the great wings beating still
Above the staggering girl, her thighs caressed
By the dark webs, her nape caught in his bill,
He holds her helpless breast upon his breast.

How can those terrified vague fingers push
The feathered glory from her loosening thighs?
And how can body, laid in that white rush,
But feel the strange heart beating where it lies?

A shudder in the loins engenders there
The broken wall, the burning roof and tower
And Agamemnon dead.
                              Being so caught up,
So mastered by the brute blood of the air,
Did she put on his knowledge with his power
Before the indifferent beak could let her drop?

FROM 'OEDIPUS AT COLONUS'

Endure what life God gives and ask no longer span;
Cease to remember the delights of youth, travel-
        wearied aged man;
Delight becomes death-longing if all longing else be
        vain.

Even from that delight memory treasures so,
Death, despair, division of families, all entanglements
    of mankind grow,
As that old wandering beggar and these God-hated
    children know.

In the long echoing street the laughing dancers throng,
The bride is carried to the bridegroom's chamber
    through torchlight and tumultuous song;
I celebrate the silent kiss that ends short life or long.

Never to have lived is best, ancient writers say;
Never to have drawn the breath of life, never to have
    looked into the eye of day;
The second best's a gay goodnight and quickly turn
    away.

'THE WINDING STAIR' AND OTHER POEMS

*I*n the opening poem here Yeats shows how easily he has absorbed the new movement in verse, using all the breaks and intrusions of natural speech, while at the same time hanging his words on an exquisite low-keyed rhythm structure and half rhymes. 'In Memory of Eva Gore-Booth and Constance Markiewicz' is his final tribute to the two beautiful young girls he had known in his youth in Sligo when they rode to the hounds and astonished the countryside by their beauty.

In his 1931 poem 'Coole Park and Ballylee' he conjures up again his memory of that great house where the two cultures of Anglo-Ireland and Gaelic Ireland met under Lady Gregory's regime. Here he puts his friends Hyde, Synge, Hugh Lane and the others in context.

We were the last romantics – chose for theme
Traditional sanctity and loveliness.

IN MEMORY OF EVA GORE-BOOTH
AND CON MARKIEWICZ

The light of evening, Lissadell,
Great windows open to the south,
Two girls in silk kimonos, both
Beautiful, one a gazelle.
But a raving autumn shears
Blossom from the summer's wreath;
The older is condemned to death,
Pardoned, drags out lonely years
Conspiring among the ignorant.
I know not what the younger dreams—
Some vague Utopia – and she seems,
When withered old and skeleton-gaunt,
An image of such politics.
Many a time I think to seek
One or the other out and speak
Of that old Georgian mansion, mix
Pictures of the mind, recall
That table and the talk of youth,

Two girls in silk kimonos, both
Beautiful, one a gazelle.

Dear shadows, now you know it all,
All the folly of a fight
With a common wrong or right.
The innocent and the beautiful
Have no enemy but time;
Arise and bid me strike a match
And strike another till time catch;
Should the conflagration climb,
Run till all the sages know.
We the great gazebo built,
They convicted us of guilt;
Bid me strike a match and blow.
   October 1927

COOLE PARK AND BALLYLEE, 1931

Under my window-ledge the waters race,
Otters below and moor-hens on the top,
Run for a mile undimmed in Heaven's face
Then darkening through 'dark' Raftery's 'cellar' drop,
Run underground, rise in a rocky place
In Coole demesne, and there to finish up
Spread to a lake and drop into a hole.
What's water but the generated soul?

Upon the border of that lake's a wood
Now all dry sticks under a wintry sun,
And in a copse of beeches there I stood,
For Nature's pulled her tragic buskin on
And all the rant's a mirror of my mood:
At sudden thunder of the mounting swan
I turned about and looked where branches break
The glittering reaches of the flooded lake.

Another emblem there! That stormy white
But seems a concentration of the sky;

And, like the soul, it sails into the sight
And in the morning's gone, no man knows why;
And is so lovely that it sets to right
What knowledge or its lack had set awry,
So arrogantly pure, a child might think
It can be murdered with a spot of ink.

Sound of a stick upon the floor, a sound
From somebody that toils from chair to chair;
Beloved books that famous hands have bound,
Old marble heads, old pictures everywhere;
Great rooms where travelled men and children found
Content or joy; a last inheritor
Where none has reigned that lacked a name and fame
Or out of folly into folly came.

A spot whereon the founders lived and died
Seemed once more dear than life; ancestral trees,
Or gardens rich in memory glorified
Marriages, alliances and families
And every bride's ambition satisfied.
Where fashion or mere fantasy decrees
We shift about – all that great glory spent –
Like some poor Arab tribesman and his tent.

We were the last romantics – chose for theme
Traditional sanctity and loveliness;
Whatever's written in what poets name
The book of the people; whatever most can bless
The mind of man or elevate a rhyme;
But all is changed, that high horse riderless,
Though mounted in that saddle Homer rode
Where the swan drifts upon a darkening flood.

FOR ANNE GREGORY
(Lady Gregory's Niece, *Ed.*)

'Never shall a young man,
Thrown into despair

By those great honey-coloured
Ramparts at your ear,
Love you for yourself alone
And not your yellow hair.'

'But I can get a hair-dye
And set such colour there,
Brown, or black, or carrot,
That young men in despair
May love me for myself alone
And not my yellow hair.'

'I heard an old religious man
But yesternight declare
That he had found a text to prove
That only God, my dear,
Could love you for yourself alone
And not your yellow hair.'

BYZANTIUM

The unpurged images of day recede;
The Emperor's drunken soldiery are abed;
Night resonance recedes, night-walkers' song
After great cathedral gong;
A starlit or a moonlit dome disdains
All that man is,
All mere complexities,
The fury and the mire of human veins.

Before me floats an image, man or shade,
Shade more than man, more image than a shade;
For Hades' bobbin bound in mummy-cloth
May unwind the winding path;
A mouth that has no moisture and no breath
Breathless mouths may summon;
I hail the superhuman;
I call it death-in-life and life-in-death.

Miracle, bird or golden handiwork,
More miracle than bird or handiwork.
Planted on the star-lit golden bough,
Can like the cocks of Hades crow,
Or, by the moon embittered, scorn aloud
In glory of changeless metal
Common bird or petal
And all complexities of mire or blood.

At midnight on the Emperor's pavement flit
Flames that no faggot feeds, nor steel has lit,
Nor storm disturbs, flames begotten of flame,
Where blood-begotten spirits come
And all complexities of fury leave,
Dying into a dance,
An agony of trance,
An agony of flame that cannot singe a sleeve.

Astraddle on the dolphin's mire and blood,
Spirit after spirit! The smithies break the flood,
The golden smithies of the Emperor!
Marbles of the dancing floor
Break bitter furies of complexity,
Those images that yet
Fresh images beget,
That dolphin-torn, that gong-tormented sea.

1930

The Last Poems

*I*n his last years Yeats had a sudden revival of his nationalist feeling. The attack by Alfred Noyes on Roger Casement's moral life (Casement had been hanged for treason in 1916) infuriated Yeats into replying with a number of ballads written with a distinctive anti-English flavour.

These poems, including one on his first hero Parnell, were written in ballad form. He was far too fine a poet, however, to indulge himself in polemic, and the power of these patriotic verses is balanced by the savage doubts that run through 'Parnell's Funeral', where he wonders:

> Come, fix upon me that accusing eye.
> I thirst for accusation. All that was sung,
> All that was said in Ireland is a lie.

He has explained what he wanted his poem 'The Gyres' to symbolize:

> In this book and elsewhere, I have used towers, and one tower in particular, as symbols and have compared their winding stairs to the philosophical gyres, but it is hardly necessary to interpret what comes from the main track of thought and expression.

In 'The Statues' he wonders about the nature of beauty and claims for his own people a special place in the preservation of the principles underlying it. In 'The Circus Animals' Desertion', as he senses death approaching, he recalls his old themes, Oisin, The Countess Cathleen and Cuchulain, which had brought him to the summit of his art. Now he would have to find another source, for these figures had become his circus animals, looked on by him as an old trainer might regard the wonders he brought to life before an audience of his youth. As age comes on he must turn to his inner self for inspiration.

Now that my ladder's gone,
I must lie down where all the ladders start,
In the foul rag-and-bone shop of the heart.

In his last poem, 'Under Ben Bulben', written a few months before his death,
he celebrates once more the monk and the roisterer, the hard-riding country
gentleman and the peasant – the elements from which he felt the character of
the country could be formed.

That we in coming days may be
Still the indomitable Irishry.

PARNELL'S FUNERAL

I

Under the Great Comedian's tomb the crowd.
A bundle of tempestuous cloud is blown
About the sky; where that is clear of cloud
Brightness remains; a brighter star shoots down;
What shudders run through all that animal blood?
What is this sacrifice? Can someone there
Recall the Cretan barb that pierced a star?

Rich foliage that the starlight glittered through,
A frenzied crown, and where the branches sprang
A beautiful seated boy; a sacred bow;
A woman, and an arrow on a string;
A pierced boy, image of a star laid low.
That woman, the Great Mother imaging,
Cut out his heart. Some master of design
Stamped boy and tree upon Sicilian coin.

An age is the reversal of an age:
When strangers murdered Emmet, Fitzgerald, Tone,
We lived like men that watch a painted stage.
What matter for the scene, the scene once gone:
It had not touched our lives. But popular rage,
Hysterica passio dragged this quarry down.

None shared our guilt; nor did we play a part
Upon a painted stage when we devoured his heart.

Come, fix upon me that accusing eye.
I thirst for accusation. All that was sung,
All that was said in Ireland is a lie
Bred out of the contagion of the throng,
Saving the rhyme rats hear before they die.
Leave nothing but the nothings that belong
To this bare soul, let all men judge that can
Whether it be an animal or a man.

II

The rest I pass, one sentence I unsay.
Had de Valéra eaten Parnell's heart
No loose-lipped demagogue had won the day,
No civil rancour torn the land apart.

Had Cosgave eaten Parnell's heart, the land's
Imagination had been satisfied,
Or lacking that, government in such hands,
O'Higgins its sole statesman had not died.

Had even O'Duffy – but I name no more –
Their school a crowd, his master solitude;
Through Jonathan Swift's dark grove he passed, and
      there
Plucked bitter wisdom that enriched his blood.

THE GYRES

The Gyres! the gyres! Old Rocky Face, look forth;
Things thought too long can be no longer thought,
For beauty dies of beauty, worth of worth,
And ancient lineaments are blotted out.
Irrational streams of blood are staining earth;
Empedocles has thrown all things about;
Hector is dead and there's a light in Troy;

We that look on but laugh in tragic joy.

What matter though numb nightmare ride on top,
And blood and mire the sensitive body stain?
What matter? Heave no sigh, let no tear drop,
A greater, a more gracious time has gone;
For painted forms or boxes of make-up
In ancient tombs I sighed, but not again;
What matter? Out of cavern comes a voice,
And all it knows is that one word 'Rejoice!'

Conduct and work grow coarse, and coarse the soul,
What matter? Those that Rocky Face holds dear,
Lovers of horses and of women, shall,
From marble of a broken sepulchre,
Or dark betwixt the polecat and the owl,
Or any rich, dark nothing disinter
The workman, noble and saint, and all things run
On that unfashionable gyre again.

THE GHOST OF ROGER CASEMENT

O what has made that sudden noise?
What on the threshold stands?
It never crossed the sea because
John Bull and the sea are friends;
But this is not the old sea
Nor this the old seashore.
What gave that roar of mockery,
That roar in the sea's roar?
The ghost of Roger Casement
Is beating on the door.

John Bull has stood for Parliament,
A dog must have his day,
The country thinks no end of him,
For he knows how to say,
At a beanfeast or a banquet,
That all must hang their trust

Upon the British Empire,
Upon the Church of Christ.
The ghost of Roger Casement
Is beating on the door.

John Bull has gone to India
And all must pay him heed,
For histories are there to prove
That none of another breed
Has had a like inheritance,
Or sucked such milk as he,
And there's no luck about a house
If it lack honesty.
The ghost of Roger Casement
Is beating on the door.

I poked about a village church
And found his family tomb
And copied out what I could read
In that religious gloom;
Found many a famous man there;
But fame and virtue rot.
Draw round, beloved and bitter men,
Draw round and raise a shout;
The ghost of Roger Casement
Is beating on the door.

COME GATHER ROUND ME, PARNELLITES

Come gather round me, Parnellites,
And praise our chosen man;
Stand upright on your legs awhile,
Stand upright while you can,
For soon we lie where he is laid,
And he is underground;
Come fill up all those glasses
And pass the bottle round.

And here's a cogent reason,

And I have many more,
He fought the might of England
And saved the Irish poor,
Whatever good a farmer's got
He brought it all to pass;
And here's another reason,
That Parnell loved a lass.

And here's a final reason,
He was of such a kind
Every man that sings a song
Keeps Parnell in his mind.
For Parnell was a proud man,
No prouder trod the ground,
And a proud man's a lovely man,
So pass the bottle round.

The Bishops and the Party
That tragic story made,
A husband that had sold his wife
And after that betrayed;
But stories that live longest
Are sung above the glass,
And Parnell loved his country,
And Parnell loved his lass.

THE MUNICIPAL GALLERY REVISITED

I

Around me the images of thirty years:
An ambush; pilgrims at the water-side;
Casement upon trial, half hidden by the bars,
Guarded; Griffith staring in hysterical pride;
Kevin O'Higgins' countenance that wears
A gentle questioning look that cannot hide
A soul incapable of remorse or rest;
A revolutionary soldier kneeling to be blessed;

II

An Abbot or Archbishop with an upraised hand
Blessing the Tricolour. 'This is not,' I say,
'The dead Ireland of my youth, but an Ireland
The poets have imagined, terrible and gay.'
Before a woman's portrait suddenly I stand,
Beautiful and gentle in her Venetian way.
I met her all but fifty years ago
For twenty minutes in some studio.

III

Heart-smitten with emotion I sink down,
My heart recovering with covered eyes;
Wherever I had looked I had looked upon
My permanent or impermanent images:
Augusta Gregory's son; her sister's son,
Hugh Lane, 'onlie begetter' of all these;
Hazel Lavery living and dying, that tale
As though some ballad-singer had sung it all;

IV

Mancini's portrait of Augusta Gregory,
'Greatest since Rembrandt,' according to John Synge;
A great ebullient portrait certainly;
But where is the brush that could show anything
Of all that pride and that humility?
And I am in despair that time may bring
Approved patterns of women or of men
But not that selfsame excellence again.

V

My mediaeval knees lack health until they bend,
But in that woman, in that household where
Honour had lived so long, all lacking found.
Childless I thought, 'My children may find here
Deep-rooted things,' but never foresaw its end,

And now that end has come I have not wept;
No fox can foul the lair the badger swept –

VI

(An image out of Spenser and the common tongue).
John Synge, I and Augusta Gregory, thought
All that we did, all that we said or sang
Must come from contact with the soil, from that
Contact everything Antaeus-like grew strong.
We three alone in modern times had brought
Everything down to that sole test again,
Dream of the noble and the beggar-man.

VII

And here's John Synge himself, that rooted man,
'Forgetting human words,' a grave deep face.
You that would judge me, do not judge alone
This book or that, come to this hallowed place
Where my friends' portraits hang and look thereon;
Ireland's history in their lineaments trace;
Think where man's glory most begins and ends,
And say my glory was I had such friends.

THE STATUES

Pythagoras planned it. Why did the people stare?
His numbers, though they moved or seemed to move
In marble or in bronze, lacked character.
But boys and girls, pale from the imagined love
Of solitary beds, knew what they were,
That passion could bring character enough,
And pressed at midnight in some public place
Live lips upon a plummet-measured face.

No! Greater than Pythagoras, for the men
That with a mallet or a chisel modelled these
Calculations that look but casual flesh, put down

All Asiatic vague immensities,
And not the banks of oars that swam upon
The many-headed foam at Salamis.
Europe put off that foam when Phidias
Gave women dreams and dreams their looking-glass.

One image crossed the many-headed, sat
Under the tropic shade, grew round and slow,
No Hamlet thin from eating flies, a fat
Dreamer of the Middle Ages. Empty eyeballs knew
That knowledge increases unreality, that
Mirror on mirror mirrored is all the show.
When gong and conch declare the hour to bless
Grimalkin crawls to Buddha's emptiness.

When Pearse summoned Cuchulain to his side,
What stalked through the Post Office? What intellect,
What calculation, number, measurement, replied?
We Irish, born into that ancient sect
But thrown upon this filthy modern tide
And by its formless spawning fury wrecked,
Climb to our proper dark, that we may trace
The lineaments of a plummet-measured face.
        April 9, 1938

WHY SHOULD NOT OLD MEN BE MAD?

Why should not old men be mad?
Some have known a likely lad
That had a sound fly-fisher's wrist
Turn to a drunken journalist;
A girl that knew all Dante once
Live to bear children to a dunce;
A Helen of social welfare dream,
Climb on a wagonette to scream.
Some think it a matter of course that chance
Should starve good men and bad advance,
That if their neighbours figured plain,
As though upon a lighted screen,

No single story would they find
Of an unbroken happy mind,
A finish worthy of the start.
Young men know nothing of this sort,
Observant old men know it well;
And when they know what old books tell,
And that no better can be had,
Know why an old man should be mad.

THE CIRCUS ANIMALS' DESERTION

I

I sought a theme and sought for it in vain,
I sought it daily for six weeks or so.
Maybe at last, being but a broken man,
I must be satisfied with my heart, although
Winter and summer till old age began
My circus animals were all on show,
Those stilted boys, that burnished chariot,
Lion and woman and the Lord knows what.

II

What can I but enumerate old themes?
First that sea-rider Oisin led by the nose
Through three enchanted islands, allegorical dreams,
Vain gaiety, vain battle, vain repose,
Themes of the embittered heart, or so it seems,
That might adorn old songs or courtly shows;
But what cared I that set him on to ride,
I, starved for the bosom of his faery bride?

And then a counter-truth filled out its play,
The Countess Cathleen was the name I gave it:
She, pity-crazed, had given her soul away,
But masterful Heaven had intervened to save it.
I thought my dear must her own soul destroy,
So did fanaticism and hate enslave it,

And this brought forth a dream and soon enough
This dream itself had all my thought and love.

And when the Fool and Blind Man stole the bread
Cuchulain fought the ungovernable sea;
Heart-mysteries there, and yet when all is said
It was the dream itself enchanted me:
Character isolated by a deed
To engross the present and dominate memory.
Players and painted stage took all my love,
And not those things that they were emblems of.

III

Those masterful images because complete
Grew in pure mind, but out of what began?
A mound of refuse or the sweepings of a street,
Old kettles, old bottles, and a broken can,
Old iron, old bones, old rags, that raving slut
Who keeps the till. Now that my ladder's gone,
I must lie down where all the ladders start,
In the foul rag-and-bone shop of the heart.

UNDER BEN BULBEN

I

Swear by what the sages spoke
Round the Mareotic Lake
That the Witch of Atlas knew,
Spoke and set the cocks a-crow.

Swear by those horsemen, by those women
Complexion and form prove superhuman,
That pale, long-visaged company
That air in immortality
Completeness of their passions won;
Now they ride the wintry dawn
Where Ben Bulben sets the scene.

Here's the gist of what they mean.

II

Many times man lives and dies
Between his two eternities,
That of race and that of soul,
And ancient Ireland knew it all.
Whether man die in his bed
Or the rifle knocks him dead,
A brief parting from those dear
Is the worst man has to fear.
Though grave-diggers' toil is long,
Sharp their spades, their muscles strong,
They but thrust their buried men
Back in the human mind again.

III

You that Mitchel's prayer have heard,
'Send war in our time, O Lord!'
Know that when all words are said
And a man is fighting mad,
Something drops from eyes long blind,
He completes his partial mind,
For an instant stands at ease,
Laughs aloud, his heart at peace.
Even the wisest man grows tense
With some sort of violence
Before he can accomplish fate,
Know his work or choose his mate.

IV

Poet and sculptor, do the work,
Nor let the modish painter shirk
What his great forefathers did,
Bring the soul of man to God,
Make him fill the cradles right.

Measurement began our might:
Forms a stark Egyptian thought,
Forms that gentler Phidias wrought.
Michael Angelo left a proof
On the Sistine Chapel roof,
Where but half-awakened Adam
Can disturb globe-trotting Madam
Till her bowels are in heat,
Proof that there's a purpose set
Before the secret working mind:
Profane perfection of mankind.

Quattrocento put in paint
On backgrounds for a God or Saint
Gardens where a soul's at ease;
Where everything that meets the eye,
Flowers and grass and cloudless sky,
Resemble forms that are or seem
When sleepers wake and yet still dream,
And when it's vanished still declare,
With only bed and bedstead there,
That heavens had opened.

          Gyres run on;
When that greater dream had gone
Calvert and Wilson, Blake and Claude,
Prepared a rest for the people of God,
Palmer's phrase, but after that
Confusion fell upon our thought.

v

Irish poets, learn your trade,
Sing whatever is well made,
Scorn the sort now growing up
All out of shape from toe to top,
Their unremembering hearts and heads
Base-born products of base beds.
Sing the peasantry, and then
Hard-riding country gentlemen,

The holiness of monks, and after
Porter-drinkers' randy laughter;
Sing the lords and ladies gay
That were beaten into the clay
Through seven heroic centuries;
Cast your mind on other days
That we in coming days may be
Still the indomitable Irishry.

VI

Under bare Ben Bulben's head
In Drumcliff churchyard Yeats is laid.
An ancestor was rector there
Long years ago, a church stands near,
By the road an ancient cross.
No marble, no conventional phrase;
On limestone quarried near the spot
By his command these words are cut:

> *Cast a cold eye*
> *On life, on death.*
> *Horseman, pass by!*

September 4, 1938

Epilogue

*I*n May 1989 I stood at Yeats's grave under Ben Bulben's head in Drumcliff Churchyard, Co. Sligo. The great mountain running along the skyline, seemed without depth, hung like a stage canvas on the horizon, its grey-brown and green colours continually changing form, as shadows like light lace drifted across its face. The 'ancient cross' beside Drumcliff church (mentioned in Verse VI of the last poem) commemorates the spot where Columba, poet and saint, built one of his monasteries before his exile to Iona in 563. His church and monastic settlement in Iona are still a place of pilgrimage and worship and his marvellous Latin hymns still sung there.

A poem written in exile shows that Columba never forgot his native coast and the sea around Drumcliff:

> That I may hear the thunder of the crowding waves
> Upon the rocks.
> That I might hear the roar by the side of the church
> of the surrounding sea.

There is much of Yeats in the stern purpose of Columba and of his gift for building institutions which would outlast his life. It seems appropriate now that he should lie beside the sea, so beloved by the saint, whose immediate forebears would have held to that pagan culture which would nourish Yeats's imagination throughout his life.

Index